THE COMPLETE RESULTS & LINE-UPS OF THE INTERCONTINENTAL CUP 1960-2004

AND THE

FIFA CLUB WORLD CUP 2000-2022

Dirk Karsdorp

British Library Cataloguing in Publication Data
A catalogue record for this book is available from the British Library

ISBN: 978-1-86223-491-8

Copyright © 2022, SOCCER BOOKS LIMITED (01472 696226)
72 St. Peter's Avenue, Cleethorpes, DN35 8HU, United Kingdom
Web site   www.soccer-books.co.uk
e-mail   info@soccer-books.co.uk

All rights are reserved. No part of this publication may be reproduced, stored in a retrieval system or transmitted, in any form or by any means, electronic, mechanical, photocopying, recording, or otherwise, without the prior written permission of Soccer Books Limited.

Printed in the UK by 4edge Ltd.

1960 Intercontinental Cup

The 1960 Intercontinental Cup was the inaugural edition of the match-up between the reigning European football champions and the reigning South American football champions. The idea was born of discussions between Pierre Delauney, UEFA secretary and José Ramón de Freitas, CONMEBOL secretary.

The two-legged tie was contested between Spanish club Real Madrid CF (1959-60 European Cup winner) and Uruguayan club CA Peñarol Montevideo (1960 Copa Libertadores winner). The first match-up ended with Real Madrid CF holding CA Peñarol Montevideo to a 0-0 draw in Montevideo and soundly winning 5-1 in the return leg in Madrid.

03-07-1960   Estadio Centenario, Montevideo:
              CA Peñarol Montevideo - Real Madrid CF   0-0
CA Peñarol Montevideo: Luis María MAIDENA Silveira, William Ruben MARTÍNEZ Carreras, Walter AGUERRE, Santiago Raimundo PINO Ferreyra, Mílton Alves da Silva "SALVADOR" (BRA), Néstor GONÇALVES Martinicorena, Luis Alberto CUBILLA Almeida, Carlos Abel LINAZZA (ARG), Juan Eduardo HOHBERG, Alberto Pedro SPENCER Herrera (ECU), Carlos Ariel BORGES. (Coach: Roberto SCARONE Rivera).
Real Madrid CF: Rogelio Antonio DOMÍNGUEZ López (ARG), Marcos Alonso Imaz "MARQUITOS", Enrique Pérez Díaz "PACHÍN", José María VIDAL Bravo, José Emilio SANTAMARÍA Iglesias, José María ZÁRRAGA Martín, Darcy Silveira dos Santos "CANÁRIO" (BRA), Luis DEL SOL Cascajares, Alfredo Stéfano DI STÉFANO Laulhé, Ferenc PUSKÁS (HUN), Manuel "MANOLÍN" Bueno Cabral. (Coach: Miguel MUÑOZ Mozún).
Referee: José Luis PRADDAUDE (ARG)   Attendance: 71,872

04-09-1960   Santiago Bernabéu, Madrid:
              Real Madrid CF – CA Peñarol Montevideo   5-1 (4-0)
Real Madrid CF: Rogelio Antonio DOMÍNGUEZ López (ARG), Marcos Alonso Imaz "MARQUITOS", Enrique Pérez Díaz "PACHÍN", José María VIDAL Bravo, José Emilio SANTAMARÍA Iglesias, José María ZÁRRAGA Martín, Jesús "Chus" HERRERA Alonso, Luis DEL SOL Cascajares, Alfredo Stéfano DI STÉFANO Laulhé, Ferenc PUSKÁS (HUN), Francisco GENTO López. (Coach: Miguel MUÑOZ Mozún).
CA Peñarol Montevideo: Luis María MAIDENA Silveira, William Ruben MARTÍNEZ Carreras, Santiago Raimundo PINO Ferreyra, Francisco MAJEWSKI, Walter AGUERRE, Mílton Alves da Silva "SALVADOR" (BRA), Luis Alberto CUBILLA Almeida, Carlos Abel LINAZZA (ARG), Juan Eduardo HOHBERG, Alberto Pedro SPENCER Herrera (ECU), Carlos Ariel BORGES. (Coach: Roberto SCARONE Rivera).
Goals: Real Madrid CF: 1-0 Ferenc PUSKÁS (2'), 2-0 Alfredo Stéfano DI STÉFANO Laulhé (3'), 3-0 Ferenc PUSKÁS (8'), 4-0 Jesús "Chus" HERRERA Alonso (40'), 5-0 Francisco GENTO López (54').
CA Peñarol Montevideo: 5-1 Alberto Pedro SPENCER Herrera (80').
Referee: Kenneth George (Ken) ASTON (ENG)   Attendance: 90,000

*** **Real Madrid CF won the Cup** ***

1961 Intercontinental Cup

The 1961 Intercontinental Cup was played between Uruguyan club CA Peñarol Montevideo, winners of the 1961 Copa Libertadores, and Portuguese club Sport Lisboa e Benfica, winners of the 1960-61 European Cup. CA Peñarol Montevideo won the Intercontinental Cup for the first time.

Despite Peñarol's comfortable victory in the second leg in Montevideo, a play-off was required as the rules at the time awarded 2 points for each victory and both teams had won one game each.

04-09-1961   Estádio da Luz, Lisboa:
                Sport Lisboa e Benfica – CA Peñarol Montevideo   1-0 (0-0)
Sport Lisboa e Benfica: Alberto da COSTA PEREIRA, ÂNGELO Martins Gaspar, Mário JOÃO Sousa Alves, José António Conceição NETO, António da Cruz Pinto SARAIVA, Fernando da Conceição CRUZ, JOSÉ AUGUSTO Pinto de Almeida, Joaquim SANTANA Silva Guimarães, José Pinto Carvalho Santos ÁGUAS, Mário Esteves COLUNA, Domiciano Barrocal Gomes CAVÉM. (Coach: Béla GUTTMAN (HUN)).
CA Peñarol Montevideo: Luis María MAIDENA Silveira, Edgardo Nilson GONZÁLEZ, William Ruben MARTÍNEZ Carreras, Walter AGUERRE, Núber CANO, Néstor GONÇÁLVEZ Martinicorena, Luis Alberto CUBILLA Almeida, Alberto Pedro SPENCER Herrera (ECU), Angel Rubén CABRERA Santana, José Francisco SASÍA Lugo, Ernesto Sebastián LEDESMA. (Coach: Roberto SCARONE Rivera).
Goal: SL Benfica: 1-0 Mário Esteves COLUNA (60').
Referee: Othmar HUBER (SUI)   Attendance: 40,000

17-09-1961   Estadio Centenario, Montevideo:
                CA Peñarol Montevideo – Sport Lisboa e Benfica   5-0 (4-0)
CA Peñarol Montevideo: Luis María MAIDENA Silveira, Edgardo Nilson GONZÁLEZ, William Ruben MARTÍNEZ Carreras, Walter AGUERRE, Núber CANO, Néstor GONÇÁLVEZ Martinicorena, Luis Alberto CUBILLA Almeida, Ernesto Sebastián LEDESMA, José Francisco SASÍA Lugo, Alberto Pedro SPENCER Herrera (ECU), Juan Víctor JOYA Cordero (PER). (Coach: Roberto SCARONE Rivera).
Sport Lisboa e Benfica: Alberto da COSTA PEREIRA, ÂNGELO Martins Gaspar, Mário JOÃO Sousa Alves, José António Conceição NETO, António da Cruz Pinto SARAIVA, Fernando da Conceição CRUZ, JOSÉ AUGUSTO Pinto de Almeida, Joaquim SANTANA Silva Guimarães, António da Silva MENDES, Mário Esteves COLUNA, Domiciano Barrocal Gomes CAVÉM. (Coach: Béla GUTTMAN (HUN)).
Goals: CA Peñarol Montevideo: 1-0 José Francisco SASÍA Lugo (10' penalty), 2-0 Juan Víctor JOYA Cordero (18'), 3-0 Juan Víctor JOYA Cordero (28'), 4-0 Alberto Pedro SPENCER Herrera (42'), 5-0 Alberto Pedro SPENCER Herrera (58').
Referee: Carlos Nay FOINO (ARG)   Attendance: 56,358

Play-off

19-09-1961   Estadio Centenario, Montevideo:
                CA Peñarol Montevideo – Sport Lisboa e Benfica   2-1 (2-1)
CA Peñarol Montevideo: Luis María MAIDENA Silveira, Edgardo Nilson GONZÁLEZ, William Ruben MARTÍNEZ Carreras, Walter AGUERRE, Núber CANO, Néstor GONÇÁLVEZ Martinicorena, Luis Alberto CUBILLA Almeida, Ernesto Sebastián LEDESMA, José Francisco SASÍA Lugo, Alberto Pedro SPENCER Herrera (ECU), Juan Víctor JOYA Cordero (PER). (Coach: Roberto SCARONE Rivera).
Sport Lisboa e Benfica: Alberto da COSTA PEREIRA, ÂNGELO Martins Gaspar, Fernando da Conceição CRUZ, José António Conceição NETO, HUMBERTO da Silva Fernandes, Mário Esteves COLUNA, JOSÉ AUGUSTO Pinto de Almeida, EUSÉBIO da Silva Ferreira, José Pinto Carvalho Santos ÁGUAS, Domiciano Barrocal Gomes CAVÉM, António SIMÕES da Costa. (Coach: Béla GUTTMAN (HUN)).
Goals: CA Peñarol Montevideo: 1-0 José Francisco SASÍA Lugo (6'), 2-1 José Francisco SASÍA Lugo (41' penalty).
SL Benfica: 1-1 EUSÉBIO da Silva Ferreira (35').
Referee: José Luis PRADDAUDE (ARG)   Attendance: 60,241

*** CA Peñarol Montevideo won the Cup ***

1962 Intercontinental Cup

The 1962 Intercontinental Cup was played between Brazilian club Santos FC, winners of the 1962 Copa Libertadores, and Portuguese club Sport Lisboa e Benfica, winners of the 1961-62 European Cup. Santos FC won the Intercontinental Cup for the first time.

The tie is remembered for pitching Brazilian player Pelé against Portuguese player Eusébio, two of the leading players of the 1960s, who played against each other on only three occasions. Many consider that the second leg of the tie, Santos FC's 2-5 win in Lisbon, in which Pelé scored a hat-trick, as the greatest performance ever seen in the competition.

19-09-1962   Maracaña Stadium, Rio de Janeiro: Santos FC – S.L. Benfica 3-2 (1-0)
Santos FC: Gylmar dos Santos Neves "GILMAR", Antônio LIMA dos Santos, Raul Donazar CALVET, José Ely de Miranda "ZITO", MAURO Ramos de Oliveira, DALMO Gaspar, DORVAL Rodrigues, MENGÁLVIO Petro Figueiró, Antônio Wilson Vieira Honório "COUTINHO", Edson Arantes do Nascimento "PELÉ", José Macia "PEPE". (Coach: Luís Alonso Pérez "LULA").
Sport Lisboa e Benfica: JOSÉ Bartolomeu Barrocal RITA dos Mártires, ÂNGELO Martins Gaspar, RAÚL Martins Machado, Domiciano Barrocal Gomes CAVÉM, Fernando da Conceição CRUZ, HUMBERTO da Silva Fernandes, Mário Esteves COLUNA, JOSÉ AUGUSTO Pinto de Almeida, Joaquim SANTANA Silva Guimarães, EUSÉBIO da Silva Ferreira, António SIMÕES da Costa. (Coach: Fernando RIERA Bauzá (CHI)).
Goals: Santos FC: 1-0 Edson Arantes do Nascimento "PELÉ" (31'), 2-1 Antônio Wilson Vieira Honório "COUTINHO" (64'), 3-1 Edson Arantes do Nascimento "PELÉ" (86').
SL Benfica: 1-1 Joaquim SANTANA Silva Guimarães (58'), 3-2 Joaquim SANTANA Silva Guimarães (87').
Referee: Rubén CABRERA (PAR)   Attendance: 85,459

11-10-1962   Estádio da Luz, Lisboa: Sport Lisboa e Benfica - Santos FC 2-5 (0-2)
Sport Lisboa e Benfica: Alberto da COSTA PEREIRA, JACINTO José Martins Godinho Santos, RAÚL Martins Machado, HUMBERTO da Silva Fernandes, Fernando da Conceição CRUZ, Domiciano Barrocal Gomes CAVÉM, Mário Esteves COLUNA, JOSÉ AUGUSTO Pinto de Almeida, Joaquim SANTANA Silva Guimarães, EUSÉBIO da Silva Ferreira, António SIMÕES da Costa. (Coach: Fernando RIERA Bauzá (CHI)).
Santos FC: Gylmar dos Santos Neves "GILMAR", OLAVO Martins de Oliveira, Raul Donazar CALVET, DALMO Gaspar, MAURO Ramos de Oliveira, Antônio LIMA dos Santos, DORVAL Rodrigues, José Ely de Miranda "ZITO", Antônio Wilson Vieira Honório "COUTINHO", Edson Arantes do Nascimento "PELÉ", José Macia "PEPE". (Coach: Luís Alonso Pérez "LULA").
Goals: SL Benfica: 1-5 EUSÉBIO da Silva Ferreira (87'), 2-5 Joaquim SANTANA Silva Guimarães (89').
FC Santos: 0-1 Edson Arantes do Nascimento "PELÉ" (17'), 0-2 Edson Arantes do Nascimento "PELÉ" (28'), 0-3 Antônio Wilson Vieira Honório "COUTINHO" (49'), 0-4 Edson Arantes do Nascimento "PELÉ" (64'), 0-5 José Macia "PEPE" (77').
Referee: Pierre SCHWINTÉ (FRA)   Attendance: 73,000

*** Santos FC won the Cup ***

1963 Intercontinental Cup

The 1963 Intercontinental Cup was contested between 1962-63 European Cup winners AC Milan and 1963 Copa Libertadores winners Santos FC. It was the fourth edition of the competition.

The first leg was played in Milan on 16th October 1963 where Milan won 4-2. The return leg was held on 14th November 1963 in Rio de Janeiro. Santos FC won this second match 4-2, but not without great deal of controversy due to the refereeing by Juan Regis Brozzi. Milan led 2-0 at half-time and looked to be comfortably in control of the tie. However, the behaviour of the Santos players changed in the second half; they became extremely aggressive towards their opponents, with the referee failing to punish their foul play. As Milan's Gianni Rivera commented afterwards, "Each time we touched the ball, the referee stopped us. Inconceivable. Unchained spectators, people on the pitch, everything happened".

Goalkeeper Ghezzi and striker Rivera both sustained injuries from second-half challenges and Santos scored four goals, three of which were from free-kicks. There were later rumours that the referee had been bribed by the Santos management during the half-time break while other commentators cited the relevance of referee's profession. He was, in fact, a travel agent, who was often in contact with Brazilian teams when they travelled to Argentina for games!

As both teams had won one game each, a play-off game was required. The game took place two days later at the Maracaña with Brozzi again named as the referee in spite of Milan's complaints. The game began in the same manner as the previous match had ended, with Santos FC pushing forward and attacking strongly but also continuing their aggressive play. Once again, their fouls went largely unpunished and it was no surprise when, after half an hour, Brozzi awarded Santos a penalty kick for what many viewed as simulation by Dorval Rodrigues. Milan captain, Cesare Maldini, was subsequently sent off for his protests but the penalty was converted by Dalmo Gaspar to give Santos the lead. Milan's subsequent attacks proved fruitless so Santos ran out winners to retain the trophy following a controversial but memorable final!

16-10-1963   San Siro, Milano: AC Milan - Santos FC 4-2 (2-0)
AC Milan: Giorgio GHEZZI, Mario DAVID, Mario TREBBI, Ambrogio PELAGALLI, Cesare MALDINI, Giovanni TRAPATTONI, Bruno MORA, Giovanni LODETTI, José João ALTAFINI (BRA), Gianni RIVERA, AMARILDO Tavares da Silveira (BRA). (Coach: Luis Antonio CARNIGLIA (ARG)).
Santos FC: Gylmar dos Santos Neves "GILMAR", Antônio LIMA dos Santos, Theodorico HAROLDO de Oliveira, Raul Donazar CALVET, Geraldo Antônio Martins "GERALDINHO", José Ely de Miranda "ZITO", MENGÁLVIO Pedro Figueiró, DORVAL Rodrigues, Antônio Wilson Vieira Honório "COUTINHO", Edson Arantes do Nascimento "PELÉ", José Macia "PEPE". (Coach: Luís Alonso Pérez "LULA").
Goals: AC Milan: 1-0 Giovanni TRAPATTONI (4'), 2-0 AMARILDO Tavares da Silveira (15'), 3-1 AMARILDO Tavares da Silveira (67'), 4-1 Bruno MORA (82').
FC Santos: 2-1 Edson Arantes do Nascimento "PELÉ" (59'), 4-2 Edson Arantes do Nascimento "PELÉ" (87' penalty).
Referee: Alfred HABERFELLNER (AUT)   Attendance: 51,917

14-11-1963   Maracaña, Rio de Janeiro: Santos FC - AC Milan 4-2 (0-2)
Santos FC: Gylmar dos Santos Neves "GILMAR", ISMAEL Mafra Cabral, DALMO Gaspar, MAURO Ramos de Oliveira, Theodorico HAROLDO de Oliveira, Antônio LIMA dos Santos, MENGÁLVIO Pedro Figueiró, DORVAL Rodrigues, Antônio Wilson Vieira Honório "COUTINHO", ALMIR "PERNAMBUQUINHO" Moraes de Albuquerque, José Macia "PEPE". Coach: Luís Alonso Pérez "LULA").
AC Milan: Giorgio GHEZZI, Mario DAVID, Mario TREBBI, Ambrogio PELAGALLI, Cesare MALDINI, Giovanni TRAPATTONI, Bruno MORA, Giovanni LODETTI, José João ALTAFINI (BRA), Gianni RIVERA, AMARILDO Tavares da Silveira (BRA). (Coach: Luis Antonio CARNIGLIA (ARG)).
Goals: Santos FC: 1-2 José Macia "PEPE" (50'), 2-2 ALMIR "PERNAMBUQUINHO" Moraes de Albuquerque (60'), 3-2 Antônio LIMA dos Santos (63'), 4-2 José Macia "PEPE" (67').
AC Milan: 0-1 José João ALTAFINI (12'), 0-2 Bruno MORA (17').
Referee: Juan Regis BROZZI (ARG)   Attendance: 132,758

Play-off

16-11-1963   Maracaña, Rio de Janeiro: Santos FC - AC Milan   1-0 (1-0)
Santos FC: Gylmar dos Santos Neves "GILMAR", ISMAEL Mafra Cabral, DALMO Gaspar, MAURO Ramos de Oliveira, Theodorico HAROLDO de Oliveira, Antônio LIMA dos Santos, MENGÁLVIO Pedro Figueiró, DORVAL Rodrigues, Antônio Wilson Vieira Honório "COUTINHO", ALMIR "PERNAMBUQUINHO" Moraes de Albuquerque, José Macia "PEPE". (Coach: Luís Alonso Pérez "LULA").
AC Milan: Luigi BALZARINI (40' Dario BARLUZZI), Ambrogio PELAGALLI, Mario TREBBI, Victor BENÍTEZ Morales (PER), Cesare MALDINI, Giovanni TRAPATTONI, Bruno MORA, Giovanni LODETTI, José João ALTAFINI (BRA), AMARILDO Tavares da Silveira (BRA), Giuliano FORTUNATO. (Coach: Luis Antonio CARNIGLIA (ARG)).
Goal: FC Santos: 1-0 DALMO Gaspar (26' penalty).
Referee: Juan Regis BROZZI (ARG)   Attendance: 120.421
Sent-off : 34' Cesare MALDINI, 44' ISMAEL Mafra Cabral.

*** Santos FC won the Cup ***

1964 Intercontinental Cup

The 1964 Intercontinental Cup was played during September 1964 between CA Independiente Avellaneda, winners of the Copa Libertadores 1964, and FC Internazionale Milano, winners of the 1963-64 European Cup.

The first leg was held in Argentina and was won 1-0 by CA Independiente Avellaneda. Two weeks later, FC Internazionale Milano won the return leg, 2-0. As each team had won one match, a play-off was held, played at a neutral venue in Madrid, with FC Internazionale Milano winning following extra-time.

09-09-1964   Independiente Stadium, Avellaneda:
                CA Independiente Avellaneda - FC Internazionale Milano   1-0 (0-0)
CA Independiente Avellaneda: Miguel Ángel SANTORO, Roberto Carlos FERREIRO, Tomás ROLÁN, David ACEVEDO, Juan Carlos GUZMÁN, Jorge Alberto MALDONADO, Raúl Emilio BERNAO, Osvaldo Luis MURA, Pedro PROSPITTI, Mario RODRÍGUEZ Varela, Raúl Armando SAVOY. (Coach: Manuel Ernesto GIÚDICE).
FC Internazionale Milano: Giuliano SARTI, Tarcisio BRUGNICH, Giacinto FACCHETTI, Carlo TAGNIN, Aristide GUARNERI, Armando PICCHI, JAIR da Costa (BRA), Alessandro MAZZOLA, JOAQUÍN PEIRÓ Lucas (ESP), LUIS SUÁREZ Miramontes (ESP), Mario CORSO. (Coach: Helenio HERRERA Gavilán (ARG)).
Goal: CA Independiente Avellaneda: 1-0 Mario RODRÍGUEZ Varela (59').
Referee: ARMANDO Nunes Castanheira da Rosa MÁRQUES (BRA)
Attendance: 65,000

23-09-1964   Stadio San Siro, Milano:
                FC Internazionale Milano - CA Independiente Avellaneda   2-0 (2-0)
FC Internazionale Milano: Giuliano SARTI, Tarcisio BURGNICH, Giacinto FACCHETTI, Saul MALATRASI, Aristide GUARNERI, Armando PICCHI, JAIR da Costa (BRA), Alessandro MAZZOLA, Aurelio MILANI, LUIS SUÁREZ Miramontes (ESP), Mario CORSO. (Coach: Helenio HERRERA Gavilán (ARG)).
CA Independiente Avellaneda: Miguel Ángel SANTORO, David ACEVEDO, Raúl DECARÍA, Jorge Alberto MALDONADO, Roberto Carlos FERREIRO, José Andrés PAFLIK, Luis Ernesto SUÁREZ, Osvaldo Luis MURA, Pedro PROSPITTI, Mario RODRÍGUEZ Varela, Raúl Armando SAVOY. (Coach: Manuel Ernesto GIÚDICE).
Goals: FC Internazionale Milano: 1-0 Alessandro MAZZOLA (8'), 2-0 Mario CORSO (39').
Referee: Gyula GERE (HUN)   Attendance: 50,164
Sent-off: 76' Roberto Carlos FERREIRO.

Play-off

26-09-1964   Santiago Bernabéu, Madrid (ESP):
FC Internazionale Milano - CA Independiente Avellaneda   1-0 (0-0, 0-0) **(AET)**
FC Internazionale Milano: Giuliano SARTI, Saul MALATRASI, Giacinto FACCHETTI, Carlo TAGNIN, Aristide GUARNERI, Armando PICCHI, Angelo DOMENGHINI, JOAQUÍN PEIRÓ Lucas (ESP), Aurelio MILANI, LUIS SUÁREZ Miramontes (ESP), Mario CORSO. (Coach: Helenio HERRERA Gavilán (ARG)).
CA Independiente Avellaneda: Miguel Ángel SANTORO, Juan Carlos GUZMÁN, Raúl DECARÍA, David ACEVEDO, José Andrés PAFLIK, Jorge Alberto MALDONADO, Raúl Emilio BERNAO, Pedro PROSPITTI, Luis Ernesto SUÁREZ, Mario RODRÍGUEZ Varela, Raúl Armando SAVOY. (Coach: Manuel Ernesto GIÚDICE).
Goal: FC Internazionale Milano: 1-0 Mario CORSO (110').
Referee: José María ORTIZ DE MENDÍBIL (ESP)   Attendance: 25,000

*** FC Internazionale Milano won the Cup ***

1965 Intercontinental Cup

The 1965 Intercontinental Cup was played during September 1965 between CA Independiente Avellaneda, winners of the Copa Libertadores 1965, and FC Internazionale Milano, winners of the 1964-65 European Cup. Both teams had retained their continental titles so this was a rematch of the previous year's competition.

The first leg was held in Italy, and was comfortably won 3-0 by Internazionale. The return match was played seven days later, in Argentina, and ended in a goalless draw so Internazionale retained the trophy.

08-09-1965   Stadio San Siro, Milano:
FC Internazionale Milano - CA Independiente Avellaneda   3-0 (2-0)
FC Internazionale Milano: Giuliano SARTI, Tarcisio BURGNICH, Giacinto FACCHETTI, Gianfranco BEDIN, Aristide GUARNERI, Armando PICCHI, JAIR da Costa (BRA), Alessandro MAZZOLA, JOAQUÍN PEIRÓ Lucas (ESP), LUIS SUÁREZ Miramontes (ESP), Mario CORSO. (Coach: Helenio HERRERA Gavilán (ARG)).
CA Independiente Avellaneda: Miguel Ángel SANTORO, Ricardo Elvio PAVONI Cúneo (URU), Rubén Marino NAVARRO, David ACEVEDO, Juan Carlos GUZMÁN, Roberto Carlos FERREIRO, Raúl Emilio BERNAO, Vicente DE LA MATA, Roque AVALLAY, Mario RODRÍGUEZ Varela, Raúl Armando SAVOY. (Coach: Manuel Ernesto GIÚDICE).
Goals: FC Internazionale Milano: 1-0 JOAQUÍN PEIRÓ Lucas (3'), 2-0 Alessandro MAZZOLA (23'), 3-0 Alessandro MAZZOLA (61').
Referee: Rudolf KREITLEIN (FRG)   Attendance: 75,000

15-09-1965   La Doble Visera, Avellaneda:
CA Independiente Avellaneda - FC Internazionale Milano   0-0
CA Independiente Avellaneda: Miguel Ángel SANTORO, Rubén Marino NAVARRO, Ricardo Elvio PAVONI Cúneo (URU), Tomás Rolan BARRIOS, Juan Carlos GUZMÁN, Roberto Carlos FERREIRO, Raúl Emilio BERNAO, Osvaldo Luis MURA, Roque AVALLAY, Miguel Ángel MORI, Raúl Armando SAVOY. (Coach: Manuel Ernesto GIÚDICE).
FC Internazionale Milano: Giuliano SARTI, Tarcisio BURGNICH, Giacinto FACCHETTI, Gianfranco BEDIN, Aristide GUARNERI, Armando PICCHI, JAIR da Costa (BRA), Alessandro MAZZOLA, JOAQUÍN PEIRÓ Lucas (ESP), LUIS SUÁREZ Miramontes (ESP), Mario CORSO. (Coach: Helenio HERRERA Gavilán (ARG)).
Referee: Arturo YAMASAKI (PER)   Attendance: 80,000

*** FC Internazionale Milano won the Cup ***

1966 Intercontinental Cup

The 1966 Intercontinental Cup was played between Uruguayan club CD Peñarol Montevideo, winners of the Copa Libertadores 1966, and European Champions, Real Madrid CF, in a repeat of the 1960 competition.

In the first match, held in Montevideo, Peñarol beat Real Madrid 2-0 while in the second leg, held in Madrid, Peñarol defeated the Spanish side by the same score to comfortably win their second Intercontinental Cup title.

12-10-1966   Estadio Centenario, Montevideo:
              CA Peñarol Montevideo - Real Madrid CF   2-0 (1-0)
CA Peñarol Montevideo: Ladislao MAZURKIEWICZ Iglesias, Omar CAETANO Otero, Pio Tabaré GONZÁLEZ Buttini, Néstor GONÇÁLVEZ Martinicorena, Juan Vicente LEZCANO López (PAR), Luis Alberto VARELA, Julio César ABBADIE Gismero, Julio César CORTÉS Lagos, Alberto Pedro SPENCER Herrera (ECU), Pedro Virgilio ROCHA Franchetti, Juan Víctor JOYA Cordero (PER). (Coach: Roque Gastón MÁSPOLI Arbelvide).
Real Madrid CF: Antonio Rodrigo BETANCORT Barrera, Enrique Pérez Díaz "PACHÍN", Manuel SANCHIS Martinéz, Félix RUIZ Gabari, Pedro Eugenio DE FELIPE Cortés, Ignacio ZOCO Esparza, Fernando Rodríguez SERENA, AMANCIO Amaro Varela, José Martínez Sánchez "PIRRI", Manuel VELÁZQUEZ Villaverde, Manuel "MANOLÍN" Bueno Cabral. (Coach: Miguel MUÑOZ Mozún).
Goals: CA Peñarol Montevideo: 1-0 Alberto Pedro SPENCER Herrera (39'), 2-0 Alberto Pedro SPENCER Herrera (82').
Referee: Claudio VICUÑA (CHI)   Attendance: 58,324
Sent-off: 68' Enrique Pérez Díaz "PACHÍN".

26-10-1966   Estadio Santiago Bernabéu, Madrid:
              Real Madrid CF – CA Peñarol Montevideo   0-2 (0-2)
Real Madrid CF: Antonio Rodrigo BETANCORT Barrera, Antonio CALPE Hernández, Manuel SANCHIS Martinéz, José Martínez Sánchez "PIRRI", Pedro Eugenio DE FELIPE Cortés, Ignacio ZOCO Esparza, Fernando Rodríguez SERENA, AMANCIO Amaro Varela, Ramón Moreno GROSSO, Manuel VELÁZQUEZ Villaverde, Francisco GENTO López. (Coach: Miguel MUÑOZ Mozún).
CA Peñarol Montevideo: Ladislao MAZURKIEWICZ Iglesias, Pio Tabaré GONZÁLEZ Buttini, Omar CAETANO Otero, Néstor GONÇÁLVEZ Martinicorena, Juan Vicente LEZCANO López (PAR), Luis Alberto VARELA, Julio César ABBADIE Gismero, Julio César CORTÉS Lagos, Alberto Pedro SPENCER Herrera (ECU), Pedro Virgilio ROCHA Franchetti, Juan Víctor JOYA Cordero (PER). (Coach: Roque Gastón MÁSPOLI Arbelvide).
Goals: CA Peñarol Montevideo: 0-1 Pedro Virgilio ROCHA Franchetti (28' penalty), 0-2 Alberto Pedro SPENCER Herrera (37').
Referee: Concetto LO BELLO (ITA)   Attendance: 71,063

*** CA Peñarol Montevideo won the Cup ***

1967 Intercontinental Cup

The 1967 Intercontinental Cup was played between the winners of the 1966-67 European Cup, Celtic FC Glasgow, and Racing Club de Avellaneda, winners of the 1967 Copa Libertadores.

The first leg was played in Glasgow, with Celtic winning 1-0. However, the game itself was marred by incessant fouling by Racing Club's players in addition to accusations of spitting. The return match in Argentina was just as acrimonious, with Celtic's Ronnie Simpson unable to play after being struck by an object thrown from the crowd just before the start of the match. He was badly dazed and had to be replaced by John Fallon. Celtic once again took the lead, but Racing Club fought back to win the game 2-1. As both teams were level on two points after two legs, a play-off was required and this took place at a neutral venue in Montevideo, Uruguay.

The game proved a shambles as Racing Club's continued their cynical fouling and the Celtic players lost all composure and discipline in what has become known as the "Battle of Montevideo". The Paraguayan referee was clearly out of his depth and stopped the match after 23 minutes to warn both captains via an interpreter that players would be sent off should the foul play not stop. However, this warning was ignored and the match erupted 14 minutes later when Jimmy Johnstone was hacked down by Juan Rulli. A melee ensued between various opposing players, John Clark approached both Rulli and Alfio Basile with his fists up, striking a pose reminiscent of a bare-knuckle boxer, and Uruguayan riot police had to intervene on the pitch several times. Six players were sent off in all, four from Celtic and two from Racing Club. Celtic's Bertie Auld refused to leave the field after being "sent off" and ended up playing for the whole game! Racing Club scored the only goal of the game in the second half, winning the game 1-0 and the Intercontinental Cup series, becoming the first Argentinian holders of the trophy.

18-10-1967   Hampden Park, Glasgow:
              Celtic FC Glasgow - Racing Club de Avellaneda   1-0 (0-0)
Celtic FC Glasgow: Ronnie SIMPSON, Jim CRAIG, Tommy GEMMELL, Bobby
MURDOCH, Billy McNEILL, John CLARK, Jimmy JOHNSTONE, Bobby LENNOX, Willie
WALLACE, Bertie AULD, John HUGHES. (Coach: Jock STEIN).
Racing Club de Avellaneda: Agustín Mario CEJAS, Roberto Alfredo PERFUMO, Rubén
Oswaldo DÍAZ Figueras, Oscar Raimundo MARTÍN, Miguel Ángel MORI, Alfio BASILE,
Norberto RAFFO, Juan Carlos RULLI, Juan Carlos CÁRDENAS, Juan José RODRÍGUEZ,
Humberto Dionisio MASCHIO. (Coach: Juan José PIZZUTI).
Goal: Celtic FC Glasgow: 1-0 Billy McNEILL (67').
Referee: Juan GARDEAZÁBAL Garay (ESP)   Attendance: 83,437

01-11-1967   Estadio Presidente Juan Domingo Perón, Avellaneda:
              Racing Club de Avellaneda - Celtic FC Glasgow   2-1 (1-1)
Racing Club de Avellaneda: Agustín Mario CEJAS, Roberto Alfredo PERFUMO, Nelson
CHABAY (URU), Oscar Raimundo MARTÍN, Juan Carlos RULLI, Alfio BASILE, Norberto
RAFFO, João Rodrigo Esteves CARDOSO (BRA), Juan Carlos CÁRDENAS, Juan José
RODRÍGUEZ, Humberto Dionisio MASCHIO. (Coach: Juan José PIZZUTI).
Celtic FC Glasgow: John FALLON, Jim CRAIG, Tommy GEMMELL, Bobby MURDOCH,
Billy McNEILL, John CLARK, Jimmy JOHNSTONE, Willie WALLACE, Stevie
CHALMERS, Willie O'NEILL, Bobby LENNOX. (Coach: Jock STEIN).
Goals: Racing Club de Avellaneda: 1-1 Norberto RAFFO (32'), 2-1 Norberto RAFFO (48').
Celtic FC Glasgow: 0-1 Tommy GEMMELL (20' penalty).
Referee: Esteban MARINO (URU)   Attendance: 70,000

Play-off

04-11-1967   Estadio Centenario, Montevideo (URU):
              Racing Club de Avellaneda - Celtic FC Glasgow   1-0 (0-0)
Racing Club de Avellaneda: Agustín Mario CEJAS, Roberto Alfredo PERFUMO, Nelson
CHABAY (URU), Oscar Raimundo MARTÍN, Juan Carlos RULLI, Alfio BASILE, Norberto
RAFFO, Juan Carlos CÁRDENAS, João Rodrigo Esteves CARDOSO (BRA), Juan José
RODRÍGUEZ, Humberto Dionisio MASCHIO. (Coach: Juan José PIZZUTI).
Celtic FC Glasgow: John FALLON, Jim CRAIG, Tommy GEMMELL, Bobby MURDOCH,
Billy McNEILL, John CLARK, Jimmy JOHNSTONE, Bobby LENNOX, Willie WALLACE,
Bertie AULD, John HUGHES. (Coach: Jock STEIN).
Goal: Racing Club de Avellaneda: 1-0 Juan Carlos CÁRDENAS (55').
Referee: Rodolfo PÉREZ Osorio (PAR)   Attendance: 65,172
Sent-off: 42' Alfio BASILE, 42' Bobby LENNOX, 8' Jimmy JOHNSTONE, 74' John
HUGHES, 78' Juan Carlos RULLI, 88' Bertie AULD.

*** Racing Club de Avellaneda won the Cup ***

1968 Intercontinental Cup

The 1968 Intercontinental Cup was played between the winners of the 1967-68 European Cup, Manchester United FC, and CA Estudiantes de La Plata, winners of the 1968 Copa Libertadores.

The first leg was held at the Estadio Boca Juniors, in Buenos Aires, as Estudiantes' ground was deemed unsuitable. Nevertheless, Estudiantes won the first leg 1-0. The return match was held three weeks later at Old Trafford, in Manchester and finished as a 1-1 draw, earning Estudiantes their first Intercontinental Cup title.

25-09-1968   Estadio Boca Juniors, Buenos Aires:
CA Estudiantes de La Plata - Manchester United FC   1-0 (1-0)
CA Estudiantes de La Plata: Alberto José POLETTI, Oscar Miguel MALBERNAT Candela, Ramón Alberto AGUIRRE Suárez, Raúl Horacio MADERO, José Hugo MEDINA, Carlos Salvador BILARDO Digiano, Carlos Oscar PACHAMÉ, Néstor Rubén TOGNERI, Felipe RIBAUDO, Marcos Norberto CONIGLIARO, Juan Ramón VERÓN. (Coach: Osvaldo Juan ZUBELDÍA).
Manchester United FC: Alex STEPNEY, Tony DUNNE (IRL), Francis BURNS (SCO), Pat CRERAND (SCO), Bill FOULKES, Nobby STILES, Willie MORGAN (SCO), David SADLER, Denis LAW (SCO), Bobby CHARLTON, George BEST (NIR). (Coach: Alexander Matthew (Matt) BUSBY (SCO)).
Goal: CA Estudiantes de La Plata: 1-0 Marcos Norberto CONIGLIARO (28').
Referee: Hugo SOSA Miranda (PAR)   Attendance: 25,134
Sent-off: 79' Nobby STILES.

16-10-1968   Old Trafford, Manchester:
Manchester United FC - CA Estudiantes de La Plata   1-1 (0-1)
Manchester United FC: Alex STEPNEY, Tony DUNNE (IRL), Shay BRENNAN (IRL), Pat CRERAND (SCO), Bill FOULKES, David SADLER, Willie MORGAN (SCO), Brian KIDD, Bobby CHARLTON, Denis LAW (SCO) (43' Carlo SARTORI (ITA)), George BEST (NIR). (Coach: Alexander Matthew (Matt) BUSBY (SCO)).
CA Estudiantes de La Plata: Alberto José POLETTI, Oscar Miguel MALBERNAT Candela, Ramón Alberto AGUIRRE Suárez, Raúl Horacio MADERO, José Hugo MEDINA, Carlos Salvador BILARDO, Carlos Oscar PACHAMÉ, Néstor Rubén TOGNERI, Felipe RIBAUDO (71' Juan Michael ECHECOPAR Di Santo), Marcos Norberto CONIGLIARO, Juan Ramón VERÓN. (Coach: Osvaldo Juan ZUBELDÍA).
Goals: Manchester United FC: 1-1 Willie MORGAN (90').
CA Estudiantes de La Plata: 0-1 Juan Ramón VERÓN (6').
Referee: Konstantin ZECEVIC (YUG)   Attendance: 63,428
Sent-off: 89' George BEST, 89' José Hugo MEDINA.

*** CA Estudiantes de La Plata won the Cup ***

1969 Intercontinental Cup

The 1969 Intercontinental Cup was played between AC Milan, the winners of the 1968-69 European Cup, and CA Estudiantes de La Plata, winners of the 1969 Copa Libertadores. It was the 10th edition of the competition.

The first leg was played in Milan and the home side won 3-0. The return leg was held two weeks later in Buenos Aires. Despite suffering a 2-1 defeat, Milan won the title on aggregate.

The return match was yet another tie played in South America which became infamous for the violent conduct employed by the home team (most of which was ignored by the supposedly neutral referee), and this game was subsequently dubbed "The Bombonera Massacre" in Italy. The Estudiantes players showed their intent during the warm-up as they fired balls at the Milan players and the Italian team was also pelted with missiles from the crowd. Once play commenced, Eduardo Manera manhandled goalkeeper Fabio Cudicini and was then accused of biting Saul Malatrasi! Aguirre Suárez felled Pierino Prati with a challenge which left the Italian player concussed and followed this up by fracturing the nose of Néstor Combin with an elbow. The Estudiantes goalkeeper, Alberto Poletti, then repeatedly punched Gianni Riviera to the ground. Following the match, the semi-conscious Combin (who was born in Argentina but played for France) was even arrested by the police for draft-dodging! The outcry following the match had immediate ramifications, in part due to Argentina's ongoing bid to host the World Cup in 1978. Many of the team's players were arrested, Poletti was handed a life ban and imprisoned for a month along with his teammate, Manera. Suárez was banned from international fixtures for five years. This brutal and chaotic match is also at least partly to blame for a subsequent boycott of the tournament by many European teams.

08-10-1969   Stadio San Siro, Milano:
              AC Milan - CA Estudiantes de La Plata   3-0 (2-0)
AC Milan: Fabio CUDICINI, Saul MALATRASI, Angelo ANQUILLETTI, Roberto ROSATO, Karl-Heinz SCHNELLINGER (FRG), Giovanni LODETTI, Gianni RIVERA, Romano FOGLI, Angelo SORMANI, Néstor COMBIN (FRA) (65' Giorgio ROGNONI), Pierino PRATI. (Coach: Nereo ROCCO).
CA Estudiantes de La Plata: Alberto José POLETTI, Ramón Alberto AGUIRRE Suárez, José Hugo MEDINA, Raúl Horacio MADERO, Oscar Miguel MALBERNAT Candela, Carlos Salvador BILARDO, Néstor Rubén TOGNERI, Juan Michael ECHECOPAR Di Santo (60' Felipe RIBAUDO), Eduardo Raúl FLORES, Marcos Norberto CONIGLIARO, Juan Ramón VERÓN. (Coach: Osvaldo Juan ZUBELDÍA).
Goals: AC Milan: 1-0 Angelo SORMANI (8'), 2-0 Néstor COMBIN (44'), 3-0 Angelo SORMANI (73').
Referee: Roger MACHIN (FRA)   Attendance: 60,675

22-10-1969   La Bombonera, Buenos Aires:
              CA Estudiantes de La Plata - AC Milan   2-1 (2-1)
CA Estudiantes de La Plata: Alberto José POLETTI, Eduardo Luján MANERA, Ramón Alberto AGUIRRE Suárez, Raúl Horacio MADERO, Oscar Miguel MALBERNAT Candela, Carlos Salvador BILARDO (55' Juan Michael ECHECOPAR Di Santo), Daniel ROMEO, Néstor Rubén TOGNERI, Marcos Norberto CONIGLIARO, Juan Alberto TAVERNA, Juan Ramón VERÓN. (Coach: Osvaldo Juan ZUBELDÍA).
AC Milan: Fabio CUDICINI, Saul MALATRASI (53' Luigi MALDERA), Angelo ANQUILLETTI, Romano FOGLI, Roberto ROSATO, Karl-Heinz SCHNELLINGER (FRG), Giavanni LODETTI, Gianni RIVERA, Angelo SORMANI, Néstor COMBIN (FRA), Pierino PRATI (31' Giorgio ROGNONI). (Coach: Nereo ROCCO).
Goals: CA Estudiantes de La Plata: 1-1 Marcos Norberto CONIGLIARO (43'), 2-1 Ramón Alberto AGUIRRE Suárez (44').
AC Milan: 0-1 Gianni RIVERA (30').
Referee: Domingo MASSARO (CHI)   Attendance: 45,000

*** AC Milan won the Cup ***

1970 Intercontinental Cup

The 1970 Intercontinental Cup was played between the winners of the 1969-70 European Cup, SC Feyenoord Rotterdam, and CA Estudiantes de La Plata, winners of the 1970 Copa Libertadores.

The first leg was held in Buenos Aires and ended in a 2-2 draw. The return leg was held in Rotterdam, which Feyenoord won 1-0.

This was the first Intercontinental Cup title for Feyenoord in their first appearance in the competition. It was the third consecutive final for Estudiantes de La Plata, having won in 1968 and lost in 1969.

26-08-1970   La Bombonera, Buenos Aires:
CA Estudiantes de La Plata - SC Feyenoord Rotterdam   2-2 (2-1)
CA Estudiantes de La Plata: Néstor Martín ERREA, Rubén Oscar PAGNANINI, Néstor Rubén TOGNERI, Oscar Miguel MALBERNAT Candela, Hugo SPADARO, Carlos Salvador BILARDO (84' Jorge Raúl SOLARI), Carlos Oscar PACHAMÉ, Juan Michael ECHECOPAR Di Santo (84' Christian RUDZKY), Marcos Norberto CONIGLIARO, Eduardo Raúl FLORES, Juan Ramón VERÓN. (Coach: Osvaldo Juan ZUBELDÍA).
SC Feyenoord Rotterdam: Eddy TREYTEL, Piet ROMEIJN, Theo VAN DUIVENBODE, Franz HASIL (AUT), Rinus ISRAËL, Theo LASEROMS, Wim JANSEN, Henk WERY, Ove KINDVALL (SWE), Willem VAN HANEGEM (73' Johan BOSKAMP), Coen MOULIJN. (Coach: Ernst HAPPEL (AUT)).
Goals: CA Estudiantes de La Plata: 1-0 Juan Michael ECHECOPAR Di Santo (6'), 2-0 Juan Ramón VERÓN (12').
SC Feyenoord: 2-1 Ove KINDVALL (21'), 2-2 Willem VAN HANEGEM (67').
Referee: Rudolf (Rudi) GLÖCKNER (GDR)   Attendance: 50,500

09-09-1970   De Kuip, Rotterdam:
SC Feyenoord Rotterdam - CA Estudiantes de La Plata   1-0 (0-0)
SC Feyenoord Rotterdam: Eddy TREYTEL, Piet ROMEIJN, Theo VAN DUIVENBODE, Franz HASIL (AUT) (46' Johan BOSKAMP), Rinus ISRAËL, Theo LASEROMS, Wim JANSEN, Henk WERY, Ove KINDVALL (SWE), Willem VAN HANEGEM, Coen MOULIJN (61' Joop VAN DAELE). (Coach: Ernst HAPPEL (AUT)).
CA Estudiantes de La Plata: Oscar PEZZANO, Hugo SPADARO, Néstor Rubén TOGNERI, Oscar Miguel MALBERNAT Candela, José Hugo MEDINA, Carlos Salvador BILARDO, Carlos Oscar PACHAMÉ, Eduardo Raúl FLORES, Héctor Daniel ROMEO (61' Rubén Oscar PAGNANINI), Marcos Norberto CONIGLIARO (51' Christian RUDZKY), Juan Ramón VERÓN. (Coach: Osvaldo Juan ZUBELDÍA).
Goal: SC Feyenoord: 1-0 Joop VAN DAELE (63').
Referee: Alberto TEJADA Burga (PER)   Attendance: 63,475

*** SC Feyenoord Rotterdam won the Cup ***

1971 Intercontinental Cup

The 1971 Intercontinental Cup was played between the runners-up of the 1970-71 European Cup, Panathinaikos AO Athina (replacing European Cup winners AFC Ajax who declined to participate), and Club Nacional Montevideo, winners of the 1971 Copa Libertadores.

The first leg was held at Karaiskakis Stadium, home of Olympiacos FC Piraeus, as the home ground of Panathinaikos was deemed to be unsuitable, and the match finished as a 1-1 draw. During the game, Julio César Araújo Morales broke the leg of Yannis Tomaras in a bad challenge and was sent off. The return match was held 13 days later and Montevideo beat Panathiakos 2-1 to win their first Intercontinental Cup trophy 3-2 on aggregate. Argentine striker Luis Artime proved to be the key player, scoring all three goals of Montevideo's goals over the two games.

15-12-1971   Karaiskakis Stadium, Piraeus:
              Panathinaikos AO Athina - Club Nacional Montevideo   1-1 (0-0)
Panathinaikos AO Athina: Takis IKONOMOPOULOS, Yannis TOMARAS (62' Giorgos VLACHOS), Anthimos KAPSIS, Frangiskos SOURPIS, Kostas ATHANASSOPOULOS, Kostas ELEFTHERAKIS, Totis FILAKOURIS, Mitsos DIMITRIOU, Sakis KOUVAS, Antonis ANTONIADIS, Mimis DOMAZOS. (Coach: Ferenc PUSKÁS (HUN)).
Club Nacional Montevideo: Haílton Corrêa de Arruda "MANGA" (BRA), Juan Carlos MASNIK Hornos, Ángel Oscar BRUNELL Sosa, Ildo Enrique MANEIRO Ghezzi, Julio Walter MONTERO Castillo, Juan Carlos BLANCO Estradé, Luis Ignacio UBIÑA Olivera, Víctor Rodolfo ESPÁRRAGO Videla (80' Juan José DUARTE), Luis Alberto CUBILLA Almeida, Luis ARTIME (ARG), Julio César Araújo MORALES. (Coach: Washington ETCHAMENDI Sosa).
Goals: Panathinaikos AO: 1-0 Totis FILAKOURIS (48').
Club Nacional Montevideo: 1-1 Luis ARTIME (50').
Referee: José Favilli NETO (BRA)   Attendance: 35,000
Sent-off: 61' Julio César Araújo MORALES.

28-12-1971   Estadio Centenario, Montevideo:
              Club Nacional Montevideo - Panathinaikos AO Athina   2-1 (1-0)
Club Nacional Montevideo: Haílton Corrêa de Arruda "MANGA" (BRA), Luis Ignacio UBIÑA Olivera, Ángel Oscar BRUNELL Sosa, Juan Carlos MASNIK Hornos, Juan Carlos BLANCO, Julio Walter MONTERO Castillo, Ildo Enrique MANEIRO, Víctor Rodolfo ESPÁRRAGO Videla, Luis Alberto CUBILLA Almeida (..' Juan Martín MUJICA Ferreira), Luis ARTIME (ARG), Juan Carlos MAMELLI (ARG) (..' Ruben Laudelino BAREÑO Silva). (Coach: Washington ETCHAMENDI Sosa).
Panathinaikos AO Athina: Takis IKONOMOPOULOS, Victor MITROPOULOS, Anthimos KAPSIS, Frangiskos SOURPIS, Kostas ATHANASSOPOULOS, Aristidis KAMARAS (..' Totis FILAKOURIS), Mimis DOMAZOS, Kostas ELEFTHERAKIS, Mitsos DIMITRIOU, Antonis ANTONIADIS, Sakis KOUVAS. (Coach: Ferenc PUSKÁS (HUN)).
Goals: Club Nacional Montevideo: 1-0 Luis ARTIME (34'), 2-0 Luis ARTIME (74').
Panathinaikos AO: 2-1 Totis FILAKOURIS (89').
Referee: William Joseph MULLAN (SCO)   Attendance: 63,000

*** Club Nacional Montevideo won the Cup ***

1972 Intercontinental Cup

The 1972 Intercontinental Cup was played between the winners of the 1971-72 European Cup, AFC Ajax Amsterdam, and CA Independiente Avellaneda, winners of the 1972 Copa Libertadores.

The first leg was held in Avellaneda and ended in a 1-1 draw, with Johan Cruijff scoring for the Dutch team. Three weeks later in the return leg in Amsterdam, the hugely talented Ajax team proved much too strong for their Argentine opponents and won 3-0 to earn their first Intercontinental Cup trophy.

06-09-1972   Independiente Stadium, Avellaneda:
           CA Independiente Avellaneda - AFC Ajax Amsterdam   1-1 (0-1)
CA Independiente Avellaneda: Miguel Ángel SANTORO, Eduardo Antonio COMMISSO, Miguel Ángel LÓPEZ, Francisco Pedro Manuel SÁ, Ricardo Elvio PAVONI Cúneo (URU), José Omar PASTORIZA, Alejandro Estanislao SEMENEWICZ, Miguel Ángel RAIMONDO (70' Carlos Alberto BULLA), Agustín Alberto BALBUENA, Eduardo Andrés MAGLIONI, Dante MIRCOLI. (Coach: Pedro Rodolfo DELLACHA).
AFC Ajax Amsterdam: Heinz STUY, Horst BLANKENBURG (FRG), Wim SUURBIER, Barry HULSHOFF, Ruud KROL, Arie HAAN, Johan NEESKENS, Gerrie MÜHREN, Sjaak SWART, Johan CRUIJFF (30' Arnold MÜHREN), Piet KEIZER. (Coach: Stefan KOVÁCS (ROM)).
Goals: CA Independiente Avellaneda: 1-1 Francisco Pedro Manuel SÁ (82').
AFC Ajax: 0-1 Johan CRUIJFF (7').
Referee: Tofiq BAKHRAMOV (URS)   Attendance: 45,000

28-09-1972   Olympisch Stadion, Amsterdam:
           AFC Ajax Amsterdam - CA Independiente Avellaneda   3-0 (1-0)
AFC Ajax Amsterdam: Heinz STUY, Horst BLANKENBURG (FRG), Wim SUURBIER, Barry HULSHOFF, Ruud KROL, Arie HAAN, Johan NEESKENS, Gerrie MÜHREN, Sjaak SWART (61' Johnny REP), Johan CRUIJFF, Piet KEIZER. (Coach: Stefan KOVÁCS (ROM)).
CA Independiente Avellaneda: Miguel Ángel SANTORO, Eduardo Antonio COMMISSO, Miguel Ángel LÓPEZ, Francisco Pedro Manuel SÁ, Ricardo Elvio PAVONI Cúneo (URU), José Omar PASTORIZA, Alejandro Estanislao SEMENEWICZ, Luis GARISTO Pan (URU) (73' Manuel Rosendo MAGÁN Romero), Agustín Alberto BALBUENA, Eduardo Andrés MAGLIONI, Dante MIRCOLI (64' Carlos Alberto BULLA). (Coach: Pedro Rodolfo DELLACHA).
Goals: AFC Ajax: 1-0 Johan NEESKENS (12'), 2-0 Johnny REP (65'), 3-0 Johnny REP (78').
Referee: José ROMEI Cañete (PAR)   Attendance: 46,511

*** AFC Ajax won the Cup ***

1973 Intercontinental Cup

The 1973 Intercontinental Cup was played in Rome on 28th November 1973 between FC Juventus Torino, runners-up of the 1972-73 European Cup, and CA Independiente Avellaneda, winners of the 1973 Copa Libertadores. The match was Juventus' first appearance into the competition and Independiente's fourth appearance. Despite initially refusing to participate in the competition, FC Juventus replaced AFC Ajax as UEFA's representative team after European Champions, Ajax, declined the opportunity to play as they didn't want contest a possible meeting in South America – officially for financial reasons!

In the event, a single match was played instead of a two-legged final as held in previous years because Juventus simply refused to travel to Buenos Aires. The club's condition for playing in the competition was that it must be a single match played in Rome and the Independiente executives grudgingly accepted these terms. The match ended in a 1-0 win for Independiente, marking the club's first Intercontinental Cup and the third to be won by an Argentine club.

28-11-1973   Stadio Olimpico, Roma:
              FC Juventus Torino - CA Independiente Avellaneda 0-1 (0-0)
FC Juventus Torino: Dino ZOFF, Luciano SPINOSI (74' Silvio LONGOBUCCO), Sandro SALVADORE, Francesco MORINI, Gianpietro MARCHETTI, Franco CAUSIO, Antonello CUCCUREDDU, Claudio GENTILE, José João ALTAFINI (BRA), Pietro ANASTASI, Roberto BETTEGA (74' Fernando VIOLA). (Coach: Cestmír VYCPÁLEK (TCH)).
CA Independiente Avellaneda: Miguel Ángel SANTORO, Eduardo Antonio COMMISSO, Miguel Ángel LÓPEZ, Francisco Pedro Manuel SÁ, Ricardo Elvio PAVONI Cúneo (URU) (YC), Miguel Ángel RAIMONDO, Rubén GALVÁN, Ricardo Enrique BOCHINI, Agustín Alberto BALBUENA, Eduardo Andrés MAGLIONI, Ricardo Daniel BERTONI (83' Alejandro Estanislao SEMENEWICZ). (Coach: Roberto Oscar FERREIRO).
Goal: CA Independiente Avellaneda: 0-1 Ricardo Enrique BOCHINI (79').
Referee: Alfred (Fred) DELCOURT (BEL)   Attendance: 22,489

*** CA Independiente Avellaneda won the Cup ***

1974 Intercontinental Cup

The 1974 Intercontinental Cup was played between the runners-up of the 1973-74 European Cup, Club Atlético de Madrid and CA Independiente Avellaneda, winners of the 1974 Copa Libertadores. The winners of the European Cup, FC Bayern München, declined to participate in the competition.

The first leg was held in Buenos Aires and finished up as a 1-0 victory for Independiente. The second leg was held in Madrid four weeks later and game finished 2-0 to Atlético so the Spaniards won the tie 2-1 on aggregate. In doing so, Atlético became the only team to win the Intercontinental Cup without ever winning their own continental championship.

12-03-1975   Estadio Libertadores de América, Buenos Aires:
             CA Independiente Avellaneda – Club Atlético de Madrid   1-0 (1-0)
CA Independiente Avellaneda: José Alberto PÉREZ, Eduardo Antonio COMMISSO, Francisco Pedro Manuel SÁ, Ricardo Elvio PAVONI Cúneo (URU), Miguel Ángel LÓPEZ, Aldo Fernando RODRÍGUEZ (57' Alejandro Estanislao SEMENEWICZ), Rubén GALVÁN, Ricardo Enrique BOCHINI, Agustín Alberto BALBUENA, Percy ROJAS Montero (PER), Ricardo Daniel BERTONI (83' Luis Alberto GIRIBET). (Coach: Roberto Oscar FERREIRO).
Club Atlético de Madrid: Miguel REINA Santos, Francisco Delgado MELO, Ramón Armando HEREDIA Ruarte (ARG), José Luis CAPÓN González, Domingo BENEGAS Jiménez (PAR), ADELARDO Rodríguez Sánchez, EUSEBIO Bejarano Vilaro, Javier "IRURETA" Iruretagoyena Amaino, ALBERTO Fernández Fernández (46' Heraldo BEZERRA Nuñez), José Eulogio GÁRATE Ormaechea, Rubén Hugo AYALA Sanabria (ARG). (Coach: Luis ARAGONÉS Suárez).
Goal: CA Independiente Avellaneda: 1-0 Agustín Alberto BALBUENA (34').
Referee: Charles George Reinier KORVER (HOL) Attendance: 60,000

10-04-1975   Estadio Vicente Calderón, Madrid:
             Club Atlético de Madrid - CA Independiente Avellaneda   2-0 (1-0)
Club Atlético de Madrid: José Luis PACHECO Gómez, Francisco Delgado MELO, Ramón Armando HEREDIA Ruarte (ARG), EUSEBIO Bejarano Vilaro, José Luis CAPÓN González, ADELARDO Rodríguez Sánchez, Javier "IRURETA" Iruretagoyena Amaino, ALBERTO Fernández Fernández (27' Ignacio María SALCEDO Sánchez), Francisco AGUILAR Fernández, José Eulogio GÁRATE Ormaechea, Rubén Hugo AYALA Sanabria (ARG). (Coach: Luis ARAGONÉS Suárez).
CA Independiente Avellaneda: José Alberto PÉREZ, Eduardo Antonio COMMISSO, Miguel Ángel LÓPEZ, Osvaldo Miguel CARRICA, Ricardo Elvio PAVONI Cúneo (URU), Hugo José SAGGIORATO, Rubén GALVÁN, Ricardo Enrique BOCHINI, Agustín Alberto BALBUENA, Percy ROJAS Montero (PER) (62' Aldo Fernando RODRÍGUEZ), Ricardo Daniel BERTONI. (Coach: Roberto Oscar FERREIRO).
Goals: Atlético de Madrid: 1-0 Javier "IRURETA" Iruretagoyena Amaino (34'), 2-0 Rubén Hugo AYALA Sanabria (86').
Referee: Carlos ROBLES (CHI)   Attendance: 65,000

*** Club Atlético de Madrid won the Cup ***

1975 Intercontinental Cup

No competition was played this year as winners of the 1974-75 European Cup, FC Bayern München, and CA Independiente Avellaneda, winners of the 1975 Copa Libertadores could not agree when it should be played.

1976 Intercontinental Cup

The 1976 Intercontinental Cup was played between the winners of the 1975-76 European Cup, FC Bayern München, and Cruzeiro EC Belo Horizonte, winners of the 1976 Copa Libertadores.

The first leg was held in München and finished with a 2-0 win for Bayern, in a game during which the snow-covered pitch would have presented a special challenge for the Brazilian team! The return leg was held in rather different conditions in Belo Horizonte and finished as a goalless draw.

This was the first Intercontinental Cup win for Bayern München.

23-11-1976   Olympiastadion, München:
           FC Bayern München – Cruzeiro EC Belo Horizonte   2-0 (0-0)
FC Bayern München: Sepp MAIER, Björn ANDERSSON (SWE), Franz BECKENBAUER, Hans-Georg SCHWARZENBECK, Udo HORSMANN, Bernd DÜRNBERGER, Conny TORSTENSSON (SWE), Jupp KAPELLMANN, Uli HOENEß, Gerd MÜLLER, Karl-Heinz RUMMENIGGE. (Coach: Dettmar CRAMER).
Cruzeiro EC: RAUL Guiherme Plassmann, Manoel Rezende de Mattos Cabral "NELINHO", José Francisco de MORAIS, OSIRIS de Paiva, VANDERLEI Lázaro, ZE CARLOS, Wilson da Silva PIAZZA, Jair Ventura Filho "JAIRZINHO", EDUARDO Fernandes Amorim, Vanderlei Eustáquio de Oliveira "PALHINHA", João Soares Almeida Filho "JOÁOZINHO" (80' DIRCEU LOPES Mendes). (Coach: Alfredo "ZEZÉ" MOREIRA Júnior).
Goals: FC Bayern München: 1-0 Gerd MÜLLER (80'), 2-0 Jupp KAPELLMANN (82').
Referee: Luis PESTARINO (ARG)   Attendance: 22.000

21-12-1976   Mineirão, Belo Horizonte: Cruzeiro EC - FC Bayern München   0-0
Cruzeiro EC Belo Horizonte: RAUL Guiherme Plassmann, José Francisco de MORAIS, OSIRIS de Paiva, Wilson da Silva PIAZZA (30' EDUARDO Fernandes Amorim), Manoel Rezende de Mattos Cabral "NELINHO", VANDERLEI Lázaro, DIRCEU LOPES Mendes (46' Pablo Justo FORLÁN Lamarque (URU)), José "ZÉ" CARLOS Bernardo, Jair Ventura Filho "JAIRZINHO", Vanderlei Eustáquio de Oliveira "PALHINHA", João Soares Almeida Filho "JOÁOZINHO". (Coach: Alfredo "ZEZÉ" MOREIRA Júnior).
FC Bayern München: Sepp MAIER, Björn ANDERSSON (SWE), Franz BECKENBAUER, Hans-Georg SCHWARZENBECK, Udo HORSMANN, Sepp WEIß, Conny TORSTENSSON (SWE), Jupp KAPELLMANN, Uli HOENEß, Gerd MÜLLER, Karl-Heinz RUMMENIGGE (85' Fred ARBINGER). (Coach: Dettmar CRAMER).
Referee: Patrick (Pat) PARTRIDGE (ENG)   Attendance: 123,715

*** FC Bayern München won the Cup ***

1977 Intercontinental Cup

The 1977 Intercontinental Cup was played between the runners-up of the 1976-77 European Cup, Borussia Mönchengladbach, and CA Boca Juniors Buenos Aires, winners of the 1977 Copa Libertadores. Liverpool FC, the reigning European Champions declined to participate in the competition.

Due to problems with scheduling the games, the 1977 Intercontinental Cup was not played until 1978, with the second leg eventually played more than four months after the first game in Buenos Aires. The first leg in Buenos Aires ended in a 2-2 draw but Boca Juniors won the second leg in Karlsruhe with a 3-0 scoreline to win the tie 5-2 on aggregate.

This was the first Intercontinental Cup win for CA Boca Juniors Buenos Aires.

21-03-1978   La Bombonera, Buenos Aires:
         CA Boca Juniors Buenos Aires - Borussia Mönchengladbach 2-2 (1-2)
CA Boca Juniors Buenos Aires: Osvaldo Norberto SANTOS González, Vicente Alberto PERNÍA, Francisco Pedro Manuel SÁ, Roberto MOUZO, Miguel Ángel BORDÓN, Jorge José BENÍTEZ (46' Jorge Daniel RIBOLZI), Rubén José SUÑÉ, Maria Nicasio ZANABRIA, Ernesto Enrique MASTRÁNGELO, Daniel Severino PAVÓN (64' Carlos Alberto ÁLVAREZ), Carlos Horacio SALINAS. (Coach: Juan Carlos LORENZO).
Borussia Mönchengladbach: Wolfgang KLEFF, Berti VOGTS, Horst WOHLERS, Wilfried HANNES, Winfried SCHÄFER, Herbert WIMMER (56' Dietmar DANNER), Rainer BONHOF, Carsten NIELSEN (DEN), Karl DEL' HAYE, Christian KULIK, Ewald LIENEN. (Coach: Udo LATTEK).
Goals: CA Boca Juniors Buenos Aires: 1-0 Ernesto Enrique MASTRÁNGELO (16'), 2-2 Jorge Daniel RIBOLZI (51').
Borussia Mönchengladbach: 1-1 Wilfried HANNES (24'), 1-2 Rainer BONHOF (29').
Referee: Nikola Milanov DOUDINE (BUL)   Attendance: 60.000

01-08-1978   Wildparkstadion, Karlsruhe:
         Borussia Mönchengladbach - CA Boca Juniors Buenos Aires   0-3 (0-3)
Borussia Mönchengladbach: Wolfgang KNEIB, Norbert RINGELS, Horst WOHLERS (46' Winfried SCHÄFER), Wilfried HANNES, Berti VOGTS, Hans-Günter BRUNS, Carsten NIELSEN, Christian KULIK, Allan SIMONSEN (DEN), Helmut LAUSEN (72' Ewald LIENEN), Rudi GORES. (Coach: Udo LATTEK).
CA Boca Juniors Buenos Aires: Hugo Orlando GATTI, Vicente Alberto PERNÍA, José Luis TESARE, Rubén José SUÑÉ, José María SUÁREZ, Miguel Ángel BORDÓN, Maria Nicasio ZANABRIA, Carlos Horacio SALINAS, Ernesto Enrique MASTRÁNGELO, José Luis SALDAÑO (46' Carlos José VEGLIO), Darío Luis FELMAN. (Coach: Juan Carlos LORENZO).
Goals: CA Boca Juniors Buenos Aires: 0-1 Darío Luis FELMAN (2'), 0-2 Ernesto Enrique MASTRÁNGELO (33'), 0-3 Carlos Horacio SALINAS (37').
Referee: Roque Tito CERULLO (URU)   Attendance: 38.000

*** CA Boca Juniors Buenos Aires won the Cup ***

1978 Intercontinental Cup

No competition was played this year as both winners and runners-up of the 1974-75 European Cup (Liverpool FC and Club Brugge KV respectively) refused to play against the Copa Libertadores winners, CA Boca Juniors Buenos Aires.

1979 Intercontinental Cup

The 1979 Intercontinental Cup was played between Club Olimpia Asunción, winners of the 1979 Copa Libertadores, and Malmö FF, runners-up of the 1978-79 European Cup. Nottingham Forest FC, the European Champions, declined to participate in the competition.

The first leg was held in Malmö and ended in a 1-0 win for Olimpia. The second leg was played more than three months later in Asunción and the home team won 2-1 to lift the trophy 3-1 on aggregate. Club Olimpia Asunción were the first Paraguayan team to win the Intercontinental Cup.

18-11-1979   Malmö Stadion, Malmö:
                Malmö FF – Club Olimpia Asunción   0-1 (0-1)
Malmö FF: Jan MÖLLER, Roland ANDERSSON, Kent JÖNSSON, Ingemar ERLANDSSON, Robert PRYTZ, Tommy HANSSON, Anders LJUNGBERG, Claes MALMBERG (46' Tommy ANDERSSON), Mats ARVIDSSON, Thomas SJÖBERG, Jan-Olov KINNVALL. (Coach: Bob HOUGHTON (ENG)).
Club Olimpia Asunción: Ever Hugo ALMEIDA Almada, Rubén Roberto PAREDES Vera, Miguel Ángel PIAZZA Rivera (URU), Flaminio SOSA Ovelar, Alicio Ignacio SOLALINDE Miers, Carlos Alberto KIESE Wiesner, Rogelio Wilfrido DELGADO Casco, Ernesto Luis TORRES Torreani, Eduardo ORTIZ Sanabria (46' Osvaldo AQUINO), Mauro CÉSPEDES, Evaristo ISASI Colmán. (Coach: Luis Alberto CUBILLA Almeida (URU)).
Goal: Club Olimpia Asunción: 0-1 Evaristo ISASI Colmán (41').
Referee: Patrick (Pat) PARTRIDGE (ENG)   Attendance: 4.811

02-03-1980   Estadio Defensores del Chaco, Asuncion:
                Club Olimpia Asunción - Malmö FF   2-1 (1-0)
Club Olimpia Asunción: Ever Hugo ALMEIDA Almada, Alicio Ignacio SOLALINDE Miers, Rubén Roberto PAREDES Vera, Flaminio SOSA Ovelar, Daniel DI BARTOLOMEO (ARG), Ernesto Luis TORRES Torreani, Carlos Alberto KIESE Wiesner, Hugo Ricardo TALAVERA Valdez (50' Miguel Maria MICHELAGIOLI Ayala), Evaristo ISASI Colmán, Carlos Alfredo YALUK (46' Rogelio DELGADO), Osvaldo AQUINO. (Coach: Luis Alberto CUBILLA Almeida (URU)).
Malmö FF: Jan MÖLLER, Roland ANDERSSON, Tim PARKIN (ENG), Kent JÖNSSON, Mats ARVIDSSON, Magnus ANDERSSON, Anders OHLSSON (65' Tommy HANSSON), Robert PRYTZ, Ingemar ERLANDSSON, Thomas SJÖBERG (65' Claes MALMBERG), Tommy ANDERSSON. (Coach: Bob HOUGHTON (ENG)).
Goals: Club Olimpia Asunción: 1-0 Alicio Ignacio SOLALINDE Miers (39' penalty), 2-1 Miguel Maria MICHELAGIOLI Ayala (71').
Malmö FF: 1-1 Ingemar ERLANDSSON (46').
Referee: Juan Daniel CARDELLINO de San Vicente (URU)
Attendance: 47,000

*** Club Olimpia Asunción won the Cup ***

1980 Intercontinental Cup

Toyota became the major sponsor of the Intercontinental Cup in 1980 and the format was changed so both teams travelled played a single-game final in Japan each year.

The 1980 Intercontinental Cup (officially, the '1980 Toyota European / South American Cup') was played between Club Nacional Montevideo, winners of the 1980 Copa Libertadores, and Nottingham Forest FC, winners of the 1979-80 European Cup.

The match ended in a 1-0 win for Club Nacional Montevideo, the second time the Uruguayan team had won trophy. Their first win was in 1971.

15-02-1981 National Stadium, Tokyo (JPN):
Club Nacional Montevideo - Nottingham Forest FC   1-0 (1-0)
Club Nacional Montevideo: Rodolfo Sergio RODRÍGUEZ Rodríguez, José Hermes MOREIRA, Washington GONZÁLEZ, Víctor Rodolfo ESPÁRRAGO Videla, Daniel ENRÍQUEZ, Juan Carlos BLANCO Peñalba, Alberto Viller BICA Alonso, Roberto Arsenio LUZARDO Correa, Waldemar VICTORINO, Denís Alfredo MILAR Otero, Julio César Araújo MORALES. (Coach: Juan Martín MUJICA Ferreira).
Nottingham Forest FC: Peter SHILTON, Viv ANDERSON, Frank GRAY (SCO), Stuart GRAY, Larry LLOYD, Kenny BURNS (SCO), Martin O'NEILL (NIR), Raimondo PONTE (SUI) (67' Peter WARD), Trevor FRANCIS, Ian WALLACE (SCO), John ROBERTSON (SCO). (Coach: Brian CLOUGH).
Goal: Club Nacional Montevideo: 1-0 Waldemar VICTORINO (10').
Referee: Avraham KLEIN (ISR)   Attendance: 62,000

*** Club Nacional Montevideo won the Cup ***

1981 Intercontinental Cup

The 1981 Intercontinental Cup (officially, the '1981 Toyota European / South American Cup') was played between Liverpool FC, winners of the 1980-81 European Cup, and CR Flamengo Rio de Janeiro, winners of the 1981 Copa Libertadores. It was the first time that Flamengo had qualified to play in the Intercontinental Cup and it was also the first time that Liverpool had appeared after they had declined to take part in the 1977 and 1978 competitions.

The match finished 3-0 to Flamengo who secured their first victory in the Intercontinental Cup. Interestingly, this was the fourth successive victory by a South American team.

13-12-1981   National Stadium, Tokyo (JPN):
              Liverpool FC - CR Flamengo Rio de Janeiro 0-3 (0-3)
Liverpool FC: Bruce GROBBELAAR (ZIM), Phil NEAL, Alan HANSEN (SCO), Ray KENNEDY, Mark LAWRENSON (IRL), Phil THOMPSON, Craig JOHNSTON, Terry McDERMOTT (51' David JOHNSON), Kenny DALGLISH (SCO), Sammy LEE, Graeme SOUNESS (SCO). (Coach: Bob PAISLEY).
CR Flamengo Rio de Janeiro: RAUL Guilherme Plassmann, José LEANDRO de Souza Ferreira, Leovegildo Lins da Gama JÚNIOR, Jorge Luís ANDRADE da Silva, José Carlos Nepomuceno MOZER, Mário Caetano Filho "MARINHO", Milton Queiroz da Paixão "TITA", ADÍLIO de Oliveira Gonçalves, João Batista NUNES de Oliveira, Arthur Antines Coimbra "ZICO", Antônio Nunes "LICO". (Coach: Paulo César CARPEGIANI).
Goals: CR Flamengo: 0-1 João Batista NUNES de Oliveira (13'), 0-2 ADÍLIO de Oliveira Gonçalves (33'), 0-3 João Batista NUNES de Oliveira (41').
Referee: Mario Lamberto Rubio VÁZQUEZ (MEX)   Attendance: 62,000

*** CR Flamengo Rio de Janeiro won the Cup ***

1982 Intercontinental Cup

The 1982 Intercontinental Cup (officially, the '1982 Toyota European / South American Cup') was played in Tokyo between Aston Villa FC, winners of the 1981-82 European Cup, and CA Peñarol Montevideo, winners of the 1982 Copa Libertadores. It was Aston Villa's first appearance into the competition, whereas it was Peñarol's fourth appearance following victories in 1961 and 1966 and a defeat in 1960.

The South American domination of the Intercontinental Cup continued with a fifth successive victory as CA Peñarol Montevideo won 2-0 to secure their third success in the competition.

12-12-1982   National Stadium, Tokyo (JPN):
                CA Peñarol Montevideo - Aston Villa FC   2-0 (1-0)
CA Peñarol Montevideo: Gustavo Daniel FERNÁNDEZ Figuerón, Víctor Hugo DIOGO Silva, Juan Vicente MORALES, Miguel Angel BOSSIO Bastianini, Nelson Daniel GUTIÉRREZ Luongo, Walter Daniel OLIVERO Prada, Venancio Ariel RAMOS Villanueva, Mario Daniel SARALEGUI Iriarte, Fernando MORENA Belora, JAIR Gonçalves Prates (BRA), Walkir SILVA Castellanos. (Coach: Víctor Hugo BAGNULO Fernández).
Aston Villa FC: Jimmy RIMMER, Mark JONES, Garry WILLIAMS, Dennis MORTIMER, Allan EVANS (SCO), Ken McNAUGHT (SCO), Des BREMNER (SCO), Gary SHAW, Peter WITHE, Gordon COWANS, Tony MORLEY. (Coach: Tony BARTON).
Goals: CA Peñarol Montevideo: 1-0 JAIR Gonçalves Prates (27'), 2-0 Walkir SILVA Castellanos (68').
Referee: Jesus Luís Paulino SILES Calderón (CRC)   Attendance: 63,000

*** CA Peñarol Montevideo won the Cup ***

1983 Intercontinental Cup

The 1983 Intercontinental Cup (officially, the '1983 Toyota European / South American Cup') was played in Tokyo between Hamburger SV, winners of the 1982-83 European Cup, and Grêmio Foot-Ball Porto Alegrense, winners of the 1983 Copa Libertadores. The was the first time that either team had played in the competition.

Grêmio Foot-Ball won 2-1 after extra-time to secure their first victory in the Intercontinental Cup – the sixth successive victory by a South American team.

11-12-1983   National Stadium, Tokyo (JPN):
                Hamburger SV - Grêmio Foot-Ball Porto Alegrense   1-2 (0-1, 1-1) **(AET)**
Hamburger SV: Uli STEIN (YC73), Bernd WEHMEYER, Michael SCHRÖDER, Jürgen GROH, Ditmar JAKOBS, Holger HIERONYMUS, Jimmy HARTWIG (YC90+14), Wolfgang ROLFF, Wolfram WUTTKE, Felix MAGATH, Allan HANSEN (DEN). (Coach: Ernst HAPPEL (AUT)). (Not used sub: Uwe HAIN (YC)).
Grêmio Foot-Ball Porto Alegrense: Geraldo Pereira de Matos Filho "MAZARÓPI" (YC75), PAULO ROBERTO Curtis Costa, PAULO CÉSAR MAGALHÃES, Henrique Valmir da Conceição "CHINA", Hugo Eduardo DE LEÓN Rodríguez (URU) (YC90+23), Jorge BAIDEK, RENATO "GAÚCHO" Portaluppi (YC90+13), OSVALDO Luiz Vital (78' Paulo Afonso BONAMIGO), José TARCISO de Souza, Paulo Cézar Lima "CAJU" (70' CAIO Ribeiro Decoussau (YC81)), MÁRIO SÉRGIO Pontes de Paiva. (Coach: VALDIR Ataualpa Ramirez ESPINOSA).
Goals: Hamburger SV: 1-1 Michael SCHRÖDER (86').
Grêmio Football: 0-1 RENATO "GAÚCHO" Portaluppi (38'), 1-2 RENATO "GAÚCHO" Portaluppi (94').
Referee: Michel VAUTROT (FRA)   Attendance: 62,000

*** Grêmio Foot-Ball Porto Alegrense won the Cup ***

1984 Intercontinental Cup

The 1984 Intercontinental Cup (officially, the '1984 Toyota European / South American Cup' for sponsorship reasons) was played in Tokyo between Liverpool FC, winners of the 1983-84 European Cup, and CA Independiente Avellaneda, winners of the 1984 Copa Libertadores.

Independiente were appearing in their sixth Intercontinental Cup, but had only won the competition once in 1973, losing on the other four occasions. Liverpool were making their second appearance in the competition, after their loss in 1981.

The match finished in a 1-0 victory to CA Independiente Avellaneda to secure their second win in the Intercontinental Cup. It was the seventh successive victory by a South American team.

09-12-1984   National Stadium, Tokyo (JPN):
Liverpool FC - CA Independiente Avellaneda   0-1 (0-1)
Liverpool FC: Bruce GROBBELAAR (ZIM), Phil NEAL, Alan HANSEN (SCO), Gary GILLESPIE (SCO), alan KENNEDY, John WARK (SCO) (76' Ronnie WHELAN (IRL)), Craig JOHNSTON, Jan MØLBY (DEN) (YC42), Steve NICOL (SCO), Ian RUSH (WAL), Kenny DALGLISH (SCO). (Coach: Joe FAGAN).
CA Independiente Avellaneda: Carlos Mario GOYÉN Prieto (URU), Néstor Rolando CLAUSEN (YC72), Enzo Héctor TROSSERO, Hugo Eduardo VILLAVERDE (74' Pedro Damián MONZÓN), Carlos Alberto ENRIQUE, Ricardo Omar GIUSTI, Claudio Oscar MARANGONI, Ricardo Enrique BOCHINI, Jorge Luis BURRUCHAGA, José Alberto PERCUDANI, Alejandro Esteban BARBERÓN. (Coach: José Omar PASTORIZA).
Goal: CA Independiente Avellaneda: 0-1 José Alberto PERCUDANI (6').
Referee: Romualdo ARPPI Filho (BRA).   Attendance: 62,000

*** CA Independiente Avellaneda won the Cup ***

1985 Intercontinental Cup

The 1985 Intercontinental Cup (officially, the '1985 Toyota European / South American Cup' for sponsorship reasons) was played in Tokyo between FC Juventus Torino, winners of the 1984-85 European Cup, and AA Argentinos Juniors, winners of the 1985 Copa Libertadores.

This game is regarded by some as the best Intercontinental Cup Final due to the skilful play of both teams. Juventus began the game as firm favourites to win but the performance of Argentinos Juniors surprised everybody and the match finished 2-2 following extra time. Juventus won the subsequent penalty shoot-out 4-2 which meant that the Bianconeri became the first football team to have won all the official continental competitions as well as the world title.

08-12-1985   National Stadium, Tokyo (JPN):
             FC Juventus Torino - AA Argentinos Juniors   2-2 (0-0, 2-2) **(AET)**
FC Juventus Torino: Stefano TACCONI, Luciano FAVERO, Antonio CABRINI, Massimo BONINI (SMR), Sergio BRIO, Gaetano SCIREA (64' Stefano PIOLI), Massimo MAURO (YC) (78' Massimo BRIASCHI), Lionello MANFREDONIA, Aldo SERENA, Michel PLATINI (FRA) (YC), Michael LAUDRUP (DEN). (Coach: Giovanni TRAPATTONI).
AA Argentinos Juniors: Enrique Bernardo VIDALLÉ, José Luis PAVONI, Adrián DOMENECH, Sergio Daniel BATISTA, Carmelo Daniel VILLALBA, Jorge Mario OLGUÍN, José Antonio CASTRO, Mario Hernán VIDELA (YC), Claudio BORGHI (YC), Emilio Nicolás COMMISSO (82' Renato CORSI (YC)), Carlos Adolfo EREROS (117' Juan José LÓPEZ). (Coach: José Antonio YUDICA).
Goals: FC Juventus: 1-1 Michel PLATINI (63' penalty), 2-2 Michael LAUDRUP (82').
AA Argentinos Juniors: 1-0 Carlos Adolfo EREROS (55'), 2-1 José Antonio CASTRO (75').
Referee: Volker ROTH (FRG)   Attendance: 62.000
Penalties: 1 Sergio BRIO   1 Jorge Mario OLGUÍN
             2 Antonio CABRINI   * Sergio Daniel BATISTA
             3 Aldo SERENA   2 Juan José LÓPEZ
             * Michael LAUDRUP   * José Luis PAVONI
             4 Michel PLATINI

*** FC Juventus Torino won the Cup ***

1986 Intercontinental Cup

The 1986 Intercontinental Cup (officially, the '1986 Toyota European / South American Cup' for sponsorship reasons) was played in Tokyo between FC Steaua Bucureşti, winners of the 1985-86 European Cup, and CA River Plate Buenos Aires, winners of the 1986 Copa Libertadores.

River Plate won the game by a single goal in their first appearance in the competition.

14-12-1986   National Stadium, Tokyo (JPN):
                         CA River Plate Buenos Aires – FC Steaua Bucureşti   1-0 (1-0)
CA River Plate Buenos Aires: Nery Alberto PUMPIDO, Jorge Manuel GORDILLO, Oscar Alfredo RUGGERI, Américo Rubén GALLEGO, Alejandro Alfredo MONTENEGRO (YC), Nelson Daniel GUTIÉRREZ Luongo (URU), Antonio ALZAMENDI Casas (URU), Héctor Adolfo ENRIQUE (YC), Juan Gilberto FUNES Baldovino, Norberto Osvaldo ALONSO, Roque Raúl ALFARO (68' Daniel Adolfo SPERANDÍO). (Coach: Héctor Rodolfo VEIRA).
FC Steaua Bucureşti: Dumitru STÂNGACIU, Stefan IOVAN, Ilie BARBULESCU (60' Mihail MAJEARU), Tudorel STOICA, Adrian BUMBESCU (YC), Miodrag BELODEDICI, Marius LACATUS, Lucian BALAN, Victor PITURCA, Gabi BALINT, Anton WEISENBACHER. (Coach: Anghel IORDANESCU).
Goal: CA River Plate Buenos Aires: 1-0 Antonio ALZAMENDI Casas (28').
Referee: José Luis MARTÍNEZ Bazán (URU)   Attendance: 62.000

*** CA River Plate Buenos Aires won the Cup ***

1987 Intercontinental Cup

The 1987 Intercontinental Cup (officially, the '1987 Toyota European / South American Cup' for sponsorship reasons) was played in Tokyo between FC Porto, winners of the 1986-87 European Cup, and CA Peñarol Montevideo, winners of the 1987 Copa Libertadores. Due to heavy falling snow, the pitch became a mud bath and playing conditions were very difficult for both teams.

Peñarol couldn't add to their tally of three victories (1961, 1966 and 1982) as Porto won a tight game 2-1 with the decisive goal scored in extra time in the club's first appearance in the competition.

14-12-1987   National Stadium, Tokyo (JPN):
                 FC Porto – CA Peñarol Montevideo   2-1 (1-0, 1-1) **(AET)**
FC Porto: Józef MLYNARCZYK (POL), JOÃO Domingos da Silva PINTO, Augusto Soares INÁCIO, António dos Santos Ferreira ANDRÉ, António José LIMA PEREIRA, Geraldo Dutra Pereira "GERALDÃO" (BRA), JAIME Fernandes MAGALHÃES, Rabah MADJER (ALG), Fernando Mendes Soares GOMES, António Augusto Gomes de SOUSA, RUI Gil Soares de BARROS (61' Joaquim Carvalho de Azevedo "QUIM"). (Coach: Tomislav IVIC (YUG)).
CA Peñarol Montevideo: Eduardo PEREIRA Martínez, José Oscar HERRERA Corominas (95' Jorge Miguel GONÇÁLVEZ Rojo), Alfonso Enrique DOMINGUEZ Maidana, José Batlle PERDOMO Teixeira, Marcelo Gustavo ROTTI Vanuchi, Obdulio TRASANTE, Daniel Alejandro VIDAL, Eduardo DA SILVA Díaz, Diego Vicente AGUIRRE Camblor, Ricardo Lindolfo VIERA Andrade, Jorge Daniel CABRERA (46' Gustavo Cristian MATOSAS Paidón (ARG)). (Coach: Óscar Washington TABÁREZ Silva).
Goals: FC Porto: 1-0 Fernando Mendes Soares GOMES (42'), 2-1 Rabah MADJER (109').
CA Peñarol Montevideo: 1-1 Ricardo Lindolfo VIERA Andrade (80').
Referee: Franz WÖHRER (AUT)   Attendance: 45,000

*** FC Porto won the Cup ***

1988 Intercontinental Cup

The 1988 Intercontinental Cup (officially, the '1988 Toyota European / South American Cup' for sponsorship reasons) was played in Tokyo between PSV Eindhoven, winners of the 1987-88 European Cup, and Club Nacional Montevideo, winners of the 1988 Copa Libertadores.

Club Nacional Montevideo won 7-6 on penalties after the match had ended 2-2 following extra time and it took no fewer than 20 penalties to decide the result! This was Club Nacional's third appearance in the competition and they kept up their 100% record following previous victories in 1971 and 1981.

01-12-1988   National Stadium, Tokyo (JPN):
            Club Nacional Montevideo - PSV Eindhoven   2-2 (1-0, 1-1) **(AET)**
Club Nacional Montevideo: Jorge Fernando SERÉ Dulcini, Tony César GÓMEZ, Hugo Eduardo DE LÉON Rodríguez, Daniel Felipe REVÉLEZ Pereira (YC), José Luis PINTOS SALDANHA (YC), Yubert LEMOS Morais, Santiago Javier OSTOLAZA Sosa, Jorge Daniel CARDACCIO (113' José Daniel CARREÑO Izquierdo), William CASTRO (YC70), Ernesto VARGAS Rodríguez (71' Héctor Eduardo MORÁN Correa), Juan Carlos DE LIMA del Castillo. (Coach: Roberto FLEITAS).
PSV Eindhoven: Hans VAN BREUKELEN, Eric GERETS (BEL), Adick KOOT, Ronald KOEMAN (YC), Jan HEINTZE (73' Hans GILLHAUS), Søren LERBY (DEN) (YC), Berry VAN AERLE, Gerald VANENBURG (90' Stan VALCKX), ROMÁRIO de Souza Faria (BRA), Wim KIEFT, Juul ELLERMAN (YC). (Coach: Guus HIDDINK).
Goals: Nacional Montevideo: 1-0 Santiago Javier OSTOLAZA Sosa (7'), 2-2 Santiago Javier OSTOLAZA Sosa (119').
P.S.V. Eindhoven: 1-1 ROMÁRIO de Souza Faria (75'), 1-2 Ronald KOEMAN (110' penalty).
Referee: Jesús DIAZ Palacio (COL)   Attendance: 62,000
Penalties:
1 Ronald KOEMAN	1 Yubert LEMOS Morais
* Wim KIEFT	* José Daniel CARREÑO Izquierdo
2 Hans GILLHAUS	* Héctor Eduardo MORÁN Correa
3 ROMÁRIO de Souza Faria	2 William CASTRO
* Søren LERBY	3 Hugo Eduardo DE LÉON Rodríguez
4 Juul ELLERMAN	4 Juan Carlos DE LIMA del Castillo
5 Stan VALCKX	5 Daniel Felipe REVÉLEZ Pereira
* Eric GERETS	* José Luis PINTOS SALDANHA
6 Adick KOOT	6 Santiago Javier OSTOLAZA Sosa
* Berry VAN AERLE	7 Tony César GÓMEZ

*** Club Nacional Montevideo won the Cup ***

1989 Intercontinental Cup

The 1989 Intercontinental Cup (officially, the '1989 Toyota European / South American Cup' for sponsorship reasons) was played in Tokyo between AC Milan, winners of the 1988-89 European Cup, and Atlético Nacional SA Medellín, winners of the 1989 Copa Libertadores.

Milan scored the only goal of the game during extra time to win the trophy for the second time, 20 years after their previous win in 1969.

17-12-1989   National Stadium, Tokyo (JPN):
              AC Milan –Atlético Nacional SA Medellín   1-0 (0-0, 0-0) **(AET)**

AC Milan: Giovanni GALLI, Mauro TASSOTTI, Paolo MALDINI, Diego FUSER (65' Alberigo EVANI), Alessandro COSTACURTA, Franco BARESI, Roberto DONADONI, Frank RIJKAARD (HOL), Marco VAN BASTEN (HOL), Carlo ANCELOTTI, Daniele MASSARO (70' Marco SIMONE). (Coach: Arrigo SACCHI).

Atlético Nacional SA Medellín: José René HIGUITA Zapata, Luis Fernando HERRERA Arango, Gabriel Jaime GÓMEZ Jaramillo, José Ricardo PÉREZ Morales, Geovanis CASSIANI Gómez, Andrés ESCOBAR Saldarriaga, Jaime de Jesús ARANGO Estrada (46' Gustavo Adolfo RESTREPO Vásquez), Leonel de Jesús ÁLVAREZ Zuleta, Niver ARBOLEDA Díaz (46' Albeiro USURIAGA López), Alexis Enrique GARCIA Vega, John Jairo TRÉLLEZ Valencia. (Coach: Francisco Antonio MATURANA García).

Goal: AC Milan: 1-0 Alberigo EVANI (119').

Referee: Erik FREDRIKSSON (SWE)   Attendance: 60,228

*** AC Milan won the Cup ***

1990 Intercontinental Cup

The 1990 Intercontinental Cup (officially, the '1990 Toyota European / South American Cup' for sponsorship reasons) was played in Tokyo between AC Milan, winners of the 1989-90 European Cup, and Club Olimpia Asunción, winners of the 1990 Copa Libertadores.

Milan retained the trophy following a comfortable 3-0 victory to earn their third Intercontinental Cup title.

09-12-1990   National Stadium, Tokyo (JPN):
                AC Milan - Club Olimpia Asuncion   3-0 (1-0)
AC Milan: Andrea PAZZAGLI, Mauro TASSOTTI, Franco BARESI, Alessandro COSTACURTA, Paolo MALDINI (22' Filippo GALLI), Frank RIJKAARD (HOL), Roberto DONADONI (83' Gianluca GAUDENZI), Giovanni STROPPA, Angelo CARBONE, Marco VAN BASTEN (HOL), Ruud GULLIT (HOL). (Coach: Arrigo SACCHI).
Club Olimpia Asuncion: Ever Hugo ALMEIDA Almada, Virginio CÁCERES Villalba, Silvio SUÁREZ, Remigio FERNÁNDEZ, Mario César RAMÍREZ Estigarribia (49' Herib Yamil CHAMAS), Luis Alberto MONZÓN León, Fermín BALBUENA, Adolfo Ramón JARA Heyn (67' Cristóbal CUBILLA Delgadillo), Jorge Catalino GUASCH Bazán, Adriano SAMANIEGO Giménez, RAÚL Vicente AMARILLA Vera (ESP). (Coach: Luis Alberto CUBILLA Almeida (URU)).
Goals: AC Milan: 1-0 Frank RIJKAARD (43'), 2-0 Giovanni STROPPA (61'), 3-0 Frank RIJKAARD (65').
Referee: José Roberto WRIGHT Ramiz (BRA)   Attendance: 60,228

*** AC Milan won the Cup ***

1991 Intercontinental Cup

The 1991 Intercontinental Cup (officially, the '1991 Toyota European / South American Cup' for sponsorship reasons) was played in Tokyo between FC Crvena Zvezda Beograd, winners of the 1990-91 European Cup, and CSD Colo-Colo Santiago, winners of the 1991 Copa Libertadores.

Crvena Zvezda Beograd won the game 3-0 to lift the trophy in their first appearance in the competition.

08-12-1991   National Stadium, Tokyo (JPN):
              FC Crvena Zvezda Beograd – CSD Colo-Colo Santiago   3-0 (1-0)
FC Crvena Zvezda Beograd: Zvonko MILOJEVIC, Dusko RADINOVIC, Goran VASILI-JEVIC (YC49), Miodrag BELODEDICI (ROM), Ilija NAJDOSKI, Vladimir JUGOVIC, Vlada STOSIC, Milorad RATKOVIC, Dejan SAVICEVIC (RC42), Sinisa MIHAJLOVIC (YC46), Darko PANCEV. (Coach: Vladica POPOVIC).
CSD Colo-Colo Santiago: José Daniel MORÓN (ARG), Lizardo Antonio GARRIDO Bustamante, Javier Luciano MARGAS Loyola, Miguel Mauricio RAMÍREZ Pérez (YC42) (61' Hugo Eduardo RUBIO Montecinos), Agustín Alex SALVATIERRA Concha (65' Ricardo Mariano DABROWSKI), Gabriel Rafael MENDOZA Ibarra, Eduardo Enrique VILCHES Arriagada, Marcelo Pablo BARTICCIOTTO Cicaré (ARG), Jaime Augusto PIZZARO Herrera, Patricio Nazario YÁÑEZ Candia, Rubén Ignacio MARTÍNEZ Núñez. (Coach: Mirko JOZIC (YUG)).
Goals: FC Crvena Zvezda Beograd: 1-0 Vladimir JUGOVIC (19'), 2-0 Vladimir JUGOVIC (59'), 3-0 Darko PANCEV (72').
Referee: Kurt RÖTHLISBERGER (SUI)   Attendance: 60,000

*** FC Crvena Zvezda Beograd won the Cup ***

1992 Intercontinental Cup

The 1992 Intercontinental Cup (officially, the '1992 Toyota European / South American Cup' for sponsorship reasons) was played in Tokyo between between FC Barcelona, winners of the 1991-92 European Cup, and São Paulo FC, winners of the 1992 Copa Libertadores.

It was the first appearance for both Barcelona and São Paulo in the competition and the South American team won 2-1, with both goals scored by RAÍ Souza Vieira de Oliveira

13-12-1992 National Stadium, Tokyo (JPN):
FC Barcelona - São Paulo FC   1-2 (1-1)

FC Barcelona: Andoni ZUBIZARRETA Urreta, Albert FERRER Llopis, Ronald KOEMAN (HOL), EUSEBIO Sacristán Mena, José "Mari" María BAKERO Escudero (52' Jon Andoni GOIKOETXEA Lasa (YC89)), Josep "PEP" GUARDIOLA Sala, Guillermo AMOR Martínez, Richard WITSCHGE (HOL), Michael LAUDRUP (DEN), Hristo STOICHKOV (BUL), Aitor "Txiki" BEGIRISTAIN Mujika (YC43) (81' Miguel Ángel NADAL Homar). (Coach: Johan CRUIJFF (HOL)).

São Paulo FC: Armelino Donizetti Quagliato "ZETTI", Claudemir VÍTOR Marques, Ronaldo Rodrigues de Jesus "RONALDÃO" (YC26), RONALDO LUIZ Goncalves, Marcos Evangelista de Morais "CAFU", Luís Carlos de Oliveira Preto "PINTADO", Antônio Carlos "TONINHO" CEREZO (YC58) (82' Edi Wilson Jose Dos Santos "DINHO"), ADILSON José Pinto, Luís Antônio Corrêa da Costa "MÜLLER", RAÍ Souza Vieira de Oliveira, Jorge Ferreira da Silva "PALHINHA". (Coach: TELÊ SANTANA da Silva).

Goals: FC Barcelona: 1-0 Hristo STOICHKOV (12').
São Paulo FC: 1-1 RAÍ Souza Vieira de Oliveira (27'), 1-2 RAÍ Souza Vieira de Oliveira (78').
Referee: Juan Carlos LOUSTAU (ARG)   Attendance: 60,000

*** São Paulo FC won the Cup ***

1993 Intercontinental Cup

The 1993 Intercontinental Cup (officially, the '1993 Toyota European / South American Cup' for sponsorship reasons) was played in Tokyo between AC Milan, runners-up of the 1992-93 UEFA Champions League, and São Paulo FC, winners of the 1993 Copa Libertadores.

Olympique Marseille, winners of inaugural 1992-93 UEFA Champions League, were not allowed to participate in the competition due to a match-fixing scandal involving the club. This saw them stripped of the 1992-93 French Division 1 title and banned from the 1993-94 UEFA Champions League, 1993 European Super Cup and the Intercontinental Cup. Because of these bans, UEFA Champions League runners-up, AC Milan, took the place of Marseille in both the Super Cup and the Intercontinental Cup.

It was AC Milan's fifth appearance in the competition (which they had won in 1969, 1989 and 1990) but São Paulo scored a late goal to win the match 3-2 and retain the Intercontinental Cup.

12-12-1993   National Stadium, Tokyo (JPN): AC Milan - São Paulo FC   2-3 (0-1)
AC Milan: Sebastiano ROSSI, Christian PANUCCI, Alessandro COSTACURTA, Franco BARESI, Paolo MALDINI, Roberto DONADONI, Marcel DESAILLY (FRA), Demetrio ALBERTINI (79' Mauro TASSOTTI), Daniele MASSARO, Florin RADUCIOIU (ROM) (79' Alessandro ORLANDO), Jean-Pierre PAPIN (FRA). (Coach: Fabio CAPELLO).
São Paulo FC: Armelino Donizetti Quagliato "ZETTI", Marcos Evangelista de Moraes "CAFU", VÁLBER Roel de Oliveira, Ronaldo Rodrigues de Jesus "RONALDÃO", ANDRÉ LUIZ Moreira, Antônio Carlos "TONINHO" CEREZO, Dorival Guidoni Júnior "DORIVA", LEONARDO Nascimento de Araujo, Edi Wilson Jose Santos "DINHO", Jorge Reffereia da Silva "PALHINHA" (64' Osvaldo Giroldo Júnior "JUNINHO PAULISTA"), Luís Antônio Corrêa da Costa "MÜLLER".(Coach: TELÊ SANTANA da Silva).
Goals: AC Milan: 1-1 Daniele MASSARO (48'), 2-2 Jean-Pierre PAPIN (82').
São Paulo FC: 0-1 Jorge Ferreira da Silva "PALHINHA" (19'), 1-2 Antonio Carlos "TONINHO" CEREZO (59'), 2-3 Luís Antônio Corrêa da Costa "MÜLLER" (88').
Referee: Joél QUINIOU (FRA)   Attendance: 52,275

*** São Paulo FC Won the Cup ***

1994 Intercontinental Cup

The 1994 Intercontinental Cup (officially, the '1994 Toyota European / South American Cup' for sponsorship reasons) was played in Tokyo between AC Milan, winners of the 1993-94 UEFA Champions League, and CA Vélez Sarsfield Buenos Aires, winners of the 1994 Copa Libertadores.

It was AC Milan's sixth appearance into the competition, but they were again unable to add to their tally of victories and lost the final for a second year running as Vélez Sarsfield won 2-0 to lift the trophy in their first Intercontinental Cup appearance.

01-12-1994   National Stadium, Tokyo (JPN):
                    AC Milan - CA Vélez Sarsfield Buenos Aires   0-2 (0-0)
AC Milan: Sebastiano ROSSI (YC), Mauro TASSOTTI, Franco BARESI, Alessandro COSTACURTA (RC85), Paolo MALDINI, Demetrio ALBERTINI (YC44), Roberto DONADONI, Marcel DESAILLY (FRA), Zvonimir BOBAN (CRO) (55' Marco SIMONE (YC84)), Dejan SAVICEVIC (YC27) (YUG) (86' Christian PANUCCI), Daniele MASSARO. (Coach: Fabio CAPELLO)
CA Vélez Sarsfield Buenos Aires: José Luis Félix CHILAVERT González (PAR), Héctor Alfredo ALMANDOZ (YC2), Roberto TROTTA (YC70), Víctor Hugo SOTOMAYOR, Raúl Ernesto CARDOZO, Marcelo Adrián GOMEZ (YC17), Christia Gustavo BASSEDAS, José Horacio BASUALDO, Roberto Fabián POMPEI, Omar Andrés ASAD (YC79), José Oscar FLORES Bringas. (Coach: Carlos Arsenio BIANCHI).
Goals: CA Vélez Sarsfield: 0-1 Roberto TROTTA (50' penalty), 0-2 Omar Andrés ASAD (57').
Referee: José Joaquín TORRES Cadeña (COL)   Attendance: 47,886

*** CA Vélez Sarsfield Buenos Aires won the Cup ***

1995 Intercontinental Cup

The 1995 Intercontinental Cup (officially, the '1995 Toyota European / South American Cup' for sponsorship reasons) was played in Tokyo between AFC Ajax Amsterdam, winners of the 1994-95 UEFA Champions League, and Grêmio Foot-Ball Porto Alegrense, winners of the 1995 Copa Libertadores.

It was the second Intercontinental Cup appearance for both Ajax and Grêmio (though the Dutch team had declined to appear in 1971 and 1973) and Ajax won 4-3 on penalties following a goalless draw after extra time.

28-11-1995   National Stadion, Tokyo (JPN):
AFC Ajax Amsterdam - Grêmio Foot-Ball Porto Alegrense   0-0 **(AET)**
AFC Ajax Amsterdam: Edwin VAN DER SAR, Michael REIZIGER, Danny BLIND, Frank DE BOER, Winston BOGARDE, Ronald DE BOER, Jari LITMANEN (FIN) (94' Martijn REUSER), Edgar DAVIDS (YC113), Finidi GEORGE (NGR), Patrick KLUIVERT, Marc OVERMARS (68' Nwankwo KANU (YC70) (NGR)). (Coach; Louis VAN GAAL).
Grêmio Foot-Ball Porto Alegrense: DANRLEI de Deus Hinterholz, Francisco Javier ARCE Rolón (YC18) (PAR), Catalino RIVAROLA Méndez (YC53,YC56) (PAR), ADÍLSON Dias Batista, ROGER Machado Marques, Edi Wilson Jose dos Santos "DINHO", Luís Carlos "GOIANO" Vaz da Silva (YC43), ARÍLSON Gilberto da Costa (YC54) (61' LUCIANO Williams Dias), CARLOS MIGUEL da Silva Junior (97' GÉLSON da Silva (YC109)), Arilson da Paula "PAULO" NUNES, Mário JARDEL Almeida Ribeiro (78' MAGNO Morcelin).
(Coach: Luiz Felipe SCOLARI).
Referee: David ELLERAY (ENG)   Attendance: 47,129
Penalties: * Edi Wilson Jose dos Santos "DINHO"   * Patrick KLUIVERT
              * Francisco Javier ARCE Rolón   1 Ronald DE BOER
              1 MAGNO Morcelin   2 Frank DE BOER
              2 GÉLSON da Silva   3 Finidi GEORGE
              3 ADÍLSON Dias Batista   4 Danny BLIND

*** AFC Ajax Amsterdam won the Cup ***

1996 Intercontinental Cup

The 1996 Intercontinental Cup (officially, the '1996 Toyota European / South American Cup' for sponsorship reasons) was played in Tokyo between FC Juventus Torino, winners of the 1995-96 UEFA Champions League, and CA River Plate Buenos Aires, winners of the 1996 Copa Libertadores.

It was Juventus' third appearance into the competition, after the defeat in 1973 and the victory in 1985 against Argentinos Juniors, whereas it was River Plate's second appearance, the first being their victory in 1986 over Steaua Bucuresti.

Alessandro Del Piero scored a late winner so Juventus won the Intercontinental Cup trophy a second time.

26-11-1996   National Stadion, Tokyo (JPN):
                    FC Juventus Torino - CA River Plate Buenos Aires   1-0 (0-0)
FC Juventus Torino: Angelo PERUZZI, Ciro FERRARA, Moreno TORRICELLI (YC82), Rónald Paulo MONTERO Iglesias (URU) (YC51), Sergio PORRINI (YC67), Angelo DI LIVIO, Didier DESCHAMPS (FRA), Vladimir JUGOVIC (YUG) (YC50), Zinedine ZIDANE (FRA) (YC84) (89' Alessio TACCHINARDI), Alen BOKSIC (CRO), Alessandro DEL PIERO. (Coach: Marcello LIPPI).
CA River Plate Buenos Aires: Roberto Oscar BONANO, Hernán Edgardo DÍAZ, Celso Rafael AYALA Gavilán (PAR), Eduardo BERIZZO Magnolo, Juan Pablo SORÍN, Roberto Carlos MONSERRAT, Leonardo Rubén ASTRADA (YC38), Sergio Ángel BERTI (74' Leonel Fernando GANCEDO), Enzo FRANCESCOLI Uriarte (URU), Ariel Arnaldo ORTEGA, Julio Ricardo CRUZ (83' José Marcelo SALAS Meliano (CHI)). (Coach: Ramón Ángel DÍAZ).
Goal: FC Juventus: 1-0 Alessandro DEL PIERO (81').
Referee: Márcio REZENDE de Freitas (BRA)   Attendance: 48,305

*** FC Juventus Torino won the Cup ***

1997 Intercontinental Cup

The 1997 Intercontinental Cup (officially, the '1997 Toyota European / South American Cup' for sponsorship reasons) was played in Tokyo between BV Borussia Dortmund, winners of the 1996-97 UEFA Champions League, and Cruzeiro EC Belo Horizonte, winners of the 1997 Copa Libertadores.

Borussia Dortmund won 2-0 in their debut appearance in the competition as Cruzeiro were once again unable to overcome German opponents following their 1976 defeat against Bayern München.

02-12-1997   National Stadion, Tokyo (JPN):
           BV Borussia Dortmund - Cruzeiro EC Belo Horizonte   2-0 (1-0)
BV Borussia Dortmund: Stefan KLOS, Wolfgang FEIERSINGER (AUT), Stefan REUTER (YC54), JÚLIO CÉSAR da Silva (BRA), Steffen FREUND, PAULO Manuel Carvalho de SOUSA (POR), Michael ZORC (80' Jovan KIROVSKI (USA)), Jörg HEINRICH, Andreas MÖLLER (YC18), Heiko HERRLICH (YC83), Stéphane CHAPUISAT (SUI) (75' Harry DECHEIVER (HOL)). (Coach: Nevio SCALA).
Cruzeiro EC Belo Horizonte: Nélson de Jesus Silva "DIDA", Claudemir VÍTOR Marques (YC15,RC66), Marcelo GONÇALVES Costa Lopes, JOÃO CARLOS dos Santos, Fabio Silva de Azevedo "FABINHO", Ricardo Alexandre dos Santos "RICARDINHO", ELIVÉLTON Alves Rufino, Roberto Carlos PALACIOS Mestas (PER) (64' MARCELO Silva RAMOS), CLEISSON Edson Assuncao, José Roberto Gama de Oliveira "BEBETO", Osmar DONIZETE Cândido. (Coach: Nélson "NELSINHO" Baptista Júnior).
Goals: BV Borussia Dortmund: 1-0 Michael ZORC (34'), 2-0 Heiko HERRLICH (85').
Referee: José María GARCIA-ARANDA Encinar (ESP)   Attendance: 46,953

*** BV Borussia Dortmund won the Cup ***

1998 Intercontinental Cup

The 1998 Intercontinental Cup (officially, the '1998 Toyota European / South American Cup' for sponsorship reasons) was played in Tokyo between Real Madrid CF, winners of the 1997-98 UEFA Champions League, and CR Vasco da Gama Rio de Janeiro, winners of the 1998 Copa Libertadores.

Real Madrid won the game 2-1 to earn their first victory in the competition since 1960.

01-12-1998   National Stadion, Tokyo (JPN):
            Real Madrid CF – CR Vasco da Gama Rio de Janeiro   2-1 (1-0)
Real Madrid CF: Bodo ILLGNER (GER), Christian PANUCCI (ITA), Manuel "MANOLO" SANCHÍS Hontiyuelo, FERNANDO SANZ Durán (YC73), ROBERTO CARLOS da Silva Rocha (BRA) (YC19), Clarence SEEDORF (HOL) (YC44), Fernando Ruiz HIERRO, Fernando Carlos REDONDO Neri (ARG), SÁVIO Bortolini Pimentel (BRA) (89' Davor SUKER (CRO)), Predrag MIJATOVIC (YUG) (86' Robert JARNI (CRO)), RAÚL González Blanco. (Coach: Guus HIDDINK (HOL)).
CR Vasco da Gama Rio de Janeiro: CARLOS GERMANO Schwambach Neto, VÁGNER Rogério Nunes (81' Claudemir VÍTOR Marques), ODVAN Gomes da Silva, MAURO Geraldo GALVÃO, FELIPE Jorge Loureiro, Luís Carlos Quintanilha "LUISINHO" (YC37) (86' GUILHERME de Cássio Alves), Gesiel José de Lima "NASA" (YC28), Antônio Augusto Ribeiro Reis Júnior "JUNINHO PERNAMBUCANO", RAMON Menezes Hubner (87' VÁLBER Roel de Oliveira), Osmar DONIZETE Cândido, Luiz Carlos Bombonato Goulart "LUIZÃO" (YC75). (Coach: ANTÔNIO LOPES dos Santos).
Goals: Real Madrid CF: 1-0 Gesiel José de Lima "NASA" (25' own goal), 2-1 RAÚL González Blanco (83').
CR Vasco da Gama: 1-1 Antônio Augusto Ribeiro Reis Júnior "JUNINHO PERNAMBUCANO" (56').
Referee: Mario Fernando SÁNCHEZ Yanten (CHI)   Attendance: 51,514

*** Real Madrid CF won the Cup ***

1999 Intercontinental Cup

The 1999 Intercontinental Cup (officially, the '1999 Toyota European / South American Cup' for sponsorship reasons) was played in Tokyo between Manchester United FC, winners of the 1998-99 UEFA Champions League, and SE Palmeiras São Paulo, winners of the 1999 Copa Libertadores.

Manchester United won 1-0 to lift the Intercontinental Cup for the first time. Interestingly, this was also the first time that any team from the British Isles had won the competition.

30-11-1999   National Stadion, Tokyo (JPN):
   Manchester United FC - SE Palmeiras São Paulo   1-0 (1-0)
Manchester United FC: Mark BOSNICH (AUS), Gary NEVILLE, Jaap STAM (HOL), Mikaël SILVESTRE (FRA) (YC79), Denis IRWIN (IRL), David BECKHAM, Roy KEANE (IRL), Paul SCHOLES (75' Teddy SHERINGHAM), Nicky BUTT, Ole Gunnar SOLSKJÆR (NOR) (46' Dwight YORKE (TRI)), Ryan GIGGS (WAL). (Coach: Alex FERGUSON (SCO)).
SE Palmeiras São Paulo: MARCOS Roberto Silveira Rios, Francisco Javier ARCE Rolón (PAR), Jenílson Ângelo de Souza "JÚNIOR", Raimundo Ferreira Ramos Junior "JÚNIOR BAIANO", José Vítor ROQUE JÚNIOR, Alexsandro de Souza "ALEX" (YC28), Carlos CÉSAR SAMPAIO Campos, Marcos Aurélio GALEANO (54' EVAIR Aparecido Paulino), Crizam César de Oliveira Filho "ZINHO", Arílson de PAULO NUNES (77' EULLER Elias de Carvalho), Faustino Hernán ASPRILLA Hinestroza (COL) (56' OSÉAS Reis dos Santos). (Coach: Luiz Felipe SCOLARI).
Goal: Manchester United FC: 1-0 Roy KEANE (35').
Referee: Hellmut KRUG (GER)   Attendance: 53,372

*** Manchester United FC won the Cup ***

2000 Intercontinental Cup

The 2000 Intercontinental Cup (officially, the '2000 Toyota European / South American Cup' for sponsorship reasons) was played in Tokyo between Real Madrid CF, winners of the 1999-2000 UEFA Champions League, and CA Boca Juniors Buenos Aires, winners of the 2000 Copa Libertadores.

Boca Juniors won 2-1, their second win in the competition and their first since 1977.

28-11-2000 National Stadium, Tokyo (JPN):
Real Madrid CF – CA Boca Juniors Buenos Aires   1-2 (1-2)
Real Madrid CF: Iker CASILLAS Fernández, GEREMI Sorele Fotso N'jitap (CMR) (YC89), Aitor KARANKA de la Hoz, Fernando Ruíz HIERRO, ROBERTO CARLOS da Silva Rocha (BRA), Claude MAKÉLÉLÉ (FRA) (77' Fernando MORIENTES Sánchez), José María Gutiérrez Hernández "GUTI", Iván HELGUERA Bujía (YC89), Steve McMANAMAN (ENG) (67' SÁVIO Bortolini Pimentel (BRA)), RAÚL González Blanco, Luís Felipe Madeira Caeiro FIGO (POR). (Coach: Vicente DEL BOSQUE González).
CA Boca Juniors Buenos Aires: Óscar Eduardo CÓRDOBA Arce (COL), Hugo Benjamin IBARRA (YC69), Jorge Hernán BERMÚDEZ Morales (COL), Cristián Alberto TRAVERSO, Aníbal Samuel MATELLÁN, José Horacio BASUALDO, Mauricio Alberto SERNA Valencia (COL), Juan Román RIQUELME, Sebastián Alejandro BATTAGLIA (YC89) (90+3' Nicolás Andrés BURDISSO), Marcelo Alejandro DELGADO (88' Guillermo BARROS SCHELOTTO), Martín PALERMO. (Coach: Carlos Arcesio BIANCHI).
Goals: Real Madrid CF: 1-2 ROBERTO CARLOS da Silva (12').
CA Boca Juniors Buenos Aires: 0-1 Martín PALERMO (3'), 0-2 Martín PALERMO (6').
Referee: Óscar Julian RUÍZ Acosta (COL)   Attendance: 52,511

*** CA Boca Juniors Buenos Aires won the Cup ***

2001 Intercontinental Cup

The 2001 Intercontinental Cup (officially, the '2001 Toyota European / South American Cup' for sponsorship reasons) was played in Tokyo between FC Bayern München, winners of the 2000-01 UEFA Champions League, and winners of the 2001 Copa Libertadores, CA Boca Juniors Buenos Aires, who were also defending champions.

Bayern München won a close game by a single goal scored in the second period of extra time. This was the German team's second victory in the competition in their second appearance.

27-11-2001   National Stadium, Tokyo (JPN):
      FC Bayern München – CA Boca Juniors Buenos Aires   1-0 (0-0, 0-0) **(AET)**
FC Bayern München: Oliver KAHN, Willy SAGBOL (FRA), Bixente LIZARAZU (FRA), Samuel Osei KUFFOUR (GHA) (YC29), Robert KOVAC (CRO), Nico KOVAC (CRO) (76' Carsten JANCKER), Thorsten FINK, Owen HARGRAEVES (ENG) (YC72) (76' Ciriaco SFORZA (SUI)), "GIOVANE" ÉLBER de Souza (BRA) (YC106), PAULO SÉRGIO Silvestre do Nascimento (BRA), Claudio PIZARRO (PER) (118' Pablo THIAM (GUI)). (Coach: Ottmar HITZFELD).
CA Boca Juniors Buenos Aires: Óscar Eduardo CÓRDOBA Arce (COL) (YC102), Rolando Carlos SCHIAVI (YC111), Jorge Daniel MARTÍNEZ (18' José María CALVO, 111' Ariel CARREÑO), Nicolás Andrés BURDISSO, Clemente Juan RODRÍGUEZ (YC70), Mauricio Alberto SERNA Valencia (COL) (YC5), Cristian Alberto TRAVERSO, Juan Román RIQUELME, Javier Alejandro VILLARREAL (100' Gustavo Hernán PINTO), Marcelo Alejandro DELGADO (YC19,RC46), Guillermo BARROS SCHELOTTO (YC83). (Coach: Carlos Arcesio BIANCHI).
Goal: FC Bayern München: 1-0 Samuel Osei KUFFOUR (109').
Referee: Kim Milton NIELSEN (DEN)   Attendance: 51,360

*** FC Bayern München won the Cup ***

2002 Intercontinental Cup

The 2002 Intercontinental Cup (officially, the '2002 Toyota European / South American Cup' for sponsorship reasons) was played between Real Madrid CF, winners of the 2001-02 UEFA Champions League, and Club Olimpia Asunción, winners of the 2002 Copa Libertadores. For the first time, the match was played at Yokohama's International Stadium.

This game was a special occasion for Club Olimpia and Real Madrid, as both clubs also celebrated their centenary during 2002.

Real Madrid won the match 2-0 to lift the Intercontinental Cup for the third time.

03-12-2002   International Stadium Yokohama, Yokohama:
Real Madrid CF – Club Olimpia Asunción   2-0 (1-0)
Real Madrid CF: Ilker CASILLAS Fernández, Miguel Ángel "MÍCHEL" SALGADO, Fernando Ruíz HIERRO, Iván HELGUERA Bujía, ROBERTO CARLOS da Silva Rocha (BRA) (YC89), Luís Felipe Madeira Caeiro "FIGO" (POR), Claude MAKÉLÉLÉ (FRA), Esteban Matías CAMBIASSO Deleau (ARG) (90' Francisco PAVÓN Barahona), Zinedine ZIDANE (FRA) (86' Santiago Hernán SOLARI (ARG)), RAÚL González Blanco, RONALDO Luis Nazario de Lima (BRA) (82' José Maria Gutiérrez "GUTI"). (Coach: Vicente DEL BOSQUE González).
Club Olimpia Asunción: Ricardo Javier TAVARELLI Paiva, Néstor Daniel ISASI Guillén, Nelson Fabián ZELAYA Ramírez, Juan Ramón JARA Martínez, Julio César CÁCERES López (YC34), Pedro Juan BENÍTEZ Domínguez, Julio César ENCISO Ferreira, Sergio Daniel ÓRTEMAN Rodríguez (URU), Hernán Rodrigo LÓPEZ Mora (URU), Fernando Gastón CÓRDOBA (ARG) (65' Richart Martín BÁEZ Fernández), Miguel Ángel BENÍTEZ Pavón (81' Mauro Antonio CABALLERO López). (Coach: Nery Alberto PUMPIDO (ARG)).
Goals: Real Madrid CF: 1-0 RONALDO Luis Nazario de Lima (14'), 2-0 José Maria Gutiérrez "GUTI" (84').
Referee: CARLOS Eugênio SIMON (BRA)   Attendance: 66,070

*** Real Madrid CF won the Cup ***

2003 Intercontinental Cup

The 2003 Intercontinental Cup (officially, the '2003 Toyota European / South American Cup' for sponsorship reasons) was played in Yokohama between AC Milan, winners of the 2002-03 UEFA Champions League, and CA Boca Juniors Buenos Aires, winners of the 2003 Copa Libertadores.

The match finished 1-1 after extra time and Boca Juniors won 3-1 in the penalty shoot-out to lift the Intercontinental Cup for the third time.

14-12-2003 International Stadium Yokohama, Yokohama:
AC Milan – CA Boca Juniors Buenos Aires 1-1 (1-1, 1-1) **(AET)**
AC Milan: Nelson de Jesus Silva "DIDA" (BRA), Alessandro COSTACURTA, Paolo MALDINI, Marcos Evangeliste de Moraes "CAFÚ" (BRA) (YC62), Giuseppe PANCARO, Clarence SEEDORF (HOL), Ivan Gennaro GATTUSO (102' Massimo AMBROSINI), Andrea PIRLO, Ricardo Izecson dos Santos Leite "KAKÁ" (BRA) (YC19) (77' RUI Manuel César COSTA (POR)), Andriy SHEVCHENKO (UKR), Jon Dahl TOMASSON (DEN) (69' Filippo INZAGHI). (Coach: Carlo ANCELOTTI).
CA Boca Juniors Buenos Aires: Roberto Carlos ABBONDANCIERI, Rolando Carlos SCHIAVI, Luis Amaranto PEREA Mosquera (COL) (YC6), Nicolás Andrés BURDISSO, Clemente Juan RODRÍGUEZ, Diego Daniel CAGNA, Raúl Alfredo CASCINI, Matías Abel DONNET, Sebastián Alejandro BATTAGLIA, Guillermo BARROS SCHELOTTO (73' Carlos Alberto TÉVEZ), Pedro IARLEY Lima Dantas (BRA). (Coach: Carlos Arcesio BIANCHI).
Goals: AC Milan: 1-0 Jon Dahl TOMASSON (24').
CA Boca Juniors Buenos Aires: 1-1 Matías Abel DONNET (29').
Referee: Valentin IVANOV (RUS)   Attendance: 66,757
Penalties:
* Andrea PIRLO   1 Rolando Carlos SCHIAVI
1 RUI Manuel César COSTA   * Sebastián Alejandro BATTAGLIA
* Clarence SEEDORF   2 Matías Abel DONNET
* Alessandro COSTACURTA   3 Alfredo Raúl CASCINI

*** CA Boca Juniors Buenos Aires won the Cup ***

2004 Intercontinental Cup

The 2004 Intercontinental Cup (officially, the '2004 Toyota European / South American Cup' for sponsorship reasons) was played in Yokohama between FC Porto, winners of the 2003-04 UEFA Champions League, and Once Caldas SA Manizales, winners of the 2004 Copa Libertadores. The match was played in Yokohama. FC Porto won the penalty shoot-out 8-7 to lift the trophy, after the Final had remained goalless following extra-time.

This was the last Intercontinental Cup Final as the competition was merged into the FIFA Club World Cup which featured the continental champions of not just Europe and South America, but also the other Confederations affiliated with FIFA.

12-12-2004 International Stadium Yokohama, Yokohama:
FC Porto – Once Caldas SA Manizales   0-0 **(AET)**
FC Porto: VÍTOR Manuel Martins BAÍA (104' NUNO Herlander Simões do Espírito Santos), JORGE Paulo COSTA Almeida (YC79), PEDRO EMANUEL dos Santos Martíns Silva, RICARDO Miguel Moreira da COSTA, Giourkas SEITARIDIS (GRE) (YC85), Francisco José Rodrigues da Costa "COSTINHA", Nuno Ricardo Oliveira Ribeiro "MANICHE", DIEGO Ribas da Cunha (BRA) (YC50,YC120+), Vanderlei Fernandes da Silva "DERLEI" (BRA) (69' CARLOS ALBERTO Gomes de Jesus (BRA)), Benedict "Benni" Saul McCARTHY (RSA), LUIS FABIANO Clemente (BRA) (79' Ricardo Andrade QUARESMA Bernardo). (Coach: VICTOR FERNÁNDEZ Braulio (ESP)).
Once Caldas SA Manizales: Juan Carlos HENAO Valencia, Samuel Antonio VANEGAS Luna, Miguel Ángel ROJAS Lasso, Roger CAMBINDO Ibarra (46' Édgar Heriberto CATAÑO Castrillón), John Edwin GARCÍA Jiménez, Rubén Darío VELÁSQUEZ Bermúdez, Jhon Eduis VIÁFARA Mina, Diego Alejandro ARANGO Montoya (YC33) (61' Jefrey José DÍAZ Ortiz), Elkin SOTO Jaramillo (97' Herly Enrique ALCÁZAR Vélez), Jonathan FABBRO (ARG) (YC60), Antonio DE NIGRIS Guajardo (MEX) (YC118). (Coach: Luis Fernando MONTOYA Soto).
Referee: Jorge Luis LARRIONDA Pietrafiesa (URU)   Attendance: 45.748
Penalties:

1 Samuel Antonio VANEGAS Luna	1 DIEGO Ribas da Cunha
2 Herly Enrique ALCÁZAR Vélez	2 CARLOS ALBERTO Gomes de Jesus
3 John Eduis VIÁFARA Mina	3 Ricardo Andrade QUARESMA Bernardo
4 Antonio DE NIGRIS Guajardo	* Nuno Ricardo Oliveira Ribeiro "MANICHE"
* Jonathan FABBRO	4 Benedict "Benni" Saul McCARTHY
5 Rubén Darío VELÁSQUEZ Bermúdez	5 Francisco José Rodrigues da Costa "COSTINHA"
6 Jefrey José DÍAZ Ortiz	6 JORGE Paulo COSTA Almeida
7 Édgar Heriberto CATAÑO Castrillón	7 RICARDO Miguel Moreira da COSTA
* John Edwin GARCÍA Jiménez	8 PEDRO EMANUEL dos Santos Martíns Silva

*** FC Porto won the Cup ***

2000 FIFA Club World Championship

The 2000 FIFA Club World Championship was a new competition which aimed to be a 'World Cup' for club sides. The competition was played as a tournament hosted in São Paulo and Rio de Janeiro in Brazil with matches played between 5th January and 14th January 2000.

Eight teams – two from South America, two from Europe and one each from North America, Africa, Asia and Oceania – were invited to play in the tournament. This was played with two groups of 4 teams, one group hosted in each city, and teams played their opponents once with the table-toppers qualifying for the Final. The second-placed teams in each group entered a play-off to decide third-place in the competition.

The two 'home' teams, SC Corinthians Paulista São Paulo and CR Vasco da Gama Rio de Janeiro, won their respective groups to qualify for the Final which was played at the famous Estádio do Maracaña in front of 73,000 spectators. Corinthians Paulista won the penalty shoot-out 4-3 after the game had finished goalless following extra-time. To try and make it an appealing event, the competition was very lucrative with prize money of at least $2.5 million for all competitors and the winners earning US $6 million.

The clubs invited to compete in the 2000 tournament were:

SC Corinthians Paulista (BRA) – winners of the 1998 Campeonato Brasileiro
Al-Nassr FC (KSA) – winners of the 1998 Asian Super Cup
Manchester United FC (ENG) – winners of the 1998-99 UEFA Champions League
CID Necaxa SA (MEX) – winners of the 1999 CONCACAF Champions' Cup
Raja CA Casablanca (MAR) – winners of the 1999 CAF Champions League
Real Madrid CF (ESP) – winners of the 1998 Intercontinental Cup
South Melbourne FC (AUS) – winners of the 1999 Oceania Club championship
CR Vasco da Gama (BRA) – winners of the 1998 Copa Libertadores

GROUP STAGE

GROUP A

05-01-2000   Estádio do Morumbi, São Paulo:
             Al-Nassr FC Riyadh - Real Madrid CF   1-3 (1-1)
Al-Nassr FC Riyadh: BABKR Mohammed KHOJALLI, AL DOSARI Muhaisen AL JAMAN (83' Fahad MEHALEL), Abdallah AL KARNI, Mohsin AL HARTHI, Hadi SHARIFY, Ibrahim AL SHOKIA, Fahad AL HUSSEINI (78' Hamad AL KHATHRAN), Fuad AL AMIN (YC46), Mansour AL MOUSA, Moussa SAÏB (66' Ismael TRIKI (MAR)), Ahmed BAHJA. (Coach: Milan ZIVADINOVIC (YUG)).
Real Madrid CF: Iker CASILLAS Fernández, Miguel Ángel "MÍCHEL" SALGADO Fernández, ROBERTO CARLOS da Silva Rocha (BRA), Fernando Ruiz HIERRO (YC33) (77' Aitor KARANKA de la Hoz), Christian KAREMBEU (FRA), Fernando Carlos Neri REDONDO (ARG), José María Gutiérrez Hernández "GUTI" (66' Steve McMANAMAN (ENG)), GEREMI Sorele N'Djitap Fotso (CMR), RAÚL González Blanco, SÁVIO Bortolini Pimentel (BRA) (72' Manuel SANCHÍS Hontiyuelo), Nicolas ANELKA (FRA). (Coach: Vicente DEL BOSQUE González).
Goals: Al-Nassr FC: 1-1 Fahad AL HUSSEINI (45+1' penalty).
Real Madrid CF: 0-1 Nicolas ANELKA (19'), 1-2 RAÚL González Blanco (61'), 1-3 SÁVIO Bortolini Pimentel (69' penalty).
Referee: Óscar Julián RUÍZ Acosta (COL)   Attendance: 12,000

05-01-2000   Estádio do Morumbi, São Paulo:
             SC Corinthians Paulista São Paulo – Raja CA Casablanca   2-0 (0-0)
SC Corinthians Paulista São Paulo: Nelson de Jesús da Silva "DIDA", José Sátiro do Nascimento "INDIO", JOÃO CARLOS Dos Santos, KLÉBER de Carvalho Corrêa, FÁBIO LUCIANO, Marcos André Batista Santos "VAMPETA" (86' Eduardo Cesar Daude "EDU" GASPAR), Marcelo Pereira Surcin "MARCELINHO CARIOCA" (76' MARCOS Antonio SENNA Da Silva), Freddy Eusébio RINCÓN Valencia (COL), Ricardo Luiz Pozzi Rodrigues "RICARDINHO", Luiz Carlos Bombonato Goulart "LUIZÃO" (83' Claudinei Alexandre Pires "DINEI"), EDÍLSON da Silva Ferreira. (Coach: Oswaldo DE OLIVEIRA Filho).
Raja CA Casablanca: Mustapha CHADILI (YC65), Redouane EL HAIMEUR, Talal EL KARKOURI, Hicham MISBAH (YC65), Abdellatif JRINDOU (YC13), Youssef SAFRI, Omar NEJJARY, Zakaria ABOUB, Reda EREYAHI, Mustapha MOUSTAOUDIA, Mohamed KHOUBBACHE (60' Youssef ACHAMI). (Coach: Jamal FATHI).
Goals: SC Corinthians Paulista: 1-0 LUIZÃO (50'), 2-0 FÁBIO LUCIANO (64').
Referee: Stefano BRASCHI (ITA)   Attendance: 23,000

07-01-2000   Estádio do Morumbi, São Paulo:
SC Corinthians Paulista São Paulo - Real Madrid CF   2-2 (1-1)
SC Corinthians Paulista São Paulo: Nelson de Jesús da Silva "DIDA", José Sátiro do Nascimento "INDIO", JOÃO CARLOS Dos Santos, KLÉBER de Carvalho Corrêa (YC89), FABIO LUCIANO (YC30), Marcos André Batista Santos "VAMPETA" (74' Eduardo Cesar Daude "EDU" GASPAR), Marcelo Pereira Surcin "MARCELINHO CARIOCA", Freddy Eusébio RINCÓN Valencia (COL) (YC42), Ricardo Luiz Pozzi Rodrigues "RICARDINHO" (85' MARCOS Antonio SENNA Da Silva), Luiz Carlos Bombonato Goulart "LUIZÃO" (81' Claudinei Alexandre Pires "DINEI"), EDÍLSON da Silva Ferreira. (Coach: Oswaldo DE OLIVEIRA Filho).
Real Madrid CF: Iker CASILLAS Fernández, Miguel Ángel "MÍCHEL" SALGADO Fernández (YC20), ROBERTO CARLOS da Silva Rocha (BRA) (YC84), Fernando Ruiz HIERRO, Christian KAREMBEU (FRA) (YC65), Fernando Carlos Neri REDONDO (ARG), José María Gutiérrez Hernández "GUTI" (YC45+) (70' Fernando MORIENTES Sánchez), GEREMI Sorele N'Djitap Fotso (CMR) (70' Steve McMANAMAN (ENG)), RAÚL González Blanco, SÁVIO Bortolini Pimentel (BRA), Nicolas ANELKA (FRA). (Coach: Vicente DEL BOSQUE González).
Goals: SC Corinthians Paulista: 1-1 EDÍLSON da Silva Ferreira (28'), 2-1 EDÍLSON da Silva Ferreira (64').
Real Madrid CF: 0-1 Nicolas ANELKA (19'), 2-2 Nicolas ANELKA (71').
Referee: William MATTUS Vega (CRC)   Attendance: 55,000

Nicolas ANELKA missed a penalty kick (81').

07-01-2000   Estádio do Morumbi, São Paulo:
Raja CA Casablanca – Al-Nassr FC Riyadh   3-4 (1-1)
Raja CA Casablanca: Mustapha CHADILI, Redouane EL HAIMEUR, Talal EL KARKOURI, Hicham MISBAH (YC90+3), Abdellatif JRINDOU (55' Youssef ACHAMI), Youssef SAFRI (RC75), Omar NEJJARY (32' Hamid NATER), Zakaria ABOUB (YC14), Reda EREYAHI (55' Bouchaib EL MOUBARKI), Mustapha MOUSTAOUDIA, Mohamed KHOUBBACHE (YC76). (Coach: Jamal FATHI).
Al-Nassr FC Riyadh: BABKT Mohammed KHOJALLI (29' Madhi AL DOSARI), Muhaisen AL JAMAN, Abdallah AL KARNI (71' Nassip AL GHAMDI), Mohsin AL HARTHI, Hadi SHARIFY, Ibrahim AL SHOKIA, Fahad AL HUSSEINI (76' Fahad MEHALEL), Fuad AL AMIN, Mansour AL MOUSA (YC69), Moussa SAÏB, Ahmed BAHJA. (Coach: Milan ZIVADINOVIC (YUG)).
Goals: Raja CA Casablanca: 1-1 Muhaisen AL JAMAN (24' own goal), 2-3 Bouchaib EL MOUBARKI (66'), 3-3 Talal EL KARKOURI (73').
Al-Nassr FC: 0-1 Fuad AL AMIN (4'), 1-2 Ahmed BAHJA (63'), 1-3 Fahad AL HUSSEINI (64'), 3-4 Moussa SAÏB (85').
Referee: Derek RUGG (NZL)   Attendance: 3,000

10-01-2000   Estádio do Morumbi, São Paulo:
Real Madrid CF – Raja CA Casablanca   3-2 (0-1)
Real Madrid CF: Iker CASILLAS Fernández, Miguel Ángel "MÍCHEL" SALGADO Fernández (80' Aitor KARANKA de la Hoz), ROBERTO CARLOS da Silva Rocha (BRA) (RC62), Fernando Ruiz HIERRO (YC38), Christian KAREMBEU (FRA) (YC45, YC87), Fernando Carlos Neri REDONDO (ARG), Steve McMANAMAN (ENG) (46' GEREMI Sorele N'Djitap Fotso (CMR)), José María Gutiérrez Hernández "GUTI" (RC62), RAÚL González Blanco, SÁVIO Bortolini Pimentel (BRA) (YC61), Nicolas ANELKA (FRA) (37' Fernando MORIENTES Sánchez). (Coach: Vicente DEL BOSQUE González).
Raja CA Casablanca: Mustapha CHADILI, Redouane EL HAIMEUR, Talal EL KARKOURI (YC14), Mohamed KHARBOUCH, Mohamed KHOUBBACHE, Bouchaib EL MOUBARKI (RC62), Zakaria ABOUB, Reda EREYAHI, Hamid NATER (90' Said KHERAZI), Mustapha MOUSTAOUDIA (YC70), Youssef ACHAMI (81' Tarik IZKI). (Coach: Jamal FATHI).
Goals: Real Madrid CF: 1-1 Fernando Ruiz HIERRO (49'), 2-1 Fernando MORIENTES Sánchez (53'), 3-2 GEREMI Sorele N'Djitap Fotso (83').
Raja CA Casablanca: 0-1 Youssef ACHAMI (28'), 2-2 Mustapha MOUSTAOUDIA (59').
Referee: Horacio Marcelo ELIZONDO (ARG)   Attendance: 18,000

10-01-2000   Estádio do Morumbi, São Paulo:
SC Corinthians Paulista São Paulo – Al-Nassr FC Riyadh   2-0 (1-0)
SC Corinthians Paulista São Paulo: Nelson de Jesús da Silva "DIDA", JOÃO CARLOS Dos Santos (10' ADILSON Dias BATISTA (YC49)), KLÉBER de Carvalho Corrêa, DANIEL Sabino Martins (YC20,YC67), FABIO LUCIANO, Marcos André Batista Santos "VAMPETA" (72' Claudinei Alexandre Pires "DINEI"), Marcelo Pereira Surcin "MARCELINHO CARIOCA" (YC30), Freddy Eusébio RINCÓN Valencia (COL), Ricardo Luiz Pozzi Rodrigues "RICARDINHO" (27' Eduardo Cesar Daude "EDU" GASPAR), Luiz Carlos Bombonato Goulart "LUIZÃO" (YC59), EDÍLSON da Silva Ferreira. (Coach: Oswaldo DE OLIVEIRA Filho).
Al-Nassr FC Riyadh: BABKR Mohammed KHOJALLI, Muhaisen AL JAMAN (88' Ismael TRIKI (MAR)), Abdallah AL KARNI, Mohsin AL HARTHI (YC1), Hadi SHARIFY, Ibrahim AL SHOKIA (YC84), Fahad AL HUSSEINI (41' Abdulaziz AL JANOUBI), Fuad AL AMIN, Mansour AL MOUSA, Moussa SAÏB (73' Fahad MEHALEL), Ahmed BAHJA. (Coach: Milan ZIVADINOVIC (YUG)).
Goals: SC Corinthians Paulista: 1-0 RICARDINHO (25'), 2-0 Freddy RINCÓN (81').
Referee: Dick JOL (HOL)   Attendance: 31,000

Pos	Team	Pld	W	D	L	GF	GA	GD	Pts
1	*SC Corinthians Paulista (BRA)*	*3*	*2*	*1*	*0*	*6*	*2*	*+4*	*7*
2	Real Madrid CF (ESP)	3	2	1	0	8	5	+3	7
3	Al-Nassr FC (KSA)	3	1	0	2	5	8	-3	3
4	Raja CA Casablanca (MAR)	3	0	0	3	5	9	-4	0

SC Corinthians Paulista São Paulo qualified for the Final
Real Madrid CF qualified for Third Place Play-off

GROUP B

06-01-2000   Estádio do Maracaña, Rio de Janeiro:
              Manchester United FC – ID Necaxa SA Aguascalientes   1-1 (0-1)
Manchester United FC: Mark BOSNICH (AUS), Gary NEVILLE, Denis IRVIN (IRL) (72'
Ole Gunnar SOLSKJÆR (NOR)), Mikaël SILVESTRE (FRA), Jaap STAM (HOL), David
BECKHAM (RC43), Nicky BUTT (72' Philip NEVILLE), Roy KEANE (YC16), Andy COLE
(72' Teddy SHERINGHAM (YC76)), Ryan GIGGS (WAL) (YC43), Dwight YORKE (TRI)
(YC82). (Coach: Alex FERGUSON (SCO) (RC63)).
ID Necaxa SA Aguascalientes: Hugo Alejandro PINEDA Vargas, Salvador CABRERA
Aguirre, Sergio ALMAGUER Treviño, Markus Javier LÓPEZ Winkler (YC85), José María
HIGAREDA Gálvez (83' Miguel Ángel ACOSTA Moreno), Álex Darío AGUINAGA Garzón
(ECU), Luis Ernesto PÉREZ Gómez, Hernán VIGNA (ARG) (79' Marcos Ignacio AMBRIZ
Espinoza), José MILIÁN Martínez, Agustín Javier DELGADO Chalá (ECU) (YC32), Cristián
Antonio MONTECINOS González (CHI) (YC58) (76' Sergio Marcelo VÁZQUEZ Robledo
(URU)). (Coach: Raúl ARIAS Rosas).
Goals: Manchester United FC: 1-1 Dwight YORKE (83').
CID Necaxa SA: 0-1 Cristián Antonio MONTECINOS González (15').
Referee: Horacio Marcelo ELIZONDO (ARG)   Attendance: 50,000

Álex Darío AGUINAGA Garzón missed a penalty kick (57').
Dwight YORKE missed a penalty kick (79').

06-01-2000   Estádio do Maracaña, Rio de Janeiro:
                  CR Vasco da Gama Rio de Janeiro – South Melbourne FC   2-0 (0-0)
CR Vasco da Gama Rio de Janeiro: HELTON da Silva Aruda, Jorge José de Amorim Campos
"JORGINHO", MAURO Geraldo GALVÃO, GILBERTO da Silva Melo, Raimundo Ferreira
Ramos JÚNIOR "BAIANO", Alexandre da Silva Marinano "AMARAL", FELIPE Jorge
Loureiro, Antônio Augusto Ribeiro Reis Junior "JUNINHO PERNAMBUCANO" (89'
ODVAN Gomes Silva), RAMON Menezes Hubner (YC64) (80' ALEX de OLIVEIRA
Freitas), EDMUNDO Alves de Souza Neto (YC86) (89' Paulo Sérgio Rosa "VIOLA"),
ROMÁRIO de Souza Faria. (Coach: ANTÔNIO LOPES dos Santos).
South Melbourne FC: Chris JONES, Steve IOSIFIDIS, Fausto DE AMICIS, Nick ORLIC
(YC29), Con BLATSIS, David CLARKSON, Steve PANOPOULOS (YC50), Goran
LOZANOVSKI (YC40), Robert LIPAROTI, Paul TRIMBOLI (80' John ANASTASIADIS),
Michael CURCIJA (74' Vaughan COVENY (NZL)). (Coach: Ange POSTECOGLOU).
Goals: CR Vasco da Gama: 1-0 FELIPE Jorge Loureiro (53'), 2-0 EDMUNDO Alves de Souza
Neto (86').
Referee: Dick JOL (HOL)   Attendance: 66,000

08-01-2000   Estádio do Maracaña, Rio de Janeiro:
CR Vasco da Gama Rio de Janeiro - Manchester United FC   3-1 (3-0)
CR Vasco da Gama Rio de Janeiro: HELTON da Silva Aruda, Jorge José de Amorim Campos "JORGINHO" (YC59) (69' PAULO MIRANDA de Oliveira), MAURO Geraldo GALVÃO, GILBERTO da Silva Melo, Raimundo Ferreira Ramos JÚNIOR "BAIANO" (YC61), Alexandre da Silva Marinano "AMARAL", FELIPE Jorge Loureiro, Antônio Augusto Ribeiro Reis Junior "JUNINHO PERNAMBUCANO" (79' ALEX de OLIVEIRA Freitas), RAMON Menezes Hubner (76' Gesiel José de Lima "NASA" (YC81)), EDMUNDO Alves de Souza Neto, ROMÁRIO de Souza Faria. (Coach: ANTÔNIO LOPES dos Santos).
Manchester United FC: Mark BOSNICH (AUS), Gary NEVILLE, Denis IRVIN (IRL), Mikaël SILVESTRE (FRA), Jaap STAM (HOL) (71' Jordi CRUIJFF (HOL)), Nicky BUTT, Philip NEVILLE, Roy KEANE (IRL), Ryan GIGGS (WAL) (77' Quinton FORTUNE (RSA)), Dwight YORKE (TRI), Ole Gunnar SOLSKJÆR (NOR) (46' Teddy SHERINGHAM (YC51)). (Coach: Alex FERGUSON (SCO)).
Goals: Manchester United FC: 1-3 Nicky BUTT (83').
CR Vasco da Gama: 1-0 ROMÁRIO de Souza (23'), 2-0 ROMÁRIO de Souza (24'), 3-0 EDMUNDO Alves de Souza Neto (42').
Referee: Saad Kamel MANE (KUW)   Attendance: 73,000

08-01-2000   Estádio do Maracaña, Rio de Janeiro:
ID Necaxa SA Aguascalientes - South Melbourne FC   3-1 (2-1)
ID Necaxa SA Aguascalientes: Hugo Alejandro PINEDA Vargas, Salvador CABRERA Aguirre, Sergio ALMAGUER Treviño, Markus Javier LÓPEZ Winkler (55' Marcos Ignacio AMBRIZ Espinoza), José María HIGAREDA, Álex Darío AGUINAGA Garzón (ECU), Luis Ernesto PÉREZ Gómez, Hernán VIGNA (ARG) (YC81), José MILIÁN Martínez (YC83), Agustín Javier DELGADO Chalá (ECU) (83' Sergio Marcelo VÁZQUEZ Robledo (URU)), Cristián Antonio MONTECINOS González (CHI) (46' Edgar David OLIVA Medina). (Coach: Raúl ARIAS Rosas).
South Melbourne FC: Chris JONES, Steve IOSIFIDIS (YC40), Fausto DE AMICIS, Nick ORLIC (YC76), Con BLATSIS, David CLARKSON, Steve PANOPOULOS (65' Michael CURCIJA), John ANASTASIADIS, Richie ALAGICH, Vaughan COVENY (NZL) (65' George GOUTZIOULIS), Paul TRIMBOLI (78' Jim TSEKINIS). (Coach: Ange POSTECOGLOU).
Goals: CID Necaxa SA: 0-1 Cristián Antonio MONTECINOS González (19' penalty), 0-2 Agustín Javier DELGADO Chalá (29'), 1-3 Salvador CABRERA Aguirre (79' penalty).
South Melbourne FC: 1-2 John ANASTASIADIS (45+2').
Referee: Falla N'DOYE (SEN)   Attendance: 5,000

Cristián Antonio MONTECINOS González missed a penalty kick (23').

11-01-2000   Estádio do Maracaña, Rio de Janeiro:
              Manchester United FC – South Melbourne FC   2-0 (2-0)
Manchester United FC: Raimond VAN DER GOUW (HOL) (83' Paul RACHUBKA), Danny HIGGINBOTHAM, Philip NEVILLE, Henning BERG (NOR), Ronnie WALLWORK, Jordi CRUIJFF (HOL), Johathan GREENING, Mark WILSON (77' David BECKHAM), Andy COLE, Ole Gunnar SOLSKJÆR (NOR), Quinton FORTUNE (RSA). (Coach: Alex FERGUSON (SCO)).
South Melbourne FC: Chris JONES, Steve IOSIFIDIS, Fausto DE AMICIS, Con BLATSIS, Robert LIPAROTI (31' George GOUTZIOULIS), David CLARKSON (71' Jim TSEKINIS), Steve PANOPOULOS, John ANASTASIADIS (66' Vaughan COVENY (NZL)), Goran LOZANOVSKI, Paul TRIMBOLI (YC90), Michael CURCIJA. (Coach: Ange POSTECOGLOU).
Goals: Manchester United FC: 1-0 Quinton FORTUNE (8'), 2-0 Quinton FORTUNE (20').
Referee: Stefano BRASCHI (ITA)   Attendance: 25,000

11-01-2000   Estádio do Maracaña, Rio de Janeiro:
              CR Vasco da Gama Rio de Janeiro - ID Necaxa SA Aguascalientes   2-1 (1-1)
CR Vasco da Gama Rio de Janeiro: HELTON da Silva Aruda, MAURO Geraldo GALVÃO, GILBERTO da Silva Melo, Raimundo Ferreira Ramos JÚNIOR "BAIANO" (9' ODVAN Gomes Silva), Alexandre da Silva Marinano "AMARAL" (YC75), FELIPE Jorge Loureiro, PSMAR DONIZETE Cândido (70' EDMUNDO Alves de Souza Neto), Antônio Augusto Ribeiro Reis Junior "JUNINHO PERNAMBUCANO", RAMON Menezes Hubner, ROMÁRIO de Souza Faria, PAULO MIRANDA de Oliveira. (Coach: ANTÔNIO LOPES dos Santos).
ID Necaxa SA Aguascalientes: Hugo Alejandro PINEDA Vargas, Salvador CABRERA Aguirre, Sergio ALMAGUER Treviño, Markus Javier LÓPEZ Winkler (YC65), José María HIGAREDA (YC21), Álex Darío AGUINAGA Garzón (ECU), Luis Ernesto PÉREZ Gómez, Hernán VIGNA (ARG), José MILIÁN Martínez (84' Sergio Marcelo VÁZQUEZ Robledo (URU)), Agustín Javier DELGADO Chalá (ECU), Cristián Antonio MONTECINOS González (CHI) (72' Marcos Ignacio AMBRIZ Espinoza). (Coach: Raúl ARIAS Rosas).
Goals: CR Vasco da Gama: 1-1 ODVAN Gomes Silva (14'), 1-2 ROMÁRIO de Souza Faria (69').
CID Necaxa SA: 1-0 Álex Darío AGUINAGA Garzón (4').
Referee: Óscar Julián RUÍZ Acosta (COL)   Attendance: 45,000

Pos	Team	Pld	W	D	L	GF	GA	GD	Pts
1	CR Vasco da Gama (BRA)	3	3	0	0	7	2	+5	9
2	ID Necaxa SA (MEX)	3	1	1	1	5	4	+1	4
3	Manchester United FC (ENG)	3	1	1	1	4	4	0	4
4	South Melbourne FC (AUS)	3	0	0	3	1	7	-6	0

CR Vasca da Gama qualified for the Final.
CID Necaxa SA qualified for the Third Place Play-off.

SECOND STAGE

THIRD PLACE PLAY-OFF

14-01-2000   Estádio do Maracaña, Rio de Janeiro:
Real Madrid CF –ID Necaxa SA Aguascalientes 1-1 (1-0, 1-1) **(AET)**
Real Madrid CF: Albano Benjamín BIZZARRI (ARG), Fernando Ruiz HIERRO (52' IVÁN CAMPO Ramos), Manuel SANCHÍS Hontiyuelo, Javier DORADO Bielsa, Aitor KARANKA de la Hoz, RAÚL González Blanco (66' Samuel ETO'O Fils (CMR)), Steve McMANAMAN (ENG), IVÁN HELGUERA Bujía, GEREMI Sorele N'Djitap Fotso (CMR), Fernando MORIENTES Sánchez, SÁVIO Bortolini Pimentel (BRA) (52' Perica OGNJENOVIC (YUG)). (Coach: Vicente DEL BOSQUE González).
ID Necaxa SA Aguascalientes: Hugo Alejandro PINEDA Vargas, Salvador CABRERA Aguirre, Sergio ALMAGUER Treviño, Markus Javier LÓPEZ Winkler (46' Marcos Ignacio AMBRIZ Espinoza), José María HIGAREDA, Álex Darío AGUINAGA Garzón (ECU), Luis Ernesto PÉREZ Gómez, Hernán VIGNA (ARG) (83' Edgar David OLIVA Medina), José MILIÁN Martínez, Agustín Javier DELGADO Chalá (ECU), Cristián Antonio MONTECINOS González (CHI) (46' Sergio Marcelo VÁZQUEZ Robledo (URU)). (Coach: Raúl ARIAS Rosas).
Goals: Real Madrid CF: 1-0 RAÚL González Blanco (15').
CID Necaxa SA: 1-1 Agustín Javier DELGADO Chalá (58').
Referee: Óscar Julián RUÍZ Acosta (COL)   Attendance: 35,000

Penalties:
1 Samuel ETO'O Fils   1 Sergio Marcelo VÁZQUEZ Robledo
2 IVÁN HELGUERA Bujía   * Salvador CABRERA Aguirre
* Steve McMANAMAN   2 Luis Ernesto PÉREZ Gómez
3 Fernando MORIENTES Sánchez   3 Álex Darío AGUINAGA Garzón
* Javier DORADO Bielsa   4 Agustín Javier DELGADO Chalá

FINAL

14-01-2000   Estádio do Maracaña, Rio de Janeiro:
CR Vasco da Gama - SC Corinthians Paulista   0-0 **(AET)**
CR Vasco da Gama Rio de Janeiro: HELTON da Silva Aruda, ODVAN Gomes Silva, MAURO Geraldo GALVÃO, Alexandre da Silva Marinano "AMARAL" (YC33), GILBERTO da Silva Melo, FELIPE Jorge Loureiro (YC16) (102' ALEX de OLIVEIRA Freitas), Antônio Augusto Ribeiro Reis Junior "JUNINHO PERNAMBUCANO" (96' Paulo Sérgio Rosa "VIOLA"), RAMON Menezes Hubner (111' OSMAR DONIZETE Cândido), PAULO MIRANDA de Oliveira (YC54), EDMUNDO Alves de Souza Neto (YC98), ROMÁRIO de Souza Faria. (Coach: ANTÔNIO LOPES dos Santos).
SC Corinthians Paulista São Paulo: Nelson de Jesús da Silva "DIDA", José Sátiro do Nascimento "INDIO" (YC97), ADILSON Dias BATISTA (YC75), KLÉBER de Carvalho, FABIO LUCIANO, Marcos André Batista Santos "VAMPETA" (91' GILMAR "fubá" de Lima Nascimento), Marcelo Pereira Surcin "MARCELINHO CARIOCA", Freddy Eusébio RINCÓN Valencia (COL) (YC43), Ricardo Luiz Pozzi Rodrigues "RICARDINHO" (46' Eduardo Cesar Daude "EDU" GASPAR), Luiz Carlos Bombonato Goulart "LUIZÃO" (YC113), EDÍLSON da Silva Ferreira (113' João FERNANDO "BAIANO" Nelo). (Coach: Oswaldo DE OLIVEIRA Filho).
Referee: Dick JOL (HOL)   Attendance: 73,000

Penalties:
1 Freddy Eusébio RINCÓN Valencia   1 ROMÁRIO de Souza Faria
2 João FERNANDO "BAIANO" Nelo   2 ALEX de OLIVEIRA Freitas
3 Luiz Carlos Bombonato Goulart "LUIZÃO"
                                       * GILBERTO da Silva Melo
4 Eduardo Cesar Daude "EDU" GASPAR   3 Paulo Sérgio Rosa "VIOLA"
* Marcelo Pereira Surcin "MARCELINHO CARIOCA"
                                       * EDMUNDO Alves de Souza Neto

*** SC Corinthians Paulista São Paulo won the Cup ***

2001 FIFA Club World Championship

The 2001 FIFA Club World Championship was originally scheduled to be played in Spain between 28th July and 12th August 2001 but was cancelled due to a number of factors, not least of which was the collapse of FIFA's marketing partner, ISL. Initially, FIFA planned to postpone the competition until 2003 but it was eventually cancelled outright and didn't return in any format until 2005.

The clubs invited to play in the 2001 tournament were:

RC Deportivo de La Coruña (ESP)	– winners of the 1999-2000 La Liga
Real Madrid CF (ESP)	– winners of the 1999-2000 UEFA Champions League
Galatasaray SK (TUR)	– winners of the 1999-2000 UEFA Cup and 2000 UEFA Super Cup
CA Boca Juniors Buenos Aires (ARG)	– winners of the 2000 Copa Libertadores
SE Palmeiras (BRA)	– winners of the 1999 Copa Libertadores
Los Angeles Galaxy (USA)	– winners of the 2000 CONCACAF Champions' Cup
CD Olimpia Tegucigalpa (HON)	– runner-up of the 2000 CONCACAF Champions' Cup
Accra Hearts of Oak SC (GHA)	– winners of the 2000 CAP Champions League
Zamalek SC Cairo (EGY)	– winners of the 2000 African Cup Winners' Cup
Al-Hilal Saudi FC (KSA)	– winners of the 2000 Asian Super Cup
Júbilo Iwata (JPN)	– winners of the 1999 Asian Super Cup
Wollongong Wolves FC (AUS)	– winners of the 2001 Oceania Club Championship

GROUP STAGE

GROUP A

28-07-2001   Estadio Riazor, A Coruña:
CA Boca Juniors Buenos Aires – RC Deportivo de La Coruña   **cancelled**

29-07-2001   Estadio Riazor, A Coruña:
Wollongong Wolves FC – Zamalek SC Cairo   **cancelled**

01-08-2001   Estadio Riazor, A Coruña:
RC Deportivo de La Coruña - Wollongong Wolves FC   **cancelled**

01-08-2001   Estadio Riazor, A Coruña:
Zamalek SC Cairo - CA Boca Juniors Buenos Aires   **cancelled**

04-08-2001   Estadio Multiusos de San Lázaro, Santiago de Compostela:
CA Boca Juniors Buenos Aires - Wollongong Wolves FC   **cancelled**

04-08-2001   Estadio Riazor, A Coruña:
RC Deportivo de La Coruña - Zamalek SC Cairo   **cancelled**

GROUP B

29-07-2001   Estadio Vicente Calderón, Madrid:
SE Palmeiras – CD Olimpia Tegucigalpa   **cancelled**

30-07-2001   Estadio Vicente Calderón, Madrid:
Galatasaray SK – Al-Hilal Saudi FC   **cancelled**

02-08-2001   Estadio Vicente Calderón, Madrid:
CD Olimpia Tegucigalpa - Galatasaray SK   **cancelled**

02-08-2001   Estadio Vicente Calderón, Madrid:
Al-Hilal Saudi FC - SE Palmeiras   **cancelled**

05-08-2001   Estadio Vicente Calderón, Madrid:
SE Palmeiras - Galatasaray SK   **cancelled**

05-08-2001   Estadio Santiago Bernabéu, Madrid:
CD Olimpia Tegucigalpa - Al-Hilal Saudi FC   **cancelled**

GROUP C

31-07-2001   Estadio Santiago Bernabéu, Madrid:
Real Madrid CF – Júbilo Iwata   **cancelled**

31-07-2001   Estadio Santiago Bernabéu, Madrid:
Accra Hearts of Oak SC – Los Angeles Galaxy   **cancelled**

03-08-2001   Estadio Santiago Bernabéu, Madrid:
Júbilo Iwata - Accra Hearts of Oak SC   **cancelled**

03-08-2001   Estadio Santiago Bernabéu, Madrid:
Los Angeles Galaxy - Real Madrid CF   **cancelled**

06-08-2001   Estadio Santiago Bernabéu, Madrid:
Real Madrid CF - Accra Hearts of Oak SC   **cancelled**

06-08-2001   Estadio Vicente Calderón, Madrid:
Júbilo Iwata - Los Angeles Galaxy   **cancelled**

KNOCKOUT STAGE

SEMI-FINALS

09-08-2001	Estadio Riazor, A Coruña:
Winner Group A – Winner Group B **cancelled**

09-08-2001	Estadio Santiago Bernabéu, Madrid:
Winner Group C – Best 2nd Place **cancelled**

THIRD PLACE PLAY-OFF

12-08-2001	Estadio Santiago Bernabéu, Madrid:
Loser Match 19 – Loser Match 20 **cancelled**

FINAL

12-08-2001	Estadio Santiago Bernabéu, Madrid:
Winner Match 19 – Winner Match 20 **cancelled**

2005 FIFA Club World Championship

The 2005 FIFA Club World Championship (officially, the 'FIFA Club World Championship Toyota Cup Japan 2005' for sponsorship reasons) was the second edition of the Club World Championship, and the first to be held following the integration of the Intercontinental Cup. To celebrate the merging of the two competitions, FIFA introduced a new trophy which is used to this day.

It was decided that the merged tournament should be smaller than the first FIFA Club World Championship played in 2000, which had lasted two weeks so caused great disruption to the regular seasons of the competitors, so just six clubs were invited to take part, one representing each regional football confederation.

The competition was a played as a knock-out tournament so each team played just two or three matches. The Champions of the four "weaker" confederations entered the First Round with the losers of the two games competing in a fifth place play-off. The winners of the First Round matches were then joined by the European and South American champions in the semi-finals and the losers of these two games entered a third place play-off.

The competition was played in Japan between 11th and 18th December 2005 and, in the event, the Final game became effectively the same as the old Intercontinental Cup as the Brazilian Copa Libertadores winners São Paulo FC defeated the English European Champions Liverpool FC by a single goal!

The clubs invited to play in the 2005 tournament were:

Liverpool FC (ENG)	- winners of the 2004-05 UEFA Champions League
São Paulo FC (BRA)	- winners of the 2005 Copa Libertadores
Al Ahly SC Cairo (EGY)	- winners of the 2005 CAF Champions League
Al-Ittihad Club (KSA)	- winners of the 2005 AFC Champions League
Deportivo Saprissa (CRC)	- winners of the 2005 CONCACAF Champions' Cup
Sydney FC (AUS)	- winners of the 2004-05 Oceania Club Championship

FIRST ROUND

11-12-2005 National Stadium, Tokyo:
            Al-Ittihad Club Jeddah – Al Ahly SC Cairo   1-0 (0-0)
Al-Ittihad Club Jeddah: MABROUK ZAID, AHMED Douki AL-DOSARI (YC22), REHDA Hassan TUKAR Fallatah, ADNAN Ibrahem FALATAH (YC90), HAMAD Mohsen AL-MONTASHARI, MOHAMMED AMEEN Haidar al-Aulaqi (64' IBRAHIM Suwayed AL-SHAHRANI), MANAF Eid ABUSHGEER (90' ALI AL-GARNI), Anderson Simas Luciano "TCHECO" (BRA), SAUD Ali Al KHARIRI (YC43), MOHAMMED NOOR Al-Hawsawi, Mohamed Ajay KALLON (SLE) (YC32). (Coaches: Anghel IORDANESCU (ROM) & Bruno Lucas Felix METSU (FRA)).
Al Ahly SC Cairo: ESSAM Kamal Tawfik EL HADARY, ISLAM Mahmoud Mohamed El Sayed EL SHATER (71' HOSSAM Mohamed ASHOUR Sanad Attia), AHMED EL-SAYED, WAEL GOMAA Kamel El Hooty, SHADY MOHAMED Abdel Fattah Ragab (YC38), MOHAMED BARAKAT Ahmed Bastamy, Felisberto Sebastião de Graça Amaral "GILBERTO" (ANG) (46' AHMED ABOU MOSLEM Farag, 84' OSAMA HOSNY), HASSAN MOSTAFA, MOHAMED Ali Abu El-Yazid SHAWKY, MUHAMMAD ABU TARIKA, EMAD MOTEAB Mohamed Abd El Naby Ibrahim. (Coach: MANUEL JOSÉ de Jesus da Silva (POR)).
Goal: Al-Ittihad Club: 1-0 MOHAMMED NOOR Al-Hawsawi (78').
Referee: Graham POLL (ENG)   Attendance: 28,281

12-12-2005 Toyota Stadium, Toyota City:
            Sydney FC – Deportivo Saprissa San José   0-1 (0-0)
Sydney FC: Clint BOLTON, Iain FYFE, Alvin CECCOLI (RC81), Mark MILLIGAN (YC71), Steve CORICA (83' David ZDRILIC), David CARNEY, Andrew PACKER (61' Mark RUDAN), Terry McFLYNN (YC3) (61' John BUONAVOGLIA), Saso PETROVSKI, Dwight YORKE (TRI), Kazuyoshi MIURA (JPN). (Coach: Pierre LITTBARSKI (GER)).
Deportivo Saprissa San José: José Francisco PORRAS Hidaldo (YC90), Víctor CORDERO Flores, Rónald Alfonso GONZÁLEZ Brenes (YC32), Gabriel BADILLA Segura, Jervis DRUMMOND Johnson, Try Anthony BENNETT Grant (83' José Luis LÓPEZ Ramírez), Christian BOLAÑOS Navarro, Wálter CENTENO Corea (YC77) (89' Reynaldo PARKS Pérez), Randall AZOFEIFA Corrales, Rónald GÓMEZ Gómez (YC56), Álvaro Alberto SABORÍO Chacón (90' Gerold DRUMMOND Johnson). (Coach: Hernán Evaristo MEDFORD Bryan).
Goal: Deportivo Saprissa: 0-1 Christian BOLAÑOS Navarro (47').
Referee: Toru KAMIKAWA (JPN)   Attendance: 28,538

SEMI–FINALS

14-12-2005 National Stadium, Tokyo: Al-Ittihad Club Jeddah – São Paulo FC 2-3 (1-1)
Al-Ittihad Club Jeddah: MABROUK ZAID, AHMED Douki AL-DOSARI (YC34) (67'
OSAMA Mabrook AL-HARBI Al Muwallad (YC87)), REHDA Hassan TUKAR Fallatah
(YC57), ADNAN Ibrahem FALATAH, HAMAD Mohsen AL-MONTASHARI, MANAF Eid
ABUSHGEER, Anderson Simas Luciano "TCHECO" (BRA), SAUD Ali Al KHARIRI,
IBRAHIM Suwayed AL-SHAHRANI (64' MOHAMMED AMEEN Haidar al-Aulaqi),
MOHAMMED NOOR Al-Hawsawi, Mohamed Ajay KALLON (SLE). (Coaches: Anghel
IORDANESCU (ROM) & Bruno Lucas Felix METSU (FRA)).
São Paulo FC: ROGÉRIO Mücke CENI, Cícero João de Cézare "CICINHO", José Fábio Alves
Azevedo "FABÃO", EDCARLOS Conceição Santos, Diego Alfredo LUGANO Moreno
(URU) (YC71), Jenílson Angelo de Souza "JÚNIOR", Carlos Luciano da Silva "MINEIRO"
(YC79), JOSUÉ Anunciado de Oliveira, DANILO Gabriel de Andrade (YC53), Marcio
AMOROSO dos Santos (YC66), ALOÍSIO José da Silva (89' Edinaldo Batista Líbanio
"GRAFITE"). (Coach: PAULO AUTUORI de Mello).
Goals: Al-Ittihad Club: 1-1 MOHAMMED NOOR Al- (33'), 2-3 HAMAD Mohsen AL-
MONTASHARI (68').
São Paulo FC: 0-1 Marcio AMOROSO dos Santos (16'), 1-2 Marcio AMOROSO dos Santos
(47'), 1-3 ROGÉRIO Mücke CENI (57' penalty).
Referee: Alain SARS (FRA)   Attendance: 31,510

14-12-2005 International Stadium Yokohama, Yokohama:
            Deportivo Saprissa San José – Liverpool FC 0-3 (0-2)
Deportivo Saprissa San José: José Francisco PORRAS Hidaldo, Víctor CORDERO Flores,
Rónald Alfonso GONZÁLEZ Brenes, Gabriel BADILLA Segura, Jervis DRUMMOND
Johnson, Try Anthony BENNETT Grant (46' Alonso SOLÍS Calderón), Christian BOLAÑOS
Navarro, Wálter CENTENO Corea, Randall AZOFEIFA Corrales (YC29), Rónald GÓMEZ
Gómez (76' Gerold DRUMMOND Johnson), Álvaro Alberto SABORÍO Chacón (83' Állan
Fabián ALEMÁN Ávila). (Coach: Hernán Evaristo MEDFORD Bryan).
Liverpool FC: José Manuel "PEPE" REINA Páez (ESP), Sami HYYPIÄ (FIN) (72' LUIS
Javier GARCÍA Sanz (ESP)), John Arne RIISE (NOR), José Miguel González Rey "JOSEMI"
(ESP), Djimi TRAORÉ (MLI), Jamie CARRAGHER, Steven GERRARD (64' Florent
SINAMA-PONGOLLE (FRA)), Xabier "XABI" ALONSO Olano (ESP) (79' Dietmar
HAMANN (GER)), Mohamed SISSOKO (MLI), Djibril CISSÉ (FRA), Peter CROUCH.
(Coach: Rafael "RAFA" BENÍTEZ Maudes (ESP)).
Goals: Liverpool FC: 0-1 Peter CROUCH (3'), 0-2 Steven GERRARD (32'), 0-3 Peter
CROUCH (58').
Referee: Carlos Luis CHANDÍA Alarcón (CHI)   Attendance: 43,902

FIFTH PLACE PLAY–OFF

16-12-2005   National Stadium, Tokyo: Al Ahly SC Cairo – Sydney FC   1-2 (1-1)
Al Ahly SC Cairo: NADER EL SAYED, MOHAMED ABDELWAHAB (76' FLÁVIO da Silva Amado (ANG)), EMAD EL NAHHAS (63' SHADY MOHAMED Abdel Fattah Ragab), AHMED EL-SAYED, WAEL GOMAA Kamel El Hooty (YC76), MOHAMED BARAKAT Ahmed Bastamy, HOSSAM Mohamed ASHOUR Sanad Attia (YC42), MOHAMED Ali Abu El-Yazid SHAWKY, MUHAMMAD ABU TARIKA, EMAD MOTEAB Mohamed Abd El Naby Ibrahim (YC90), OSAMA HOSNY (46' ISLAM Mahmoud Mohamed El Sayed EL SHATER). (Coach: MANUEL JOSÉ de Jesus da Silva (POR)).
Sydney FC: Clint BOLTON, Iain FYFE, Mark RUDAN (YC67), Mark MILLIGAN, Matthew BINGLEY, Steve CORICA (64' Andrew PACKER (YC71)), David CARNEY, Ufuk TALAY (78' Terry McFLYNN), Saso PETROVSKI (89' David ZDRILIC), Dwight YORKE (TRI) (YC87), Kazuyoshi MIURA (JPN). (Coach: Pierre LITTBARSKI (GER)).
Goals: Al Ahly SC Cairo: 1-1 EMAD MOTEAB Mohamed Abd El Naby Ibrahim (45').
Sydney FC: 0-1 Dwight YORKE (35'), 1-2 David CARNEY (66').
Referee: Toru KAMIKAWA (JPN)   Attendance: 15,951

THIRD PLACE PLAY–OFF

18-12-2005   International Stadium Yokohama, Yokohama:
                   Al-Ittihad Club Jeddah – Deportivo Saprissa San José   2-3 (1-1)
Al-Ittihad Club Jeddah: MABROUK ZAID, REHDA Hassan TUKAR Fallatah (69' MESIR AL-KAHTANI), OSAMA Mabrook AL-HARBI Al Muwallad (YC84), ADNAN Ibrahem FALATAH, HAMAD Mohsen AL-MONTASHARI (RC87), MANAF Eid ABUSHGEER, Anderson Simas Luciano "TCHECO" (BRA), SAUD Ali Al KHARIRI (YC90), MOHAMMED NOOR Al-Hawsawi (87' HAMZAH Saeed Idriss FALATAH), Mohamed Ajay KALLON (SLE), Joseph-Désiré JOB (CMR). (Coaches: Anghel IORDANESCU (ROM) & Bruno Lucas Felix METSU (FRA)).
Deportivo Saprissa San José: José Francisco PORRAS Hidaldo, Rónald Alfonso GONZÁLEZ Brenes (YC53) (80' Állan Fabián ALEMÁN Ávila), Juan Bautista ESQUIVEL Lobo, Gabriel BADILLA Segura (YC77), Reynaldo PARKS Pérez, Christian BOLAÑOS Navarro, Wálter CENTENO Corea, Alonso SOLÍS Calderón (64' Rónald GÓMEZ Gómez), José Luis LÓPEZ Ramírez, Álvaro Alberto SABORÍO Chacón, Gerold DRUMMOND Johnson (90' Víctor CORDERO Flores). (Coach: Hernán Evaristo MEDFORD Bryan).
Goals: Al-Ittihad Club: 1-1 Mohamed Ajay KALLON (28'), 2-1 Joseph-Désiré JOB (53' penalty).
Deportivo Saprissa: 0-1 Álvaro Alberto SABORÍO Chacón (13'), 2-2 Álvaro Alberto SABORÍO Chacón (85' penalty), 2-3 Rónald GÓMEZ (89').
Referee: Mohamed GUEZZAZ (MAR)   Attendance: 46,453

FINAL

18-12-2005   International Stadium Yokohama, Yokohama:
              São Paulo FC – Liverpool FC   1-0 (1-0)
São Paulo FC: ROGÉRIO Mücke CENI (YC90), Cícero João de Cézare "CICINHO", José Fábio Alves Azevedo "FABÃO", EDCARLOS Conceição Santos, Diego Alfredo LUGANO Moreno (URU) (YC57), Jenílson Angelo de Souza "JÚNIOR", Carlos Luciano da Silva "MINEIRO", JOSUÉ Anunciado de Oliveira, DANILO Gabriel de Andrade, Marcio AMOROSO dos Santos, ALOÍSIO José da Silva (75' Edinaldo Batista Líbanio "GRAFITE"). (Coach: PAULO AUTUORI de Mello).
Liverpool FC: José Manuel "PEPE" REINA Páez (ESP), Steve FINNAN (IRL), Sami HYYPIÄ (FIN), Jamie CARRAGHER, Harry KEWELL (AUS), Steven GERRARD, Xabier "XABI" ALONSO Olano (ESP), Mohamed SISSOKO (MLI) (79' John Arne RIISE (NOR)), Stephen WARNOCK (79' Florent SINAMA-PONGOLLE (FRA)), LUIS Javier GARCÍA Sanz (ESP), Fernando MORIENTES Sánchez (ESP) (85' Peter CROUCH). (Coach: Rafael "RAFA" BENÍTEZ Maudes (ESP)).
Goal: São Paulo FC: 1-0 Carlos Luciano da Silva "MINEIRO" (27').
Referee: Benito Armando ARCHUNDIA Téllez (MEX)   Attendance: 66,821

*** São Paulo FC won the Cup ***

2006 FIFA Club World Cup

The 2006 FIFA Club World Cup (officially, the 'FIFA Club World Cup Japan 2006 presented by Toyota' for sponsorship reasons) was played in Japan between 10th December and 17th December 2006. It was the third FIFA Club World Cup but the first to be known by this name after a change from the previous title, the FIFA Club World Championship.

The format of the competition was unchanged from 2005 so the Champions of each of the six confederations played in a knock-out tournament with a First Round being played by the AFC, CAF, CONCACAF and OFC teams, while the UEFA and CONMEBOL champions were given byes to the semi-final second round.

Brazilian side SC Internacional won their first World title, defeating Spanish club FC Barcelona 1-0 in the Final.

It was initially proposed that a team from the host nation could participate in the competition. Following the departure of Australia from the OFC to the AFC, the Oceanian champions, Auckland City FC, were actually an amateur side and were theoretically hopelessly outmatched by any of their potential opponents! It was thought that having Auckland face a play-off for a place in the quarter-finals against the reigning J.League champions (Gamba Osaka in 2006) would promote local interest yet still give the OFC Champions a chance to progress. The change would have also eliminated the fifth-place play-off which was seen as meaningless by many teams. The plan was eventually rejected for 2006, but the format of the tournament was changed to include a Japanese team from 2007 onwards.

The clubs invited to play in the 2006 tournament were:

```
FC Barcelona (ESP)            - winners of the 2005-06 UEFA Champions League
SC Internacional (BRA)        - winners of the 2006 Copa Libertadores
Al Ahly SC Cairo (EGY)        - winners of the 2006 CAF Champions League
Jeonbuk Hyundai Motors FC (KOR)
                              - winners of the 2006 AFC Champions League
CF América (MEX)              - winners of the 2006 CONCACAF Champions' Cup
Auckland City FC (NZL)        - winners of the 2006 OFC Club Championship
```

QUARTER-FINALS

10-12-2006   Toyota Stadium, Toyota City:
Auckland City FC – Al Ahly SC Cairo   0-2 (0-0)
Auckland City FC: Ross NICHOLSON, Jonathan PERRY (YC44), James PRITCHETT, Greg UHLMANN, Riki VAN STEEDEN (YC49) (52' Ben SIGMUND), Paul SEAMAN (WAL), Liam MULROONEY (ENG) (56' Teruo IWAMOTO (JPN)), Neil SYKES (ENG), Chad COOMBES, Grant YOUNG (RSA), Keryn JORDAN (RSA) (YC26) (56' Jason HAYNE (YC79)). (Coach: Allan JONES (ENG)).
Al Ahly SC Cairo: ESSAM Kamal Tawfik EL HADARY, ISLAM Mahmoud Mohamed El Sayed EL SHATER (90' AHMED SEDIK Andelhamid Mahdy), AHMED SHEDID Kenawi (89' Akwetey MENSAH (GHA)), WAEL GOMAA Kamel El Hooty, MOHAMED SEDEEK (YC22), SHADY MOHAMED Abdel Fattah Ragab, MOHAMED Ali Abu El-Yazid SHAWKY (YC89), MUHAMMAD ABU TARIKA, HOSSAM Mohamed ASHOUR Sanad Attia, EMAD MOTEAB Mohamed Abd El Naby Ibrahim (84' TAREK EL SAID), FLÁVIO da Silva Amado (ANG). (Coach: MANUEL JOSÉ de Jesus da Silva (POR)).
Goals: Al Ahly SC Cairo: 0-1 FLÁVIO da Silva Amado (51'), 0-2 MUHAMMAD ABU TARIKA (73').
Referee: Khalil Ibrahim M.Al GHAMDI (KSA)   Attendance: 29,922

11-12-2006   Olympic Stadium, Tokyo:
Jeonbuk Hyundai Motors FC – CF América Mexico City 0-1 (0-0)
Jeonbuk Hyundai Motors FC: KWOUN Sun-tae, CHOI Chul-soon (YC83) (85' KIM In-Ho), CHOI Jin-cheul (YC41), KIM Young-Sun (YC56), KIM Hyun-Su, LIM You-hwan (YC35) (83' LEE Hyun-Seung), WANG Jung-Hyun (29' Raphael José BOTTI Zacarias Sena (BRA)), JEON Kwang-Hwan, CHUNG Jung-Kwan, José "ZÉ" CARLOS Ferreira Filho (BRA), KIM Hyung-Bum. (Coach: CHOI Kang-hee).
CF América Mexico City: Francisco Guillermo OCHOA Magaña, José Antonio CASTRO González, Óscar Adrián ROJAS Castillón, Duilio César Jean Pierre DAVINO Rodríguez, Ricardo Francisco ROJAS Trujillo (CHI), FABIANO Pereira da Costa (BRA) (71' Juan Carlos MOSQUEDA Andrade), Germán VILLA Castañeda, Alejandro ARGÜELLO Roa, Claudio Javier LÓPEZ (ARG) (86' Vicente José Matías VUOSO), Salvador CABAÑAS Ortega (PAR), Cuauhtémoc Bravo BLANCO. (Coach: Luis Fernando TENA Garcuño).
Goal: CF América: 0-1 Ricardo ROJAS (79').
Referee: Jerome Kelvyn DAMON (RSA)   Attendance: 34,197

SEMI-FINALS

13-12-2006 Olympic Stadium, Tokyo:
Al Ahli SC Cairo – SC Internacional Porto Alegre 1-2 (0-1)
Al Ahly SC Cairo: ESSAM Kamal Tawfik EL HADARY (82' AMIR ABDELHAMID Mohamed), ISLAM Mahmoud Mohamed El Sayed EL SHATER (75' AHMED SEDIK Andelhamid), EMAD EL NAHHAS, WAEL GOMAA Kamel El Hooty (YC43), SHADY MOHAMED Abdel Fattah Ragab, TAREK EL SAID, HASSAN MOSTAFA (46' EMAD MOTEAB Mohamed Abd El Naby Ibrahim), MOHAMED Ali Abu El-Yazid SHAWKY, MUHAMMAD ABU TARIKA, HOSSAM Mohamed ASHOUR Sanad Attia, FLÁVIO da Silva Amado (ANG) (YC58). (Coach: MANUEL JOSÉ de Jesus da Silva (POR)).
SC Internacional Porto Alegre: CLEMER Melo da Silva, Emilio Martín HIDALGO Conde (PER) (63' RUBENS Vanderlei Tavares CARDOSO), FABIANO ELLER dos Santos, Marcos Antônio de Lima "ÍNDIO", Marcos Venâncio de Albuquerque "CEARÁ", WELLINGTON de Oliveira MONTEIRO, Edimo Ferreira Campos "EDINHO", ALEX Raphael Meschini (YC90), Fernando Lúcio da Costa "FERNANDÃO" (YC29), Pedro IARLEY Lima Dantas (82' Fabián Andrés VARGAS Rivera (COL)), ALEXANDRE "PATO" Rodrigues da Silva (65' LUIZ ADRIANO Souza da Silva). (Coach: ABEL Carlos da Silva BRAGA).
Goals: Al Ahli SC Cairo: 1-1 FLÁVIO da Silva Amado (54').
SC Internacional: 0-1 ALEXANDRE "PATO" Rodrigues da Silva (23'), 1-2 LUIZ ADRIANO Souza da Silva (72').
Referee: Mohd Subkhiddin bin MOHAMED SALLEH (MAS)   Attendance: 33,690

14-12-2006 International Stadium Yokohama, Yokohama:
CF América Mexico City – FC Barelona 0-4 (0-2)
CF América Mexico City: Francisco Guillermo OCHOA Magaña, José Antonio CASTRO González, Óscar Adrián ROJAS Castillón, Duilio César Jean Pierre DAVINO Rodríguez, Ricardo Francisco ROJAS Trujillo (CHI), FABIANO Pereira da Costa (BRA) (YC54) (74' Raúl Alvin MENDOZA Argüello), Germán VILLA Castañeda, Alejandro ARGÜELLO Roa, Claudio Javier LÓPEZ (ARG) (YC69) (74' Vicente José Matías VUOSO), Salvador CABAÑAS Ortega (PAR) (46' Cuauhtémoc Bravo BLANCO), Nelson Rafael CUEVAS Amarilla (PAR). (Coach: Luis Fernando TENA Garcuño).
FC Barcelona: VÍCTOR VALDÉS Arribas, Rafael MÁRQUEZ Álvarez (MEX), Carles PUYOL Saforcada, Gianluca ZAMBROTTA (ITA), Giovanni VAN BRONCKHORST (HOL), THIAGO MOTTA Santon Olivares (ITA) (61' Xavier Hernández i Creus "XAVI"), Anderson Luís de Souza "DECO" (POR), Andrés INIESTA Luján, Eidur GUDJOHNSEN (ISL) (66' Santiago EZQUERRO Marín), Ludovic GIULY (FRA) (74' Juliano Haus BELLETTI (BRA)), Ronaldo De Assis Moreira "RONALDINHO" (BRA). (Coach: Frank RIJKAARD (HOL)).
Goals: FC Barcelona: 0-1 Eidur GUDJOHNSEN (11'), 0-2 Rafael MÁRQUEZ Álvarez (30'), 0-3 Ronaldo De Assis Moreira "RONALDINHO" (65'), 0-4 Anderson Luís de Souza "DECO" (85').
Referee: Óscar Julián RUÍZ Acosta (COL)   Attendance: 62,316

FIFTH PLACE PLAY-OFF

15-12-2006   Olympic Stadium, Tokyo:
Auckland City FC – Jeonbuk Hyundai Motors FC Jeonju 0-3 (0-2)
Auckland City FC: Ross NICHOLSON, Jonathan PERRY (YC72), James PRITCHETT, Greg UHLMANN, Paul SEAMAN (WAL), Liam MULROONEY (ENG) (YC59) (79' Jason HAYNE), Neil SYKES (ENG) (YC74), Chad COOMBES, Grant YOUNG (RSA) (77' Paul URLOVIC), Keryn JORDAN (RSA) (YC42), Bryan LITTLE (SCO) (59' Teruo IWAMOTO (JPN) (YC90)). (Coach: Allan JONES (ENG)).
Jeonbuk Hyundai Motors FC Jeonju: KWOUN Sun-tae, CHOI Chul-soon (88' SHIN Sang-Hoon), KIM Young-Sun, KIM Hyun-Su (81' JEON Kwang-Hwan), KIM In-Ho, LIM You-hwan, CHUNG Jung-Kwan, LEE Hyun-Seung, JANG Ji-Hyun (76' KIM Young-shin), José "ZÉ" CARLOS Ferreira Filho (BRA), KIM Hyung-Bum. (Coach: CHOI Kang-hee).
Goals: Jeonbuk Hyundai Motors FC: 0-1 LEE Hyun-Seung (17'), 0-2 KIM Hyung-Bum (31'), 0-3 José "ZÉ" CARLOS Ferreira Filho (73' penalty).
Referee: Khalil Ibrahim M.Al GHAMDI (KSA)   Attendance: 23,258

THIRD PLACE PLAY-OFF

17-12-2006   International Stadium Yokohama, Yokohama:
Al Ahly SC Cairo – CF América Mexico City 2-1 (1-0)
Al Ahly SC Cairo: AMIR ABDELHAMID Mohamed, ISLAM Mahmoud Mohamed El Sayed EL SHATER (YC54) (67' AHMED SEDIK Andelhamid), EMAD EL NAHHAS, WAEL GOMAA Kamel El Hooty, SHADY MOHAMED Abdel Fattah Ragab, TAREK EL SAID (YC90), MOHAMED Ali Abu El-Yazid SHAWKY, MUHAMMAD ABU TARIKA (YC64), HOSSAM Mohamed ASHOUR Sanad Attia (65' HASSAN MOSTAFA), EMAD MOTEAB Mohamed Abd El Naby Ibrahim (75' MOHAMED SEDEEK), FLÁVIO da Silva Amado (ANG). (Coach: MANUEL JOSÉ de Jesus da Silva (POR)).
CF América Mexico City: Francisco Guillermo OCHOA Magaña, José Antonio CASTRO González, Óscar Adrián ROJAS Castillón, Duilio César Jean Pierre DAVINO Rodríguez, Ricardo Francisco ROJAS Trujillo (CHI) (YC41) (86' Raúl Alvin MENDOZA Argüello), FABIANO Pereira da Costa (BRA) (46' Cuauhtémoc Bravo BLANCO), Alejandro ARGÜELLO Roa, Juan Carlos MOSQUEDA Andrade, Vicente José Matías VUOSO (67' Claudio Javier LÓPEZ (ARG)), Salvador CABAÑAS Ortega (PAR), Nelson Rafael CUEVAS Amarilla (PAR). (Coach: Luis Fernando TENA Garcuño).
Goals: Al Ahly SC Cairo: 1-0 MUHAMMAD ABU TARIKA (42'), 2-1 MUHAMMAD ABU TARIKA (79').
CF América: 1-1 Salvador CABAÑAS Ortega (59').
Referee: Jerome Kelvyn DAMON (RSA)   Attendance: 51,641

FINAL

17-12-2006   International Stadium Yokohama, Yokohama:
SC Internacional Porto Alegre – FC Barcelona 1-0 (0-0)
SC Internacional Porto Alegre: CLEMER Melo da Silva, FABIANO ELLER dos Santos, Marcos Antônio de Lima "ÍNDIO" (YC45), Marcos Venâncio de Albuquerque "CEARÁ", WELLINGTON de Oliveira MONTEIRO, RUBENS Vanderlei Tavares CARDOSO, Edimo Ferreira Campos "EDINHO", ALEX Raphael Meschini (46' Fabián Andrés VARGAS Rivera (COL)), Fernando Lúcio da Costa "FERNANDÃO" (76' Carlos ADRIANO "GABIRU" de Souza Vieira), Pedro IARLEY Lima Dantas (YC90), ALEXANDRE "PATO" Rodrigues da Silva (61' LUIZ ADRIANO Souza da Silva). (Coach: ABEL Carlos da Silva BRAGA).
FC Barcelona: VÍCTOR VALDÉS Arribas, Rafael MÁRQUEZ Álvarez (MEX), Carles PUYOL Saforcada, Gianluca ZAMBROTTA (ITA) (46' Juliano Haus BELLETTI (BRA)), Giovanni VAN BRONCKHORST (HOL), THIAGO MOTTA Santon Olivares (ITA) (YC55) (59' Xavier Hernández i Creus "XAVI"), Anderson Luís de Souza "DECO" (POR), Andrés INIESTA Luján, Eidur GUDJOHNSEN (ISL) (88' Santiago EZQUERRO Marín), Ludovic GIULY (FRA), Ronaldo De Assis Moreira "RONALDINHO" (BRA). (Coach: Frank RIJKAARD (HOL)).
Goal: SC Internacional: 1-0 Carlos ADRIANO "GABIRU" de Souza Vieira (82').
Referee: Carlos Alberto BATRES González (GUA)   Attendance: 67,128

*** SC Internacional won the Cup ***

2007 FIFA Club World Cup

The 2007 FIFA Club World Cup (officially, the 'FIFA Club World Cup Japan 2007 presented by Toyota' for sponsorship reasons) was a football tournament played in Japan between 7th and 16th December 2007. This was the fourth edition of the competition.

Seven teams from the six confederations entered the tournament, and the Italian side AC Milan defeated CA Boca Juniors Buenos Aires from Argentina 4-2 in the Final.

The Champions of the six major continental competitions each entered the tournament alongside a seventh team which was originally planned to be the J.League Champions who were scheduled to enter a qualifying play-off against the Oceania Champions. However, Urawa Red Diamonds, a Japanese team had won the AFC Champions League in 2007. To avoid having two Japanese teams in the tournament, the Iranian runners-up in the AFC Champions League, Foolad Mobarakeh Sepahan FC instead played against the Oceanian Champions, Waitakere United, in the play-off.

The clubs invited to play in the 2007 tournament were:

AC Milan (ITA) - winners of the 2006-07 UEFA Champions League
CA Boca Juniors Buenos Aires (ARG)
  - winners of the 2007 Copa Libertadores
ES Sahel (TUN) - winners of the 2007 CAF Champions League
Urawa Red Diamonds (JPN) - winners of the 2007 AFC Champions League
CF Pachuca (MEX) - winners of the 2007 CONCACAF Champions' Cup
Waitakere United (NZL) - winners of the 2007 OFC Champions League
Foolad Mobarakeh Sepahan FC (IRN)
  - runners-up of the 2007 AFC Champions League

(Foolad Mobarakeh Sepahan FC took the place of the J.League winners as a Japanese team were winners of the AFC Champions League)

PLAY-OFF FOR QUARTER-FINALS

07-12-2007 National Stadium, Tokyo:
Foolad Mobarakeh Sepahan FC Isfahan – Waitakere United 3-1 (2-0)
Foolad Mobarakeh Sepahan FC Isfahan: Mohammad SAVARI, Seyed Hadi AGHILI Anvar, Mohsen BENGAR, Jaba MUJIRI (GEO), Hadi JAFARI Raraei, Farshad BAHADORANI, Abdul-Wahab ABU Al-HAIL Labid, Ehsan HAJSAFI (YC46), Emad MOHAMMED Ridha Raza Gharib (87' Kabir Prince BELLO (NGR)), Mahmoud KARIMI (68' Hossein KAZEMI (YC89)), Seyed Mohammad MEHDI SEYED SALEHI (60' Ebrahim LOVEINIAN). (Coach: Luka BONACIC (CRO)).
Waitakere United: Simon EADDY, Jonathan PERRY, Matt CUNNEEN, Danny HAY, Darren BAZELEY (ENG) (YC16), Graham PEARCE (YC84) (85' Commins MENAPI (SLM)), Neil SYKES (ENG) (YC31), Christopher BALE (WAL) (63' Jason HAYNE), Neil EMBLEN (ENG), Paul SEAMON (WAL) (90' Daniel KOPRIVIC), Benjamin TOTORI (SLM). (Coach: Chris MILICICH).
Goals: Foolad Mobarakeh Sepahan FC: 1-0 Emad MOHAMMED Ridha Raza Gharib (3'), 2-0 Emad MOHAMMED Ridha Raza Gharib (4'), 3-0 Abdul-Wahab ABU Al-HAIL Labid (47').
Waitakere United: 3-1 Seyed Hadi AGHILI Anvar (74' own goal).
Referee: Marco Antonio RODRÍGUEZ Moreno (MEX)   Attendance: 24,788

QUARTER-FINALS

09-12-2007 National Stadium, Tokyo: ES Sahel Sousse – CF Pachuca 1-0 (0-0)
ES Sahel Sousse: Aymen MATHLOUTHI Balbouli, Hatem BEJAOUI, Saïf GHEZAL, Radhouène FELHI, Saber BEN FREJ, Afouène GHARBI (YC60), Mohamed Ali NAFKHA, Moussa NARRY (GHA), Mohamed Amine CHERMITI, Mouritala Ola OGOUNBIYI (BEN), Mehdi BEN DHIFALLAH (YC56) (89' Mohamed SACKO (GUI)). (Coaches: Bertrand MARCHAND (FRA) & Kaïs ZOUAHI).
CF Pachuca: Miguel Ángel CALERO Rodríguez (COL), Leobardo LÓPEZ García (YC71), Julio César MANZUR Caffarena (PAR), Marvin Gabriel CABRERA Ibarra, Carlos Gerardo RODRÍGUEZ Serrano (87' Andrés CHITIVA Espinosa (COL)), Fausto Manuel PINTO Rosas, Jaime CORREA Córdoba, Damián Ariel ÁLVAREZ (YC51), Gabriel Esteban CABALLERO Schiker (90' Luis Gabriel REY Villamizar (COL)), Christian Eduardo GIMÉNEZ, Juan Carlos CACHO Gutiérrez. (Coach: Enrique Everardo MEZA Enríquez).
Goal: ES Sahel: 1-0 Moussa NARRY (85').
Referee: Mark Alexander SHIELD (AUS)   Attendance: 34,934

10-12-2007 Toyota Stadium, Toyota City:
Foolad Mobarakeh Sepahan FC Isfahan – Urawa Red Diamonds 1-3 (0-1)
Foolad Mobarakeh Sepahan FC Isfahan: Mohammad SAVARI, Seyed Hadi AGHILI Anvar, Mohsen BENGAR, Jaba MUJIRI (GEO), Hadi JAFARI Raraei (46' Saeid BAYAT), Farshad BAHADORANI (YC34), Abdul-Wahab ABU Al-HAIL Labid (78' Ebrahim LOVEINIAN), Ehsan HAJSAFI, Emad MOHAMMED Ridha Raza Gharib, Kabir Prince BELLO (NGR) (46' Mahmoud KARIMI), Seyed Mohammad MEHDI SEYED SALEHI. (Coach: Luka BONACIC (CRO)).
Urawa Red Diamonds: Ryota TSUZUKI, Keisuke TSUBOI, Marcus Tulio TANAKA, Fábio Camilo de Brito "NENÊ" (BRA), Takahito SOMA, Hajime HOSOGAI, Keita SUZUKI, Makoto HASEBE (90' Masayuki OKANO), Yuki ABE, Yuichiro NAGAI (73' Shinji ONO), WASHINGTON Stécanelo Cerqueira (BRA). (Coach: Holger OSIECK (GER)).
Goals: Foolad Mobarakeh Sepahan FC: 1-3 Mahmoud KARIMI (80').
Urawa Red Diamonds: 0-1 Yuichiro NAGAI (32'), 0-2 WASHINGTON Stécanelo Cerqueira (54'), 0-3 Seyed Hadi AGHILI Anvar (70' own goal).
Referee: Coffi Bonaventure CODJIA (BEN)   Attendance: 33,263

SEMI–FINALS

12-12-2007 National Stadium, Tokyo:
ES Sahel Sousse – CA Boca Juniors Buenos Aires 0-1 (0-1)
ES Sahel Sousse: Aymen MATHLOUTHI Balbouli, Saïf GHEZAL, Radhouène FELHI, Mehdi MERIAH (YC78), Saber BEN FREJ, Mohamed SACKO (GUI) (56' Mehdi BEN DHIFALLAH), Mejdi TRAOUI (75' Manuel GILSON SILVA Alves (CVI)), Mohamed Ali NAFKHA, Moussa NARRY (GHA) (YC90), Mohamed Amine CHERMITI, Mouritala Ola OGOUNBIYI (BEN) (10' Afouène GHARBI (YC21)). (Coaches: Bertrand MARCHAND (FRA) & Kaïs ZOUAHI).
CA Boca Juniors Buenos Aires: Mauricio Ariel CARANTA, Matías David MAIDANA, Claudio Marcelo MOREL Rodríguez (PAR), Hugo Benjamín IBARRA, Gabriel Alejandro PALETTA (ITA), Sebastián Alejandro BATTAGLIA (YC20), Neri Raúl CARDOZO (68' Álvaro Rafael GONZÁLEZ Luengo (URU)), Fabián Andrés VARGAS Rivera (COL) (YC16, RC65), Éver Maximiliano David BANEGA (90' Pablo Martín LEDESMA), Martín PALERMO Scorpino (YC90), Rodrigo Sebastián PALACIO (90' Mauro BOSELLI). (Coach: Miguel Ángel RUSSO).
Goal: CA Boca Juniors Buenos Aires: 0-1 Neri CARDOZO (37').
Referee: Claus Bo LARSEN (DEN)   Attendance: 37,255

13-12-2007   International Stadium Yokohama, Yokohama:
Urawa Red Diamonds – AC Milan 0-1 (0-0)
Urawa Red Diamonds: Ryota TSUZUKI, Keisuke TSUBOI, Marcus Tulio TANAKA (76' Nobuhisa YAMADA), Fábio Camilo de Brito "NENÊ" (BRA) (YC83), Takahito SOMA (81' Tadaaki HIRAKAWA), Hajime HOSOGAI, Keita SUZUKI, Makoto HASEBE, Yuki ABE (YC52), Yuichiro NAGAI, WASHINGTON Stécanelo Cerqueira (BRA). (Coach: Holger OSIECK (GER)).
AC Milan: Nelson de Jesús da Silva "DIDA" (BRA), Kakha KALADZE (GEO), Alessandro NESTA (YC6), Marek JANKULOVSKI (CZE) (80' Paolo MALDINI), Massimo ODDO, Gennaro GATTUSO, Clarence SEEDORF (HOL) (90' Cristian BROCCHI), Andrea PIRLO, Ricardo Izecson dos Santos Leite "KAKÁ" (BRA), Massimo AMBROSINI, Alberto GILARDINO (63' Filippo INZAGHI). (Coach: Carlo ANCELOTTI).
Goal: AC Milan: 0-1 Clarence SEEDORF (68').
Referee: Jorge Luis LARRIONDA Pietrafesa (URU)   Attendance: 67,005

THIRD PLACE PLAY–OFF

16-12-2007   International Stadium Yokohama, Yokohama:
ES Sahel Sousse – Urawa Red Diamonds 2-2 (1-1, 2-2) **(AET)**
ES Sahel Sousse: Aymen MATHLOUTHI Balbouli (90' Ahmed JAOUACHI), Saïf GHEZAL, Radhouène FELHI, Mehdi MERIAH, Saber BEN FREJ (YC87), Mejdi TRAOUI, Mohamed Ali NAFKHA, Khaled MELLITI (58' Manuel GILSON SILVA Alves (CVI)), Moussa NARRY (GHA), Mohamed Amine CHERMITI, Mehdi BEN DHIFALLAH (YC32) (90' Bassem BEN NASR). (Coaches: Bertrand MARCHAND (FRA) & Kaïs ZOUAHI).
Urawa Red Diamonds: Ryota TSUZUKI, Keisuke TSUBOI (YC4), Fábio Camilo de Brito "NENÊ" (BRA), Nobuhisa YAMADA, Takahito SOMA, Hajime HOSOGAI, Keita SUZUKI, Makoto HASEBE, Yuki ABE, Yuichiro NAGAI, WASHINGTON Stécanelo Cerqueira (BRA) (YC71). (Coach: Holger OSIECK (GER)).
Goals: ES Sahel: 1-0 Saber BEN FREJ (5' penalty), 2-2 Mohamed Amine CHERMITI (75'). Urawa Red Diamonds: 1-1 WASHINGTON Stécanelo Cerqueira (35'), 1-2 WASHINGTON Stécanelo Cerqueira (70').
Referee: Peter O'LEARY (NZL)   Attendance: 53,363

Penalties:
1 WASHINGTON Stécanelo Cerqueira   * Mohamed Ali NAFKHA
2 Yuki ABE   1 Saïf GHEZAL
3 Yuichiro NAGAI   2 Bassem BEN NASR
4 Hajime HOSOGAI   * Mejdi TRAOUI

FINAL

16-12-2007   International Stadium Yokohama, Yokohama:
CA Boca Juniors Buenos Aires – AC Milan 2-4 (1-1)
CA Boca Juniors Buenos Aires: Mauricio Ariel CARANTA, Claudio Marcelo MOREL Rodríguez (PAR), Hugo Benjamín IBARRA (YC40), Jonatan Ramón MAIDANA, Gabriel Alejandro PALETTA (ITA) (YC73), Sebastián Alejandro BATTAGLIA (YC55), Álvaro Rafael GONZÁLEZ Luengo (URU) (67' Pablo Martín LEDESMA (RC88)), Neri Raúl CARDOZO (68' Leandro GRACIÁN), Éver Maximiliano David BANEGA, Martín PALERMO Scorpino, Rodrigo Sebastián PALACIO. (Coach: Miguel Ángel RUSSO).
AC Milan: Nelson de Jesús da Silva "DIDA" (BRA), Paolo MALDINI, Kakha KALADZE (GEO) (RC77), Alessandro NESTA, Daniele BONERA, Gennaro GATTUSO (65' EMERSON Ferreira da Rosa (BRA)), Clarence SEEDORF (HOL) (87' Cristian BROCCHI), Andrea PIRLO, Ricardo Izecson dos Santos Leite "KAKÁ" (BRA) (YC62), Massimo AMBROSINI (YC22), Filippo INZAGHI (76' Marcos Evangelista de Moraes "CAFÚ" (BRA)). (Coach: Carlo ANCELOTTI).
Goals: CA Boca Juniors Buenos Aires: 1-1 Rodrigo Sebastián PALACIO (22'), 2-4 Massimo AMBROSINI (85' own goal).
AC Milan: 0-1 Filippo INZAGHI (21'), 1-2 Alessandro NESTA (50'), 1-3 Ricardo Izecson dos Santos Leite "KAKÁ" (61'), 1-4 Filippo INZAGHI (71').
Referee: Marco Antonio RODRÍGUEZ Moreno (MEX)   Attendance: 68,263

*** AC Milan won the Cup ***

2008 FIFA Club World Cup

The 2008 FIFA Club World Cup (officially, the 'FIFA Club World Cup Japan 2008 presented by Toyota' for sponsorship reasons) was the fifth FIFA Club World Cup and was played in Japan between 11th and 21st December 2008.

The Champions of the six confederations entered the tournament and, once again, a Japanese team had won the AFC Champions League so the runners-up in this competition (Adelaide United FC) took the place originally planned for the J.League Champions. In the Final, Manchester United FC defeated LDU de Quito 1-0 at the International Stadium in Yokohama to become the first British team to win the competition. It was Manchester United's second world title, following their 1999 Intercontinental Cup victory.

The fifth-place match, which had been dropped for the 2007 tournament, was reintroduced for 2008 so a total of 8 matches were played and the total prize money was increased by US $500,000 to make the additional fixture more appealing to entrants.

The clubs invited to play in the 2008 tournament were:

Manchester United FC (ENG)	- winners of the 2007-08 UEFA Champions League
LDU de Quito (ECU)	- winners of the 2008 Copa Libertadores
Al Ahly SC Cairo (EGY)	- winners of the 2008 CAF Champions League
Gamba Osaka (JPN)	- winners of the 2008 AFC Champions League
CF Pachuca (MEX)	- winners of the 2008 CONCACAF Champions' Cup
Waitakere United (NZL)	- winners of the 2007-08 OFC Champions League
Adelaide United FC (AUS)	- runners-up of the 2008 AFC Champions League

(As Gamba Osaka won the AFC Champions League, the host's spot was taken by Adelaide United FC as the highest-placed non-Japanese team in the AFC Champions League)

PLAY-OFF FOR QUARTER-FINALS

11-12-2008   National Stadium, Tokyo:
Adelaide United FC – Waitakere United 2-1 (1-1)
Adelaide United FC: Eugene GALEKOVIC, Robert CORNTHWAITE, Angelo COSTANZO, Scott JAMIESON, Daniel MULLEN, Kristian SARKIES (70' Robert YOUNIS), Travis DODD, Fabian BARBIERO (YC25), Jason SPAGNUOLO (57' Everson Arantes de Oliveira "ALEMÃO" (BRA)), Paul REID, CRISTIANO dos Santos Rodrigues (BRA). (Coach: Aurelio VIDMAR).
Waitakere United: Richard GILLESPIE, Jonathan PERRY, Jason ROWLEY, Paul SEAMON (WAL) (85' Benjamin TOTORI (SLM)), Neil SYKES (ENG), Christopher BALE (WAL) (YC78), Neil EMBLEN (ENG), Jake BUTLER (YC40), Allan PEARCE (75' ADRIANO Faria Pimenta (BRA)), Roy KRISHNA (FIJ) (YC4), Daniel KOPRIVIC (67' Kayne VINCENT). (Coach: Chris MILICICH).
Goals: Adelaide United FC: 1-1 Daniel MULLEN (39'), 2-1 Travis DODD (83').
Waitakere United: 0-1 Paul SEAMAN (34').
Referee: Mohamed Abderrezak BENOUZA (ALG)   Attendance: 19,777

QUARTER-FINALS

13-12-2008   National Stadium, Tokyo:
Al Ahly SC Cairo – CF Pachuca 2-4 (2-0, 2-2) **(AET)**
Al Ahly SC Cairo: AMIR ABDELHAMID Mohamed, AHMED EL-SAYED (YC47), WAEL GOMAA Kamel El Hooty (YC101), SHADY MOHAMED Abdel Fattah Ragab, MOHAMED BARAKAT Ahmed Bastamy, Felisberto Sebastião de Graça Amaral "duba" (ANG) (97' HUSSAIN YASSER El-Mohammadi Abdulrahman (QAT)), AHMED HASSAN Kamel Hussein (77' AHMED SEDIK Andelhamid), MUHAMMAD ABU TARIKA (YC82), AHMED FATHI Abdelmonem (91' SAYED MOAWAD Abdel Wahed), HOSSAM Mohamed ASHOUR Sanad Attia (YC98), FLÁVIO da Silva Amado (ANG). (Coach: MANUEL JOSÉ de Jesus da Silva (POR)).
CF Pachuca: Miguel Ángel CALERO Rodríguez (COL), Leobardo LÓPEZ García, Julio César MANZUR Caffarena (PAR), Carlos Gerardo RODRÍGUEZ Serrano, Fausto Manuel PINTO Rosas (46' Juan Carlos ROJAS Guerra), Paul Nicolás AGUILAR Rojas, Jaime CORREA Córdoba (46' Luis Arturo MONTES Jiménez (YC100)), Damián Ariel ÁLVAREZ (ARG), José Francisco TORRES Mezzell (USA) (70' José María CÁRDENAS López), Christian Eduardo GIMÉNEZ (ARG), Bruno MARIONI Giménez (ARG). (Coach: Enrique Everardo MEZA Enríquez).
Goals: Al Ahly SC Cairo: 1-0 Fausto Manuel PINTO Rosas (28' own goal), 2-0 FLÁVIO da Silva Amado (44').
CF Pachuca: 2-1 Luis Arturo MONTES Jiménez (47'), 2-2 Christian Eduardo GIMÉNEZ (72'), 2-3 Damián Ariel ÁLVAREZ (98'), 2-4 Christian Eduardo GIMÉNEZ (110').
Referee: Ravshan Sayfiddinovich IRMATOV (UZB)   Attendance: 30,158

14-12-2008 Toyota Stadium, Toyota City:
Adelaide United FC – Gamba Osaka Suita 0-1 (0-1)
Adelaide United FC: Eugene GALEKOVIC, Robert CORNTHWAITE, CÁSSIO José de Abreu Oliveira (BRA) (YC33) (71' Everson Arantes de Oliveira "ALEMÃO" (BRA)), Scott JAMIESON, Daniel MULLEN, Sasa OGNENOVSKI (YC21), Travis DODD, Fabian BARBIERO, DIEGO Costa Bastos Walsh (BRA) (88' Robert YOUNIS), Paul REID (YC43), CRISTIANO dos Santos Rodrigues (BRA) (77' Osama MALIK). (Coach: Aurelio VIDMAR).
Gamba Osaka Suita: Yosuke FUJIGAYA, Sota NAKAZAWA, Satoshi YAMAGUCHI, Michihiro YASUDA (YC36), Akira KAJI (YC41), Yasuhito ENDŌ, Takahiro FUTAGAWA (84' Takuya TAKEI), Hayato SASAKI (20' Ryuji BANDO, 81' Masato YAMAZAKI), Tomokazu MYOJIN, Hideo HASHIMOTO, LUCAS Severino (BRA). (Coach: Akira NISHINO).
Goal: Gamba Osaka: 0-1 Yasuhito ENDŌ (23').
Referee: Pablo Antonio POZO Quinteros (CHI)   Attendance: 38,141

SEMI-FINALS

17-12-2008   National Stadium, Tokyo: CF Pachuca – LDU de Quito 0-2 (0-2)
CF Pachuca: Miguel Ángel CALERO Rodríguez (COL) (YC45), Leobardo LÓPEZ García, Julio César MANZUR Caffarena (PAR) (YC24), Juan Carlos ROJAS Guerra, Fausto Manuel PINTO Rosas (YC27), Jaime CORREA Córdoba (46' Paul Nicolás AGUILAR Rojas (YC90)), Damián Ariel ÁLVAREZ (ARG), José Francisco TORRES Mezzell (USA) (67' Carlos Gerardo RODRÍGUEZ Serrano), Christian Eduardo GIMÉNEZ (ARG) (YC58), Bruno MARIONI Giménez (ARG), José María CÁRDENAS López (46' Luis Arturo MONTES Jiménez). (Coach: Enrique Everardo MEZA Enríquez).
LDU de Quito: José Francisco CEVALLOS Villavicencio (YC57), Norberto Carlos ARAUJO López (ARG), Renán CALLE Camacho, Diego Armando CALDERÓN Espinoza, Jayro Rolando CAMPOS León, Neicer REASCO Yano (90' Pedro Sebastián LARREA Arellano), Luis Alberto BOLAÑOS León, Patricio Javier URRUTIA Espinoza (YC50), William Francisco ARAUJO Ogonaga, Damián Alejandro MANSO (ARG) (YC33), Claudio Daniel BIELER (ARG) (78' Reinaldo Marcelino NAVIA Amador (CHI)). (Coach: Edgardo BAUZA (ARG)).
Goals: LDU de Quito: 0-1 Claudio BIELER (4'), 0-2 Luis BOLAÑOS (26').
Referee: Alberto UNDIANO MALLENCO (ESP)   Attendance: 33,366

18-12-2008   International Stadium Yokohama, Yokohama:
              Gamba Osaka Suita – Manchester United FC 3-5 (0-2)
Gamba Osaka Suita: Yosuke FUJIGAYA, Sota NAKAZAWA, Satoshi YAMAGUCHI (YC90), Akira KAJI, Yasuhito ENDŌ, Tomokazu MYOJIN, Hideo HASHIMOTO, Kodai YASUDA, LUCAS Severino (BRA), Ryuji BANDO (85' Shinichi TERADA), Masato YAMAZAKI. (Coach: Akira NISHINO).
Manchester United FC: Edwin VAN DER SAR (HOL), Gary NEVILLE, Patrice EVRA (FRA), Rio FERDINAND, Nemanja VIDIC (SRB) (69' Jonny EVANS (NIR)), ANDERSON Luís de Abreu Oliveira (BRA), Ryan GIGGS (WAL), Paul SCHOLES (67' Darren FLETCHER (SCO)), CRISTIANO RONALDO dos Santos Aveiro (POR), Luís Carlos Almeida da Cunha "NANI" (POR), Carlos Alberto TÉVEZ (ARG) (73' Wayne ROONEY). (Coach: Alex FERGUSON (SCO)).
Goals: Gamba Osaka: 1-2 Masato YAMAZAKI (74'), 2-5 Yasuhito ENDŌ (85' penalty), 3-5 Hideo HASHIMOTO (90').
Manchester United FC: 0-1 Nemanja VIDIC (28'), 0-2 CRISTIANO RONALDO dos Santos Aveiro (45'), 1-3 Wayne ROONEY (75'), 1-4 Darren FLETCHER (78'), 1-5 Wayne ROONEY (80').
Referee: Benito Armando ARCHUNDIA Téllez (MEX)   Attendance: 67,618

FIFTH PLACE PLAY–OFF

18-12-2008   International Stadium Yokohama, Yokohama:
              Al Ahly SC Cairo – Adelaide United FC 0-1 (0-1)
Al Ahly SC Cairo: AMIR ABDELHAMID Mohamed, RAMI ADEL, SAYED MOAWAD Abdel Wahed, WAEL GOMAA Kamel El Hooty, SHADY MOHAMED Abdel Fattah Ragab, MOHAMED BARAKAT Ahmed Bastamy, AHMED HASSAN Kamel Hussein (46' HUSSAIN YASSER El-Mohammadi Abdulrahman (QAT) (YC87)), MUHAMMAD ABU TARIKA (46' OSAMA HOSNY), AHMED FATHI Abdelmonem, HOSSAM Mohamed ASHOUR Sanad Attia, FLÁVIO da Silva Amado (ANG) (67' HANY Mohamed Shaaban EL EGAZI). (Coach: MANUEL JOSÉ de Jesus da Silva (POR)).
Adelaide United FC: Eugene GALEKOVIC, Robert CORNTHWAITE, Everson Arantes de Oliveira "ALEMÃO" (BRA), Scott JAMIESON, Daniel MULLEN (YC51) (54' Michael MARRONE), Sasa OGNENOVSKI, Kristian SARKIES, DIEGO Costa Bastos Walsh (BRA) (24' Jonas SALLEY (YC64)), Paul REID, CRISTIANO dos Santos Rodrigues (BRA), Robert YOUNIS (75' Osama MALIK). (Coach: Aurelio VIDMAR).
Goal: Adelaide United FC: 0-1 CRISTIANO dos Santos Rodrigues (7').
Referee: Peter O'LEARY (NZL)   Attendance: 35,154

THIRD PLACE PLAY–OFF

21-12-2008   International Stadium Yokohama, Yokohama:
               CF Pachuca – Gamba Osaka Suita 0-1 (0-1)
CF Pachuca: Miguel Ángel CALERO Rodríguez (COL) (YC15), Leobardo LÓPEZ García (YC79), Marco Iván PÉREZ Riego, Carlos Gerardo RODRÍGUEZ Serrano (YC6), Paul Nicolás AGUILAR Rojas, Jaime CORREA Córdoba, Damián Ariel ÁLVAREZ (ARG) (51' Luis Arturo MONTES Jiménez), Gabriel Esteban CABALLERO Schiker (74' Víctor Omar MAÑÓN Barrón), Christian Eduardo GIMÉNEZ (ARG), CHRISTIAN Corrêa Dionisio (BRA), José María CÁRDENAS López (46' José Francisco TORRES Mezzell (USA)).
(Coach: Enrique Everardo MEZA Enríquez).
Gamba Osaka Suita: Yosuke FUJIGAYA (YC90), Sota NAKAZAWA, Satoshi YAMAGUCHI, Michihiro YASUDA, Akira KAJI, Yasuhito ENDŌ, Tomokazu MYOJIN, Hideo HASHIMOTO, LUCAS Severino (BRA) (77' Takuya Takei), Ryuji BANDO (64' Takahiro FUTAGAWA (RC90)), Masato YAMAZAKI (YC82). (Coach: Akira NISHINO).
Goal: Gamba Osaka: 0-1 Masato YAMAZAKI (29').
Referee: Pablo Antonio POZO Quinteros (CHI)   Attendance: 62,619

FINAL

21-12-2008   International Stadium Yokohama, Yokohama:
               LDU de Quito – Manchester United FC 0-1 (0-0)
LDU de Quito: José Francisco CEVALLOS Villavicencio (YC44), Norberto Carlos ARAUJO López (ARG), Renán CALLE Camacho (YC66) (77' Vicente Paúl AMBROSI Zambrano), Diego Armando CALDERÓN Espinoza, Jayro Rolando CAMPOS León (YC36), Neicer REASCO Yano (82' Pedro Sebastián LARREA Arellano), Luis Alberto BOLAÑOS León (87' Reinaldo Marcelino NAVIA Amador (CHI)), Patricio Javier URRUTIA Espinoza, William Francisco ARAUJO Ogonaga (YC71), Damián Alejandro MANSO (ARG), Claudio Daniel BIELER (ARG) (YC2). (Coach: Edgardo BAUZA (ARG)).
Manchester United FC: Edwin VAN DER SAR (HOL), Patrice EVRA (FRA), Rio FERDINAND, Nemanja VIDIC (SRB) (RC49), RAFAEL Pereira da Silva (BRA) (85' Gary NEVILLE), ANDERSON Luís de Abreu Oliveira (BRA) (YC70) (88' Darren FLETCHER (SCO)), PARK Ji-Sung (KOR), Michael CARRICK, CRISTIANO RONALDO dos Santos Aveiro (POR), Wayne ROONEY, Carlos Alberto TÉVEZ (ARG) (51' Jonny EVANS (NIR)).
(Coach: Alex FERGUSON (SCO)).
Goal: Manchester United FC: 0-1 Wayne ROONEY (73').
Referee: Ravshan Sayfiddinovich IRMATOV (UZB)   Attendance: 68,682

*** Manchester United FC won the Cup ***

2009 FIFA Club World Cup

The 2009 FIFA Club World Cup (officially, the 'FIFA Club World Cup UAE 2009 presented by Toyota' for sponsorship reasons) was played between 9th and 19th December 2009. This was the sixth FIFA Club World Cup which, unlike the earlier competitions, was held in Abu Dhabi, United Arab Emirates. Australia, Japan and Portugal also placed bids to host the tournament, though Portugal later withdrew their application.

The Champions of the six confederations entered the tournament as did the local UAE champions Shabab Al-Ahli Club Dubai who faced the Oceanian Champions in an initial play-off.

The Final was played on 19th December 2009 and was won by the European Champions, FC Barcelona, who came from behind to win 2-1 against the South American entrants, CA Estudiantes de La Plata, after extra time. This win meant that Barcelona were the first Spanish side to win the FIFA Club World Cup, but, more impressively, also meant that they had won a total of six competitions in the 2009 calendar year, beating Liverpool FC's European record of five trophies won during 2001!

The clubs invited to play in the 2009 tournament were:

FC Barcelona (ESP) - winners of the 2008-09 UEFA Champions League
CA Estudiantes de La Plata (ARG)
                 - winners of the 2009 Copa Libertadores
TP Mazembe (DRC) - winners of the 2009 CAF Champions League
Pohang Steelers (KOR) - winners of the 2009 AFC Champions League
Atlante FC (MEX) - winners of the 2008-09 CONCACAF Champions League
Auckland City FC (NZL) - winners of the 2008-09 OFC Champions League
Shabab Al-Ahli Club Dubai (UAE)
                 - winners of the 2008-09 UAE Pro-League

PLAY-OFF FOR QUARTER-FINALS

09-12-2009   Mohammed bin Zayed Stadium, Abu Dhabi:
             Shabab Al-Ahli Club Dubai – Auckland City FC 0-2 (0-1)
Shabab Al-Ahli Club Dubai: YOUSEF Abdulla Mohamed AL ZAABI, SAAD SUROUR Masoud Surour bin Baniyas, KHALED MOHAMMED Abdulla Mohammed (84' WALEED AHMED Hassan Ahmed Al Mazam), BADER YAQOOT Nasser Al-Juraishi, HOSNY Abd Rabo Abdel Mottaleb Ibrahim (EGY), HASSAN Ali IBRAHIM Al Beloshi (54' Mehrzad MADANCHIARDEKANI (IRN)), ALI ABBAS Yasin Al Hawasin, YOUSEF JABER Naser Jaber Al Hammadi, SALEM KHAMIS Faraj Alem (YC46), ALI HUSSAIN Yousif Hassan Al Mazam (YC15) (46' MOHAMED RASHID Srour Al Naqbi), Jader Volnei Spindler "BARÉ" (BRA). (Coach: MAHDI Ali Hassan REDHA).
Auckland City FC: Jacob SPOONLEY, Ian HOGG, Ivan VICELICH, Greg UHLMANN (90' Sam CAMPBELL), Matt WILLIAMS, LEE Ki-hyung (KOR), Chad COOMBES (YC45), Daniel KOPRIVIC (CRO) (71' Keryn JORDAN (RSA)), Jason HAYNE (85' Alex FENERIDIS), Adam McGEORGE (YC33), Adam DICKINSON (ENG). (Coach: Paul POSA).
Goals: Auckland City FC: 0-1 Adam DICKINSON (45'), 0-2 Chad COOMBES (67').
Referee: CARLOS Eugênio SIMON (BRA)   Attendance: 14,856

QUARTER-FINALS

11-12-2009   Mohammed bin Zayed Stadium, Abu Dhabi:
             TP Mazembe Lubumbashi – Pohang Steelers 1-2 (1-0)
TP Mazembe Lubumbashi: Muteba KIDIABA, Miala NKULUKUTA (YC54), Bawaka MABELE (YC45), Kanyimbo TSHIZEU, Mbenza BEDI, Kazembe MIHAYO, Narcisse EKANGA (CMR) (83' Déo KANDA), Basisila LUSADISU (60' Ngandu KASONGO), Trésor MPUTU, Patou KABANGU, Dioko KALUYITUKA (82' Luyeye MVETE). (Coach: Diego GARZITTO (FRA)).
Pohang Steelers: SHIN Hwa-yong, CHOI Hyo-jin, HWANG Jae-won, KIM Hyung-il, KIM Tae-Su, KIM Jae-sung, KIM Jung-Kyum, SHIN Hyung-min (80' Go Seul-ki), DENILSON Martins Nascimento (BRA), NAMGUNG Do (56' HWANG Jin-sung), NO Byung-Jun (88' SONG Chang-Ho). (Coach: SÉRGIO Ricardo de Paiva FARIAS (BRA)).
Goals: TP Mazembe: 1-0 Mbenza BEDI (28').
Pohang Steelers: 1-1 DENILSON Martins Nascimento (50'), 1-2 DENILSON Martins Nascimento (78').
Referee: Peter O'LEARY (NZL)   Attendance: 9,627

12-12-2009 Zayed Sports City Stadium, Abu Dhabi:
Auckland City FC – Atlante FC Mexico City 0-3 (0-1)
Auckland City FC: Jacob SPOONLEY, Ian HOGG, Ivan VICELICH, Greg UHLMANN, Matt WILLIAMS, LEE Ki-hyung (KOR) (78' Milos NIKOLIC), Chad COOMBES, Daniel KOPRIVIC (CRO) (66' Grant YOUNG (RSA)), Jason HAYNE, Adam McGEORGE (YC43), Adam DICKINSON (ENG) (88' Paul URLOVIC). (Coach: Paul POSA).
Atlante FC Mexico City: Federico VILAR Baudena (ARG), Miguel Ángel MARTÍNEZ (ARG), Fernando NAVARRO Morán, Luis David VELÁZQUEZ Jiménez, Daniel ARREOLA Argüello (YC26), José Daniel Octavio GUERRERO Rodrígeuz, José Joel GONZÁLEZ Sandoval, Santiago Hernán SOLARI Poggio (ARG) (74' LUCAS Antônio SILVA de Oliveira (BRA)), Christian de Jesús BERMÚDEZ Gutiérrez, Guillermo ROJAS Rumilla, Rafael MÁRQUEZ Lugo (YC10) (86' Gabriel Ernesto PEREYRA Vázquez (ARG)). (Coach: José Guadalupe CRUZ Núñez).
Goals: Atlante FC: 0-1 Daniel ARREOLA (36'), 0-2 Christian BERMÚDEZ (69'), 0-3 Lucas SILVA (90+1')
Referee: Coffi Bonaventure CODJIA (BEN)   Attendance: 7,222

SEMI-FINALS

15-12-2009 Mohammed bin Zayed Stadium, Abu Dhabi:
Pohang Steelers – CA Estudiantes de La Plata 1-2 (0-1)
Pohang Steelers: SHIN Hwa-yong (RC77), CHOI Hyo-jin, HWANG Jae-won (YC12,YC56), KIM Hyung-il (YC90), KIM Tae-Su (YC5) (58' Kazunari OKAYAMA (JPN)), KIM Jae-sung (YC19,YC72), KIM Jung-Kyum (YC45), SHIN Hyung-min, DENILSON Martins Nascimento (BRA), NAMGUNG Do (46' KIM Myung-Joong (YC86)), NO Byung-Jun (54' PARK Hee-Chul). (Coach: SÉRGIO Ricardo de Paiva FARIAS (BRA)).
CA Estudiantes de La Plata: Damián Gonzalo ALBIL, Leandro DESÁBATO (68' Christian Ariel CELLAY), Juan Manuel DÍAZ Martínez (URU), Germán David RÉ, Clemente Juan RODRÍGUEZ, Enzo Nicolás PÉREZ, Juan Sebastián VERÓN (YC22), Maximiliano Ezequiel "MAXI" NÚÑEZ, Rodrigo BRAÑA, Leandro Damián BENÍTEZ (83' Juan Manuel SALGUEIRO Silva (URU)), Mauro BOSELLI, (Coach: Alejandro Javier SABELLA).
Goals: Pohang Steelers: 1-2 DENILSON Martins Nascimento (71').
CA Estudiantes de La Plata: 0-1 Leandro Damián BENÍTEZ (45+2'), 0-2 Leandro Damián BENÍTEZ (53').
Referee: Roberto ROSETTI (ITA)   Attendance: 22,626

16-12-2009   Zayed Sports City Stadium, Abu Dhabi:
Atlante FC Mexico City – FC Barcelona 1-3 (1-1)
Atlante FC Mexico City: Federico VILAR Baudena (ARG), Miguel Ángel MARTÍNEZ (ARG), Fernando NAVARRO Morán, Luis David VELÁZQUEZ Jiménez (YC61) (63' Gabriel Ernesto PEREYRA Vázquez (ARG)), Daniel ARREOLA Argüello, José Daniel Octavio GUERRERO Rodrígeuz (YC40), José Joel GONZÁLEZ Sandoval, Santiago Hernán SOLARI Poggio (ARG) (YC7) (56' Andrés José CAREVIC Ghelfi (ARG)), Christian de Jesús BERMÚDEZ Gutiérrez, Guillermo ROJAS Rumilla, Rafael MÁRQUEZ Lugo. (Coach: José Guadalupe CRUZ Núñez).
FC Barcelona: VÍCTOR VALDÉS Arribas, Daniel "DANI" ALVES da Silva (BRA), Rafael MÁRQUEZ Álvarez (MEX) (54' Gerard PIQUÉ i Bernabéu (YC90)), Carles PUYOL Saforcada, Éric ABIDAL (FRA), Xavier Hernández i Creus "XAVI", Andrés INIESTA Luján (76' BOJAN Krkic Pérez), Sergio BUSQUETS Burgos, Gnégnéri Yaya TOURÉ (CIV) (53' Lionel Andrés MESSI Cuccitini (ARG)), Zlatan IBRAHIMOVIC (SWE) (YC65), PEDRO Eliezer Rodríguez Ledesma. (Coach: Josep "PEP" GUARDIOLA i Sala).
Goals: Atlante FC: 1-0 Guillermo ROJAS Rumilla (5').
FC Barcelona: 1-1 Sergio BUSQUETS Burgos (35'), 1-2 Lionel Andrés MESSI Cuccitini (55'), 1-3 PEDRO Eliezer Rodríguez Ledesma (67').
Referee: CARLOS Eugênio SIMON (BRA)   Attendance: 40,955

FIFTH PLACE PLAY-OFF

16-12-2009   Zayed Sports City Stadium, Abu Dhabi:
TP Mazembe Lubumbashi – Auckland City FC 2-3 (0-1)
TP Mazembe Lubumbashi: Muteba KIDIABA (RC24), Kilitcho KASUSULA, Bawaka MABELE, Sita MILANDOU (CGO) (YC57), Mbenza BEDI, Kazembe MIHAYO, Narcisse EKANGA (CMR), Trésor MPUTU, Patou KABANGU (74' Dioko KALUYITUKA), Luyeye MVETE (26' Aimé BAKULA *goalkeeper*), Ngandu KASONGO. (Coach: Diego GARZITTO (FRA)).
Auckland City FC: Paul GOTHARD (ENG), Ian HOGG (75' Riki VAN STEEDEN), Sam CAMPBELL, James PRITCHETT, Ivan VICELICH, Matt WILLIAMS, LEE Ki-hyung (KOR), Chad COOMBES, Daniel KOPRIVIC (CRO) (YC10) (46' Daniel MORGAN), Jason HAYNE, Adam DICKINSON (ENG) (46' Grant YOUNG (RSA)). (Coach: Paul POSA).
Goals: TP Mazembe: 1-1 Ngandu KASONGO (60'), 2-1 Kilitcho KASUSULA (67').
Auckland City FC: 0-1 Jason HAYNE (29'), 2-2 Jason HAYNE (72'), 2-3 Riki VAN STEEDEN (90+4').
Referee: Benito Armando ARCHUNDIA Téllez (MEX)   Attendance: 4,200

THIRD PLACE PLAY-OFF

18-12-2009   Zayed Sports City Stadium, Abu Dhabi:
Pohang Steelers – Atlante FC Mexico City 1-1 (1-0, 1-1) **(AET)**
Pohang Steelers: SONG Dong-Jin, CHOI Hyo-jin, Kazunari OKAYAMA (JPN), KIM Hyung-il, KIM Tae-Su, KIM Jung-Kyum (YC38) (54' PARK Hee-Chul (YC80)), SHIN Hyung-min, SONG Chang-Ho (60' YOO Chang-hyun), KIM Myung-Joong (65' GO Seul-ki), DENILSON Martins Nascimento (BRA) (YC84), NO Byung-Jun. (Coach: SÉRGIO Ricardo de Paiva FARIAS (BRA)).
Atlante FC Mexico City: Federico VILAR Baudena (ARG), Miguel Ángel MARTÍNEZ (ARG), Fernando NAVARRO Morán (90' Santiago Hernán SOLARI Poggio (ARG)), Luis David VELÁZQUEZ Jiménez (YC54), Daniel ARREOLA Argüello (46' LUCAS Antônio SILVA de Oliveira (BRA)), José Daniel Octavio GUERRERO Rodrígeuz, José Joel GONZÁLEZ Sandoval, Gabriel Ernesto PEREYRA Vázquez (ARG) (90' Horacio Horacio PERALTA Saracho (URU)), Christian de Jesús BERMÚDEZ Gutiérrez, Guillermo ROJAS Rumilla, Rafael MÁRQUEZ Lugo. (Coach: José Guadalupe CRUZ Núñez).
Goals: Pohang Steelers: 1-0 DENILSON Martins Nascimento (42').
Atlante FC: 1-1 Miguel Ángel MARTÍNEZ (46').
Referee: Matthew Christopher BREEZE (AUS)   Attendance: 13,814
Penalties:
1 Santiago Hernán SOLARI Poggio   1 NO Byung-jun
* Miguel Ángel MARTÍNEZ   2 DENILSON Martins Nascimento
* Horacio Horacio PERALTA Saracho   3 SHIN Hyung-chul
2 LUCAS Antônio SILVA de Oliveira   * PARK Hee-chul
3 Federico VILAR Baudena   4 KIM Hyung-il

FINAL

19-12-2009   Zayed Sports City Stadium, Abu Dhabi:
CA Estudiantes de La Plata – FC Barcelona 1-2 (1-0, 1-1) **(AET)**
CA Estudiantes de La Plata: Damián Gonzalo ALBIL, Leandro DESÁBATO (YC119), Christian Ariel CELLAY, Juan Manuel DÍAZ Martínez (URU) (YC45), Germán David RÉ (90' Faustino Marcos Alberto ROJO (YC112)), Clemente Juan RODRÍGUEZ (YC58), Enzo Nicolás PÉREZ (YC65) (79' Maximiliano Ezequiel "MAXI" NÚÑEZ), Juan Sebastián VERÓN, Rodrigo BRAÑA (YC119), Leandro Damián BENÍTEZ (76' Matías Ariel SÁNCHEZ (YC94)), Mauro BOSELLI, (Coach: Alejandro Javier SABELLA).
FC Barcelona: VÍCTOR VALDÉS Arribas (YC118), Daniel "DANI" ALVES da Silva (BRA), Gerard PIQUÉ i Bernabéu, Carles PUYOL Saforcada, Éric ABIDAL (FRA), Xavier Hernández i Creus "XAVI", Seydou KEITA (MLI) (46' PEDRO Eliezer Rodríguez Ledesma), Sergio BUSQUETS Burgos (79' Gnégnéri Yaya TOURÉ (CIV)), Zlatan IBRAHIMOVIC (SWE), Lionel Andrés MESSI Cuccitini (ARG), Thierry HENRY (FRA) (YC82) (83' JEFFRÉN Isaac Suárez Bermúdez (VEN)). (Coach: Josep "PEP" GUARDIOLA i Sala).
Goals: CA Estudiantes de La Plata: 1-0 Mauro BOSELLI (37').
FC Barcelona: 1-1 PEDRO Eliezer Rodríguez Ledesma (89'), 1-2 Lionel Andrés MESSI Cuccitini (110').
Referee: Benito Armando ARCHUNDIA Téllez (MEX)   Attendance: 43,050

*** FC Barcelona won the Cup ***

2010 FIFA Club World Cup

The 2010 FIFA Club World Cup (officially, the 'FIFA Club World Cup UAE 2010 presented by Toyota' for sponsorship reasons) was played between 8th and 18th December 2010. It was the seventh FIFA Club World Cup and was once again hosted by the United Arab Emirates.

The Champions of the six confederations entered the tournament as did the local UAE champions Al-Wahda FC Abu Dhabi who faced the Oceanian Champions in the initial play-off.

In a landmark event, the tournament marked the first time that a team outside the traditional footballing powerhouses of Europe and South America reached the Final, as TP Mazembe of DR Congo defeated SC Internacional of Brazil at the semi-final stage. However, in the Final itself, Internazionale Milano proved too strong for their African opponents winning 3-0 to earn their third world title, previously having won the Intercontinental Cup in 1964 and 1965.

The clubs invited to play in the 2010 tournament were:

FC Internazionale Milano (ITA)	- winners of the 2009-10 UEFA Champions League
SC Internacional (BRA)	- winners of the 2010 Copa Libertadores
TP Mazembe (DRC)	- winners of the 2010 CAF Champions League
Seongnam Ilhwa Chunma FC (KOR)	- winners of the 2010 AFC Champions League
CF Pachuca (MEX)	- winners of the 2009-10 CONCACAF Champions League
Hekari United FC (PNG)	- winners of the 2009-10 OFC Champions League
Al-Wahda FC Abu Dhabi (UAE)	- winners of the 2009-10 UAE Pro-League

PLAY-OFF FOR QUARTER-FINALS

08-12-2010   Mohammed Bin Zayed Stadium, Abu Dhabi:
Al-Wahda FC Abu Dhabi – Hekari United FC Port Moresby 3-0 (2-0)
Al Wahda FC Abu Dhabi: ADEL Mohamed Ali Mohamed AL HOSANI, BASHEER Saeed Sanqour AL HAMMADI, HAIDAR Alo Ali MOHAMED, MAHMOUD KHAMIS Saeed Khamis Saeed Al Hammadi, EISA AHMED Abdul Aziz Ahmed Al Marzouqi, HAMDAN Ismael Mohammed AL KAMALI, Marcio Rodrigues "MAGRÃO" (BRA), FAHED Masoud AL-JUNAIBI (63' ABDULRAHEEM Jumaa Anbar Mubarak Alaraimi AL JUNAIBI), HUGO Henrique Assis do Nascimento (BRA) (YC31), João FERNANDO "BAIANO" Nelo (BRA) (72' Modibo DIARRA (CIV)), ISMAIL MATAR Ibrahim Khamis Al Mukaini Al Junaibi (83' AMER OMAR Abdulla Salem Bazuhair). (Coach: JOSEF HICKERSBERGER (AUT)).
Hekari United FC Port Moresby: Simione TAMANISAU (FIJ), Gideon OMOKIRIO (SLM), Pita BOLEITOGA (FIJ), Koriak UPAIGA, Alvin SINGH (FIJ), Abraham INIGA (SLM) (YC27) (79' Neil HANS), David MUTA, Malakai TIWA (FIJ), Henry FA'ARODO (SLM), Osea VAKATALESAU (FIJ), Kema JACK. (Coach: Tommy MANA).
Goals: Al-Wahda FC Abu Dhabi: 1-0 HUGO (40'), 2-0 Fernando BAIANO (44'), 3-0 Abdulraheem Al-Junaibi JUMAA (71').
Referee: Daniel Frazer BENNETT (RSA)   Attendance: 23,895

QUARTER-FINALS

10-12-2010   Mohammed Bin Zayed Stadium, Abu Dhabi:
TP Mazembe Lubumbashi – CF Pachuca 1-0 (1-0)
TP Mazembe Lubumbashi: Muteba KIDIABA, Joël KIMWAKI, Kilitcho KASUSULA, Miala NKULUKUTA, Stopila SUNZU (ZAM) (YC68,YC81), Mbenza BEDI (YC68), Kazembe MIHAYO (YC83), Narcisse EKANGA (CMR) (46' Ngandu KASONGO (YC59)), Given SINGULUMA (ZAM), Patou KABANGU (85' Mukinay TSHANI), Dioko KALUYITUKA (90' Déo KANDA). (Coach: Lamine N'DIAYE (SEN)).
CF Pachuca: Miguel Ángel CALERO Rodríguez (COL), Leobardo LÓPEZ García, Paul Nicolás AGUILAR Rojas, Javier David MUÑOZ Mustafá (ARG), Braulio LUNA Guzmán (74' Hérculez GÓMEZ Hurtado (USA)), José Francisco TORRES Mezzell (USA) (73' Edy Germán BRAMBILA Rosales), Damián Alejandro MANSO (ARG), Raúl Ascensión MARTÍNEZ Rodríguez, Carlos Alberto PEÑA Rodríguez (58' Édgar Milciades BENÍTEZ Santander (PAR)), Darío CVITANICH (ARG), Franco Faustino ARIZALA Hurtado (COL). (Coach: Pablo Alejandro MARINI (ARG)).
Goal: TP Mazembe: 1-0 Mbenza BEDI (21').
Referee: Yuichi NISHIMURA (JPN)   Attendance: 17,960

11-12-2010   Zayed Sports City Stadium, Abu Dhabi:
              Al-Wahda FC Abu Dhabi – Seongnam Ilhwa Chunma FC 1-4 (1-2)
Al Wahda FC Abu Dhabi: ADEL Mohamed Ali Mohamed AL HOSANI, BASHEER Saeed Sanqour AL HAMMADI YC88), HAIDAR Alo Ali MOHAMED (54' MOHAMED Saeed Rashed A.Saiwed AL SHEHHI), MAHMOUD KHAMIS Saeed Khamis Saeed Al Hammadi, EISA AHMED Abdul Aziz Ahmed Al Marzouqi, HAMDAN Ismael Mohammed AL KAMALI, Marcio Rodrigues "MAGRÃO" (BRA) (90' KHALID JALAL Mohamed Yousef Ibrahim Al Marzouqi), FAHED Masoud AL-JUNAIBI (64' SAEED Salem Saleh Salem AL KATHIRI), HUGO Henrique Assis do Nascimento (BRA), João FERNANDO "BAIANO" Nelo (BRA), ISMAIL MATAR Ibrahim Khamis Al Mukaini Al Junaibi. (Coach: JOSEF HICKERSBERGER (AUT)).
Seongnam Ilhwa Chunma FC: JUNG Sung-ryong, KO Jae-sung, Sasa OGNENOVSKI (AUS) (YC61), CHO Byung-kuk, JEON Gwang-Jin (45' JO Jae-cheol (YC56)), KIM Sung-hwan, HONG Chul, Maurico Alejandro MOLINA Uribe (COL) (84' KIM Jin-Yong), CHOI Sung-Kuk, CHO Dong-Geon, Dzenan RADONCIC (MNE) (69' SONG Ho-Young). (Coach: SHIN Tae-yong).
Goals: Al-Wahda FC Abu Dhabi: 1-1 João FERNANDO "BAIANO" Nelo (27').
Seongnam Ilhwa Chunma FC: 0-1 Maurico Alejandro MOLINA Uribe (4'), 1-2 Sasa OGNENOVSKI (30'), 1-3 CHOI Sung-Kuk (71'), 1-4 CHO Dong-Geon (81').
Referee: Víctor Hugo CARRILLO Casanova (PER)   Attendance: 30,625

SEMI–FINALS

14-12-2010   Mohammed Bin Zayed Stadium, Abu Dhabi:
              TP Mazembe Lubumbashi – SC Internacional Porto Alegre 2-0 (0-0)
TP Mazembe Lubumbashi: Muteba KIDIABA, Joël KIMWAKI, Kilitcho KASUSULA (YC90), Miala NKULUKUTA (YC8), Mbenza BEDI, Kazembe MIHAYO, Narcisse EKANGA (CMR), Given SINGULUMA (ZAM), Patou KABANGU (84' Déo KANDA), Dioko KALUYITUKA, Ngandu KASONGO. (Coach: Lamine N'DIAYE (SEN)).
SC Internacional Porto Alegre: RENAN Brito Soares, Fabian Guedes "BOLÍVAR", Marcos Antônio de Lima "ÍNDIO" (YC58), Claudinei Cardoso Félix da Silva "NEI", KLÉBER de Carvalho Corrêa, Pablo Horacio GUIÑAZÚ (ARG), Paulo César Fonseca do Nascimento "TINGA" (63' GIULIANO Victor de Paula), Andrés Nicolás D'ALESSANDRO (ARG), WILSON Tiago MATÍAS, ALECSANDRO Barbosa Felisbino (63' LEANDRO DAMIÃO da Silva dos Santos), RAFAEL Augusto SÓBIS do Nascimento (76' OSCAR dos Santos Emboaba Junior). (Coach: CELSO Juarez ROTH).
Goals: TP Mazembe: 1-0 Patou KABANGU (53'), 2-0 Dioko KALUYITUKA (85').
Referee: Björn KUIPERS (HOL)   Attendance: 22,131

15-12-2010 Zayed Sports City Stadium, Abu Dhabi:
Seongnam Ilhwa Chunma FC – FC Internazionale Milano 0-3 (0-2)
Seongnam Ilhwa Chunma FC: JUNG Sung-ryong, KO Jae-sung, Sasa OGNENOVSKI (AUS) (YC31), CHO Byung-kuk, KIM Sung-hwan, HONG Chul, Maurico Alejandro MOLINA Uribe (COL), JO Jae-cheol (68' JEON Gwang-Jin), CHOI Sung-Kuk (68' SONG Ho-Young), CHO Dong-Geon, Dzenan RADONCIC (MNE) (87' KIM Jin-Yong). (Coach: SHIN Tae-yong).
FC Internazionale Milano: JÚLIO CÉSAR Soares Espíndola (BRA), Ivan Ramiro CÓRDOBA Sepúlveda (COL), Javier Adelmar ZANETTI (ARG), Lucimar da Silva Ferreira "LÚCIO" (BRA), Cristian CHIVU (ROM) (79' Davide SANTON), Dejan STANKOVIC (SRB), Wesley SNEIJDER (HOL) (4' THIAGO MOTTA Santon Olivares (BRA)), Esteban Matías CAMBIASSO Deleau (ARG), Samuel ETO'O Fils (CMR), Diego Alberto MILITO (ARG) (77' Sulley Ali MUNTARI (GHA)), Goran PANDEV (MCD). (Coach: Rafael "RAFA" BENÍTEZ Maudes (ESP)).
Goals: FC Internazionale Milano: 0-1 Dejan STANKOVIC (3'), 0-2 Javier Adelmar ZANETTI (32'), 0-3 Diego Alberto MILITO LITO (73').
Referee: Roberto MORENO Salazar (PAN)   Attendance: 35,995

FIFTH PLACE PLAY–OFF

15-12-2010 Zayed Sports City Stadium, Abu Dhabi:
CF Pachuca - Al-Wahda FC Abu Dhabi 2-2 (0-1, 2-2) **(AET)**
CF Pachuca: Miguel Ángel CALERO Rodríguez (COL), Leobardo LÓPEZ García, Paul Nicolás AGUILAR Rojas (YC17) (62' Édgar Milciades BENÍTEZ Santander (PAR)), Javier David MUÑOZ Mustafá (ARG), Braulio LUNA Guzmán, Luis Arturo MONTES Jiménez, José Francisco TORRES Mezzell (USA), Damián Alejandro MANSO (ARG), Raúl Ascensión MARTÍNEZ Rodríguez (77 Darío CVITANICH (ARG)'), Hérculez GÓMEZ Hurtado (USA) (62' Juan Carlos ROJAS Guerra), Franco Faustino ARIZALA Hurtado (COL). (Coach: Pablo Alejandro MARINI (ARG)).
Al Wahda FC Abu Dhabi: ADEL Mohamed Ali Mohamed AL HOSANI, YAQOUB Yousif Matouq Mohamed AL HOSANI, BASHEER Saeed Sanqour AL HAMMADI, MAHMOUD KHAMIS Saeed Khamis Saeed Al Hammadi, EISA AHMED Abdul Aziz Ahmed Al Marzouqi, HAMDAN Ismael Mohammed AL KAMALI (YC68,YC72), FAHED Masoud AL-JUNAIBI (YC30) (64' MOHAMED Saeed Rashed A.Saiwed AL SHEHHI (YC90)), ABDULRAHEEM Jumaa Anbar Mubarek Alaraimi AL JUNAIBI, HUGO Henrique Assis do Nascimento (BRA), ISMAIL MATAR Ibrahim Khamis Al Mukaini Al Junaibi (75' OMAR Ali Omar Eissa AHMED), SAEED Salem Saleh Salem AL KATHIRI (46' Modibo DIARRA (CIV)). (Coach: JOSEF HICKERSBERGER (AUT)).
Goals: CF Pachuca: 1-2 Darío CVITANICH (82'), 2-2 Darío CVITANICH (89').
Al-Wahda FC Abu Dhabi: 0-1 ISMAIL MATAR Ibrahim Khamis Al Mukaini Al Junaib (44'), 0-2 MAHMOUD KHAMIS Saeed Khamis Saeed Al Hammadi (77').
Referee: Daniel Frazer BENNETT (RSA)   Attendance: 10,908
Penalties:
1 Darío CVITANICH   1 HUGO Henrique Assis do Nascimento
2 Leobardo LÓPEZ García   2 BASHEER Saeed Sanqour AL HAMMADI
3 Javier David MUÑOZ Mustafá   * Abdulraheem Al-Junaibi JUMAA
4 Braulio LUNA Guzmán   * Modibo DIARRA

Édgar Milciades BENÍTEZ Santander missed a penalty kick (73').

THIRD PLACE PLAY-OFF

18-12-2010 Zayed Sports City Stadium, Abu Dhabi:
SC Internacional Porto Alegre – Seongnam Ilhwa Chunma FC 4-2 (2-0)
SC Internacional Porto Alegre: RENAN Brito Soares (74' Roberto Carlos ABBONDANZIERI (ARG)), Fabian Guedes "BOLÍVAR", Marcos Antônio de Lima "ÍNDIO" (YC22), Claudinei Cardoso Félix da Silva "NEI", KLÉBER de Carvalho Corrêa, Pablo Horacio GUIÑAZÚ (ARG), Paulo César Fonseca do Nascimento "TINGA", Andrés Nicolás D'ALESSANDRO (ARG), WILSON Tiago MATÍAS (81' André Luiz Tavares "ANDREZINHO"), ALECSANDRO Barbosa Felisbino, RAFAEL Augusto SÓBIS do Nascimento (62' GIULIANO Victor de Paula). (Coach: CELSO Juarez ROTH).
Seongnam Ilhwa Chunma FC: JUNG Sung-ryong, YUN Young-sun, KO Jae-sung, KIM Sung-hwan, HONG Chul, JANG Suk-won (YC24,YC34), Maurico Alejandro MOLINA Uribe (COL), JO Jae-cheol, CHOI Sung-Kuk, CHO Dong-Geon, SONG Ho-Young (28' Dzenan RADONCIC (MNE), 43' KIM Jin-Yong, 78' JEON Gwang-Jin). (Coach: SHIN Tae-yong).
Goals: SC Internacional: 1-0 Paulo César Fonseca do Nascimento "TINGA" (15'), 2-0 ALECSANDRO Barbosa Felisbino (27'), 3-0 Andrés Nicolás D'ALESSANDRO (52'), 4-0 ALECSANDRO Barbosa Felisbino (71').
Seongnam Ilhwa Chunma FC: 4-1 Maurico Alejandro MOLINA Uribe (84'), 4-2 Maurico Alejandro MOLINA Uribe (90+3').
Referee: Michael HESTER (NZL)   Attendance: 16,563

FINAL

18-12-2010 Zayed Sports City Stadium, Abu Dhabi:
TP Mazembe Lubumbashi – FC Internazionale Milano 0-3 (0-2)
TP Mazembe Lubumbashi: Muteba KIDIABA, Joël KIMWAKI, Kilitcho KASUSULA (YC84), Miala NKULUKUTA, Mbenza BEDI (YC43), Kazembe MIHAYO, Narcisse EKANGA (CMR) (YC33), Given SINGULUMA (ZAM), Patou KABANGU, Dioko KALUYITUKA (YC12) (90' Mianga NDONGA), Ngandu KASONGO (46' Déo KANDA). (Coach: Lamine N'DIAYE (SEN)).
FC Internazionale Milano: JÚLIO CÉSAR Soares Espíndola (BRA), Ivan Ramiro CÓRDOBA Sepúlveda (COL), Javier Adelmar ZANETTI (ARG), Lucimar da Silva Ferreira "LÚCIO" (BRA), MAICON Douglas Sisenando (BRA), Cristian CHIVU (ROM) (54' Dejan STANKOVIC (SRB)), THIAGO MOTTA Santon Olivares (BRA) (YC79) (87' McDonald MARIGA (KEN), Esteban Matías CAMBIASSO Deleau (ARG), Samuel ETO'O Fils (CMR), Diego Alberto MILITO (ARG) (70' Jonathan BIABIANY (FRA)), Goran PANDEV (MCD). (Coach: Rafael "RAFA" BENÍTEZ Maudes (ESP)).
Goals: FC Internazionale Milano: 0-1 Goran PANDEV (13'), 0-2 Samuel ETO'O Fils (17'), 0-3 Jonathan BIABIANY (85').
Referee: Yuichi NISHIMURA (JPN)   Attendance: 42,174

*** FC Internazionale Milano won the Cup ***

2011 FIFA Club World Cup

The 2011 FIFA Club World Cup (officially, the 'FIFA Club World Cup Japan 2011 presented by Toyota' for sponsorship reasons) was played between 8th and 18th December 2011. It was the eighth FIFA Club World Cup and, after two years in the United Arab Emirates, the tournament returned to Japan.

The Champions of the six confederations entered the tournament as did the local Japanese champions Kashiwa Reysol who faced the Oceanian Champions in the initial play-off match.

The dominant team of the tournament were the brilliant FC Barcelona team, who defeated the AFC Champions Al-Sadd SC 4-0 in the semi-final before beating the South American Champions, Santos FC, by the same scoreline in Final.

The clubs invited to play in the 2011 tournament were:

FC Barcelona (ESP)	- winners of the 2010-11 UEFA Champions League
Santos FC (BRA)	- winners of the 2011 Copa Libertadores
ES Tunis (TUN)	- winners of the 2011 CAF Champions League
Al-Sadd SC (QAT)	- winners of the 2011 AFC Champions League
CF Monterrey (MEX)	- winners of the 2010-11 CONCACAF Champions League
Auckland City FC (NZL)	- winners of the 2010-11 OFC Champions League
Kashiwa Reysol (JPN)	- winners of the 2011 J.League Division 1

PLAY-OFF FOR QUARTER-FINALS

08-12-2011   Toyota Stadium, Toyota City:
Kashiwa Reysol – Auckland City FC 2-0 (2-0)
Kashiwa Reysol: Takanori SUGENO, Naoya KONDO (YC78), Hiroki SAKAI (67' Koki MIZUNO), Tatsuya MASUSHIMA, Wataru HASHIMOTO, Hidekazu OTANI, Leandro DOMINGUES Barbosa, JORGE WAGNER Goés Conceição (BRA), Akimi BARADA (82' Ryoichi KURISAWA), Junya TANAKA (85' Hideaki KITAJIMA), Masato KUDO. (Coach: Nélson "NELSINHO" BAPTISTA Júnior (BRA)).
Auckland City FC: Jacob SPOONLEY, Ian HOGG, ÁNGEL Luis Viña BERLANGA (ESP), James PRITCHETT, Ivan VICELICH, David MULLIGAN, Alex FENERIDIS (49' Luis Fonseca CORRALES (CRC)), ALBERT RIERA Vidal (69' Daniel KOPRIVIC (CRO)), ANDREU Guerao Mayoral (ESP), MANEL EXPÓSITO Presseguer (ESP), Adam DICKINSON (ENG) (68' Emiliano TADE (ARG)). (Coach: RAMON TRIBULIETX Santolaya (ESP)).
Goals: Kashiwa Reysol: 1-0 Junya TANAKA (37'), 2-0 Masato KUDO (40').
Referee: Nicola RIZZOLI (ITA)   Attendance: 18,754

QUARTER-FINALS

11-12-2011   Toyota Stadium, Toyota City: ES Tunis – Al-Sadd SC Doha 1-2 (0-1)
ES Tunis: Moez BEN CHÉRIFIA, Yaya BANANA (CMR), Walid HICHRI (YC64), Khalil CHEMMAM, Indrissa COULIBALY (MLI) (46' Harrison AFFUL (GHA)), Mejdi TRAOUI, Youssef MSAKNI, Khaled MOUELHI (YC75), Wajdi BOUAZZI, Yannick N'DJENG (CMR), Oussama DARRAGI (75' Khaled AYARI). (Coach: Nabil MAÂLOUL).
Al-Sadd SC Doha: MOHAMMED SAQR Ahmed, Nadir BELHADJ (ALG), LEE Jung-soo (KOR), Mohammed KASOLA (YC85), IBRAHIM MAJID Abdulmajid, Abdulla Obaid KONI (YC90), WESAM RIZIK Abdulmajid (72' TAHER Muhammad ZAKARIA), TALAL Ali AL-BLOUSHI, Mamadou Hamidou NIANG (SEN) (90' HASAN Khailad AL HAYDOS), Abdulkader KEÏTA (CIV), KHALFAN IBRAHIM Khalfan Al Khalfan (75' YOUSEF Ahmed ALI). (Coach: Jorge Daniel FOSSATI Lurachi (URU)).
Goals: ES Tunis: 1-2 Oussama DARRAGI (60').
Al-Sadd SC: 0-1 KHALFAN Ibrahim (33'), 0-2 Abdulla KONI (49').
Referee: Enrique Roberto OSSES Zencovich (CHI)   Attendance: 21,251

11-12-2011   Toyota Stadium, Toyota City:
Kashiwa Reysol – CF Monterrey 1-1 (0-0, 1-1) **(AET)**
Kashiwa Reysol: Takanori SUGENO, Naoya KONDO, Hiroki SAKAI, Tatsuya MASUSHIMA, Wataru HASHIMOTO (YC84), Hidekazu OTANI, Leandro DOMINGUES Barbosa (YC26), JORGE WAGNER Goés Conceição (BRA), Ryoichi KURISAWA (YC21), Junya TANAKA, Masato KUDO (107' Ryochei HAYASHI). (Coach: Nélson "NELSINHO" BAPTISTA Júnior (BRA)).
CF Monterrey: Jonathan Emmanuel OROZCO Martínez, Ricardo OSORIO Mendoza, Dárvin Francisco CHÁVEZ Ramírez (YC40) (91' Walter Orlando AYOVÍ Corozo (ECU)), José María BASANTA Pavone (ARG) (YC103), Hiram Ricardo MIER Alanís, Luis Ernesto PÉREZ Gómez, Jesús Eduardo ZAVALA Castañeda, Neri Raúl CARDOZO (ARG) (100' Sergio PÉREZ Moya), César Fabián DELGADO Godoy (ARG), Sergio Alejandro SANTANA Piedra (97' Jesús Aldo DE NIGRIS Guajardo), Humberto André SUAZO Pontivo (CHI). (Coach: Víctor Manuel VUCETICH Rojas).
Goals: Kashiwa Reysol: 1-0 Leandro DOMINGUES Barbosa (53').
CF Monterrey: 1-1 Humberto André SUAZO Pontivo (58').
Referee: Peter O'LEARY (NZL)   Attendance: 27,525

Penalties:
* Luis Ernesto PÉREZ Gómez   1 Leandro DOMINGUES Barbosa
1 Humberto André SUAZO   2 JORGE WAGNER Goés Conceição
2 Walter Orlando AYOVÍ Corozo   3 Ryoichi KURISAWA
* Jonathan Emmanuel OROZCO Martínez   * Junya TANAKA
3 César Fabián DELGADO Godoy   4 Ryochei HAYASHI

FIFTH PLACE PLAY-OFF

14-12-2011   Toyota Stadium, Toyota City: CF Monterrey – ES Tunis 3-2 (2-1)
CF Monterrey: Jonathan Emmanuel OROZCO Martínez, Dárvin Francisco CHÁVEZ Ramírez, José María BASANTA Pavone (ARG) (YC70), Hiram Ricardo MIER Alanís, Sergio PÉREZ Moya (YC90), Luis Ernesto PÉREZ Gómez (29' Héctor Miguel MORALES Llanes), Walter Orlando AYOVÍ Corozo (ECU), Jesús Eduardo ZAVALA Castañeda, Neri Raúl CARDOZO (ARG), Jesús Aldo DE NIGRIS Guajardo, Sergio Alejandro SANTANA Piedra (87' Severo Efraín MEZA Mayorga). (Coach: Víctor Manuel VUCETICH Rojas).
ES Tunis: Moez BEN CHÉRIFIA, Harrison AFFUL (GHA), Yaya BANANA (CMR), Walid HICHRI, Khalil CHEMMAM (54' Khaled AYARI), Indrissa COULIBALY (MLI) (YC90), Mejdi TRAOUI, Youssef MSAKNI, Khaled MOUELHI, Wajdi BOUAZZI (77' Oussama DARRAGI), Yannick N'DJENG (CMR). (Coach: Nabil MAÂLOUL).
Goals: CF Monterrey: 1-1 Hiram Ricardo MIER Alanís (39'), 2-1 Jesús Aldo DE NIGRIS Guajardo (44'), 3-1 Jesús Eduardo ZAVALA Castañeda (47').
ES Tunis: 0-1 Yannick N'DJENG (31'), 3-2 Khaled MOUELHI (76' penalty).
Referee: Ravshan Sayfiddinovich IRMATOV (UZB)   Attendance: 13,639

SEMI–FINALS

14-12-2011   Toyota Stadium, Toyota City: Kashiwa Reysol – Santos FC 1-3 (0-2)
Kashiwa Reysol: Takanori SUGENO, Naoya KONDO, Hiroki SAKAI, Tatsuya MASUSHIMA, Wataru HASHIMOTO (79' Akihiro HYODO), Hidekazu OTANI, Leandro DOMINGUES Barbosa (YC32), JORGE WAGNER Goés Conceição (BRA), Ryoichi KURISAWA (YC62), Junya TANAKA (65' Masakatsu SAWA), Masato KUDO (46' Hideaki KITAJIMA). (Coach: Nélson "NELSINHO" BAPTISTA Júnior (BRA)).
Santos FC: RAFAEL CABRAL Barbosa, Eduardo Luís Abonízio de Souza "EDU DRACENA", DANILO Luiz da Silva (90' BRUNO Henrique Fortunato AGUIAR), Severino dos Ramos DURVAL da Silva, BRUNO RODRIGO Fenelon Palomo, Marcos AROUCA da Silva, HENRIQUE Pacheco de Lima (YC72), ELANO Ralph Blumer (59' ALAN KARDEC de Souza Pereira Junior), Paulo Henrique Chagas de Lima "GANSO", Humberlito BORGES Teixeira (80' IBSON Barreto da Silva), NEYMAR da Silva Santos Júnior. (Coach: MURICY RAMALHO).
Goals: Kashiwa Reysol: 1-2 Hiroki SAKAI (54').
Santos FC: 0-1 NEYMAR da Silva Santos Júnior (19'), 0-2 Humberlito BORGES Teixeira (24'), 1-3 DANILO Luiz da Silva (63').
Referee: Nicola RIZZOLI (ITA)   Attendance: 29,173

15-12-2011   International Stadium Yokohama, Yokohama:
Al-Sadd SC Doha – FC Barcelona 0-4 (0-2)
Al-Sadd SC Doha: MOHAMMED SAQR Ahmed, Nadir BELHADJ (ALG), LEE Jung-soo (KOR), Mohammed KASOLA (YC80), IBRAHIM MAJID Abdulmajid (YC62), Abdulla Obaid KONI, WESAM RIZIK Abdulmajid, TALAL Ali AL-BLOUSHI (65' MOHAMMED Abdulrab AL YAZIDI), Mamadou Hamidou NIANG (SEN) (77' YOUSEF Ahmed ALI), Abdulkader KEÏTA (CIV) (85' HASAN Khailad AL HAYDOS), KHALFAN IBRAHIM Khalfan Al Khalfan. (Coach: Jorge Daniel FOSSATI Lurachi (URU)).
FC Barcelona: VÍCTOR VALDÉS Arribas, Carles PUYOL Saforcada, Javier Alejandro MASCHERANO (ARG), ADRIANO Correia Claro (BRA), Éric ABIDAL (FRA) (66' MAXWELL Scherrer Cabelino Andrade (BRA)), Andrés INIESTA Luján, THIAGO Alcântara do Nascimento, Seydou KEITA (MLI), DAVID VILLA Sánchez (39' Alexis Alejandro SÁNCHEZ Sánchez (CHI), 70' Joan ISAAC CUENCA López), Lionel Andrés MESSI Cuccitini (ARG), PEDRO Eliezer Rodríguez Ledesma. (Coach: Josep "PEP" GUARDIOLA i Sala).
Goals: FC Barcelona: 0-1 ADRIANO Correia Claro (25'), 0-2 ADRIANO Correia Claro (43'), 0-3 Seydou KEITA (64'), 0-4 MAXWELL Scherrer Cabelino Andrade (81').
Referee: Joel Antonio AGUILAR Chicas (SAL)   Attendance: 66,298

THIRD PLACE PLAY-OFF

18-12-2011   International Stadium Yokohama, Yokohama:
Kashiwa Reysol – Al-Sadd SC Doha 0-0 **(AET)**
Kashiwa Reysol: Takanori SUGENO, Naoya KONDO, Hiroki SAKAI, Tatsuya MASUSHIMA, Wataru HASHIMOTO, Hidekazu OTANI, JORGE WAGNER Goés Conceição (BRA), Akimi BARADA, Koki MIZUNO, Hideaki KITAJIMA (81' Ryohei HAYASHI), Junya TANAKA (75' Masakatsu SAWA). (Coach: Nélson "NELSINHO" BAPTISTA Júnior (BRA)
Al-Sadd SC Doha: MOHAMMED SAQR Ahmed, Nadir BELHADJ (ALG), LEE Jung-soo (KOR), MESAAD Ali AL HAMAD (90' TAHER Muhammad ZAKARIA), IBRAHIM MAJID Abdulmajid, Abdulla Obaid KONI, WESAM RIZIK Abdulmajid, MOHAMMED Abdulrab AL YAZIDI (83' HASAN Khailad AL HAYDOS), Mamadou Hamidou NIANG (SEN), Abdulkader KEÏTA (CIV), KHALFAN IBRAHIM Khalfan Al Khalfan (73' ALI Hasan AFIF Yahya). (Coach: Jorge Daniel FOSSATI Lurachi (URU)).
Referee: Noumandiez Désiré DOUÉ (CIV)   Attendance: 60,527

Penalties:
1 Mamadou Hamidou NIANG   1 JORGE WAGNER Goés Conceição
2 Abdulkader KEÏTA   2 Masakatsu SAWA
3 IBRAHIM MAJID Abdulmajid   * Ryohei HAYASHI
4 HASAN Khailad AL HAYDOS   3 Hidekazu OTANI
5 Nadir BELHADJ

FINAL

18-12-2011   International Stadium Yokohama, Yokohama:
Santos FC – FC Barcelona 0-4 (0-3)
Santos FC: RAFAEL CABRAL Barbosa, Eduardo Luís Abonízio de Souza "EDU DRACENA" (YC74), Leonardo Lourenço Bastos "LÉO", DANILO Luiz da Silva (31' ELANO Ralph Blumer), Severino dos Ramos DURVAL da Silva, BRUNO RODRIGO Fenelon Palomo, Marcos AROUCA da Silva, HENRIQUE Pacheco de Lima, Paulo Henrique Chagas de Lima "GANSO" (YC73) (83' IBSON Barreto da Silva), Humberlito BORGES Teixeira (79' ALAN KARDEC de Souza Pereira Junior), NEYMAR da Silva Santos Júnior. (Coach: MURICY RAMALHO).
FC Barcelona: VÍCTOR VALDÉS Arribas, Daniel "DANI" ALVES da Silva (BRA), Gerard PIQUÉ i Bernabéu (YC39) (56' Javier Alejandro MASCHERANO (ARG) (YC71)), Carles PUYOL Saforcada (85' Andreu FONTÀS Prat), Éric ABIDAL (FRA), Francesc "CESC" FÀBREGAS Soler, Xavier Hernández i Creus "XAVI", Andrés INIESTA Luján, THIAGO Alcântara do Nascimento (79' PEDRO Eliezer Rodríguez Ledesma), Sergio BUSQUETS Burgos, Lionel Andrés MESSI Cuccitini (ARG). (Coach: Josep "PEP" GUARDIOLA i Sala).
Goals: FC Barcelona: 0-1 Lionel Andrés MESSI Cuccitini (17'), 0-2 Xavier Hernández i Creus "XAVI" (24'), 0-3 Francesc "CESC" FÀBREGAS Soler (45'), 0-4 Lionel Andrés MESSI Cuccitini (82').
Referee: Ravshan Sayfiddinovich IRMATOV (UZB)   Attendance: 68,166

*** **FC Barcelona won the Cup** ***

2012 FIFA Club World Cup

The 2012 FIFA Club World Cup (officially, the 'FIFA Club World Cup Japan 2012 presented by Toyota' for sponsorship reasons) was played between 6th and 16th December 2012. It was the ninth edition of the FIFA Club World Cup and the tournament was again held in Japan.

The Champions of the six confederations entered the tournament as did the Japanese champions Sanfrecce Hiroshima who faced the Oceanian Champions Auckland City FC in the initial play-off.

The tournament was won by Brazilian club SC Corinthians Paulista who defeated Chelsea FC 1-0 in the Final to win their second world title.

The clubs invited to play in the 2012 tournament were:

Chelsea FC (ENG)	- winners of the 2011-12 UEFA Champions League
SC Corinthians Paulista (BRA)	- winners of the 2012 Copa Libertadores
Al Ahly SC Cairo (EGY)	- winners of the 2012 CAF Champions League
Ulsan Hyundai FC (KOR)	- winners of the 2012 AFC Champions League
CF Monterrey (MEX)	- winners of the 2011-12 CONCACAF Champions League
Auckland City FC (NZL)	- winners of the 2011-12 OFC Champions League
Sanfrecce Hiroshima (JPN)	- winners of the 2012 J. League Division 1

PLAY-OFF FOR QUARTER-FINALS

06-12-2012　　International Stadium Yokohama, Yokohama:
Sanfrecce Hiroshima – Auckland City FC 1-0 (0-0)
Sanfrecce Hiroshima: Shusaku NISHIKAWA, Hiroki MIZUMOTO (YC47), Kazuhiko CHIBA, Ryota MORIWAKI, Toshihiro AOYAMA, Koji MORISAKI (90' Naoki ISHIHARA), Kazuyuki MORISAKI, Mihael MIKIC (CRO) (82' HWANG Seok-ho (KOR)), Yojiro TAKAHAGI, Hisato SATO, Kohei SHIMIZU (60' Satoru YAMAGISHI (YC71)). (Coach: Hajime MORIYASU).
Auckland City FC: Tamati WILLIAMS, Takuya IWATA (JPN), ÁNGEL Luis Viña BERLANGA (ESP) (YC38), Ivan VICELICH, Andrew MILNE, Christopher BALE (WAL), Daniel KOPRIVIC (CRO) (67' Luis Fonseca CORRALES (CRC)), Alex FENERIDIS, ALBERT RIERA Vidal (ESP) (YC50), MANEL EXPÓSITO Presseguer (ESP) (77' Emiliano TADE (ARG)), Adam DICKINSON (ENG). (Coach: RAMON TRIBULIETX Santolaya (ESP)).
Goal: Sanfrecce Hiroshima: 1-0 Toshihiro AOYAMA (66').
Referee: Djamel Benmehel HAÏMOUDI (ALG)　　Attendance: 25,174

QUARTER-FINALS

09-12-2012   Toyota Stadium, Toyota City:
Ulsan Hyundai FC – CF Monterrey 1-3 (0-1)
Ulsan Hyundai FC: KIM Young-kwang, LEE Yong, KWAK Tae-hwi, KIM Chi-gon, LEE Ho, KIM Young-Sam (56' LEE Jae-sung), Juan Estiven VÉLEZ Upegui (COL), KIM Shin-wook (YC71) (78' Luis Carlos dos Santos Martins "MARANHÃO" (BRA)), Rafael dos Santos de Oliveira "RAFINHA" (BRA), LEE Keun-ho, KIM Seung-yong (71' KO Chang-Hyun). (Coach: KIM Ho-Gon).
CF Monterrey: Jonathan Emmanuel OROZCO Martínez (YC65), Severo Efraín MEZA Mayorga (YC41), Dárvin Francisco CHÁVEZ Ramírez (YC62), José María BASANTA Pavone (ARG), Hiram Ricardo MIER Alanís, Sergio PÉREZ Moya, Walter Orlando AYOVÍ Corozo (ECU), Jesús Manuel CORONA Ruiz (89' Héctor Miguel MORALES Llanes), Neri Raúl CARDOZO (ARG) (89' Abraham Darió CARREÑO Rohan), César Fabián DELGADO Godoy (ARG) (90' Edgar Iván Estuardo SOLÍS Castillón), Jesús Aldo DE NIGRIS Guajardo. (Coach: Víctor Manuel VUCETICH Rojas).
Goals: Ulsan Hyundai FC: 1-3 LEE Keun-ho (88').
CF Monterrey: 0-1 Jesús Manuel CORONA Ruiz (9'), 0-2 César Fabián DELGADO Godoy (77'), 0-3 César Fabián DELGADO Godoy (84').
Referee: Cüneyt ÇAKIR (TUR)   Attendance: 20,353

09-12-2012   Toyota Stadium, Toyota City:
Sanfrecce Hiroshima – Al Ahly SC Cairo 1-2 (1-1)
Sanfrecce Hiroshima: Shusaku NISHIKAWA (8' Takuya MASUDA), Hiroki MIZUMOTO, Kazuhiko CHIBA, Ryota MORIWAKI (46' HWANG Seok-ho (KOR)), Toshihiro AOYAMA, Koji MORISAKI, Kazuyuki MORISAKI (YC35), Mihael MIKIC (CRO), Yojiro TAKAHAGI, Hisato SATO, Kohei SHIMIZU (82' Satoru YAMAGISHI). (Coach: Hajime MORIYASU).
Al Ahly SC Cairo: SHERIF EKRAMY Ahmed, WAEL GOMAA Kamel El Hooty (YC81), AHMAD SHEDID Kenawi, MOHAMED NAGUIB Mohamed El Ghareeb, WALID SOLIMAN Said (YC12) (80' MOHAMED BARAKAT Ahmed Bastamy), HOSSAM El Sayed GHALY (34' MUHAMMAD ABU TARIKA), ABDALLAH Mahmoud EL SAID Mohamed Bekhit, AHMED FATHI Abdelmonem, HOSSAM Mohamed ASHOUR Sanad Attia (YC45), Mohamed Nagy Ismail Afash "GEDO", ELSAYED HAMDY Mahdy Hewil (71' Mahmoud Ahmed Ibrahim Hassan "TREZEGUET" (YC79)). (Coaches: HOSSAM EL BADRY & MOHAMED YOUSSEF Abdul-Razak).
Goals: Sanfrecce Hiroshima: 1-1 Hisato SATO (32').
Al Ahly SC Cairo: 0-1 ELSAYED HAMDY Mahdy Hewil (15'), 1-2 MUHAMMAD ABU TARIKA (57').
Referee: Carlos Alfredo VERA Rodríguez (ECU)   Attendance: 27,314

FIFTH PLACE PLAY-OFF

12-12-2012   Toyota Stadium, Toyota City:
Ulsan Hyundai FC – Sanfrecce Hiroshima 2-3 (1-1)
Ulsan Hyundai FC: KIM Young-kwang, LEE Yong, KWAK Tae-hwi, KIM Chi-gon (52' LEE Jae-sung), LEE Ho (YC34), KIM Young-Sam, GO Seul-ki, KIM Shin-wook, Rafael dos Santos de Oliveira "RAFINHA" (BRA), LEE Keun-ho, KIM Seung-yong (76' Luis Carlos dos Santos Martins "MARANHÃO" (BRA)). (Coach: KIM Ho-Gon).
Sanfrecce Hiroshima: Shusaku NISHIKAWA (YC90), HWANG Seok-ho (KOR) (YC66), Hiroki MIZUMOTO, Tsukasa SHIOTANI (YC89), Toshihiro AOYAMA, Koji MORISAKI, Kazuyuki MORISAKI (79' Naoki ISHIHARA), Yojiro TAKAHAGI, Satoru YAMAGISHI (75' Kohei SHIMIZU), Hironori ISHIKAWA (90' Kazuhiko CHIBA), Hisato SATO. (Coach: Hajime MORIYASU).
Goals: Ulsan Hyundai FC: 1-0 Hiroki MIZUMOTO (17' own goal), 2-3 LEE Yong (90+5').
Sanfrecce Hiroshima: 1-1 Satoru YAMAGISHI (35'), 1-2 Hisato SATO (56'), 1-3 Hisato SATO (72').
Referee: Nawaf Abdullah GHAYYATH SHUKRALLA (BRN)   Attendance: 17,581

SEMI-FINALS

12-12-2012   Toyota Stadium, Toyota City:
Al Ahly SC Cairo – SC Corinthians Paulista São Paulo 0-1 (0-1)
Al Ahly SC Cairo: SHERIF EKRAMY Ahmed (65' MAHMOUD ABOUL-SAOUD), RAMI Hisham Abdel Aziz RABIA, WAEL GOMAA Kamel El Hooty, AHMAD SHEDID Kenawi, MOHAMED NAGUIB Mohamed El Ghareeb, WALID SOLIMAN Said, ABDALLAH Mahmoud EL SAID Mohamed Bekhit (54' MUHAMMAD ABU TARIKA), AHMED FATHI Abdelmonem, HOSSAM Mohamed ASHOUR Sanad Attia, Mohamed Nagy Ismail Afash "GEDO" (80' EMAD "MOTEAB" Mohamed Abd El Naby Ibrahim), ELSAYED HAMDY Mahdy Hewil. (Coaches: HOSSAM EL BADRY & MOHAMED YOUSSEF Abdul-Razak).
SC Corinthians Paulista São Paulo: CÁSSIO Roberto Ramos, ALESSANDRO Mori Nunes, Anderson Sebastião Cardoso "CHICÃO", FÁBIO SANTOS Romeu, PAULO ANDRÉ Cren Benini, RALF de Souza Teles, José Paulo Bezerra Maciel Júnior "PAULINHO", DOUGLAS dos Santos (80' JORGE HENRIQUE de Souza), DANILO Gabriel de Andrade, José Paolo GUERRERO Gonzales (PER) (90' GUILHERME ANDRADE Silva), Marcio Passos de Albuquerque "EMERSON SHEIK" (QAT) (75' Romário Ricardo da Silva "ROMARINHO"). (Coach: Adenor Léonardo Bachi "TITE").
Goal: SC Corinthians Paulista: 0-1 José Paolo GUERRERO Gonzales (30').
Referee: Marco Antonio RODRÍGUEZ Moreno (MEX)   Attendance: 31,417

13-12-2012   International Stadium Yokohama, Yokohama:
             CF Monterrey – Chelsea FC London 1-3 (0-1)
CF Monterrey: Jonathan Emmanuel OROZCO Martínez, Severo Efraín MEZA Mayorga (83'
Abraham Darió CARREÑO Rohan), Dárvin Francisco CHÁVEZ Ramírez, José María
BASANTA Pavone (ARG), Hiram Ricardo MIER Alanís, Sergio PÉREZ Moya (57' Ricardo
OSORIO Mendoza), Walter Orlando AYOVÍ Corozo (ECU), Jesús Manuel CORONA Ruiz,
Neri Raúl CARDOZO (ARG), César Fabián DELGADO Godoy (ARG) (83' Edgar Iván
Estuardo SOLÍS Castillón), Jesús Aldo DE NIGRIS Guajardo. (Coach: Víctor Manuel
VUCETICH Rojas).
Chelsea FC London: Petr CECH (CZE), Branislav IVANOVIC (SRB), Ashley COLE, DAVID
LUIZ Moreira Marinho (BRA) (63' Frank LAMPARD), Gary CAHILL, César
AZPILICUETA Tanco (ESP), Juan Manuel MATA García (ESP) (74' PAULO Renato
Rebocho FERREIRA (POR)), OSCAR dos Santos Emboaba Junior (BRA), John "MIKEL
OBI" Michael Nchekwube Obinna (NGR), FERNANDO José TORRES Sanz (ESP) (79'
Victor MOSES (NGR)), Eden HAZARD (BEL). (Coach: Rafael "RAFA" BENÍTEZ Maudes
(ESP)).
Goals: CF Monterrey: 1-3 Jesús Aldo DE NIGRIS Guajardo (90+1').
Chelsea FC: 0-1 Juan Manuel MATA García (17'), 0-2 FERNANDO José TORRES Sanz
(46'), 0-3 Dárvin Francisco CHÁVEZ Ra (48' own goal).
Referee: Carlos Alfredo VERA Rodríguez (ECU)   Attendance: 36,648

THIRD PLACE PLAY–OFF

16-12-2012   International Stadium Yokohama, Yokohama:
             Al Ahly SC Cairo – CF Monterrey 0-2 (0-1)
Al Ahly SC Cairo: MAHMOUD ABOUL-SAOUD, RAMI Hisham Abdel Aziz RABIA,
WAEL GOMAA Kamel El Hooty (YC80), SAYED MOAWAD Abdel Wahed, MOHAMED
NAGUIB Mohamed El Ghareeb, WALID SOLIMAN Said (77' Mohamed Nagy Ismail Afash
"GEDO"), ABDALLAH Mahmoud EL SAID Mohamed Bekhit, MUHAMMAD ABU
TARIKA, AHMED FATHI Abdelmonem (62' MOHAMED BARAKAT Ahmed Bastamy),
HOSSAM Mohamed ASHOUR Sanad Attia (YC8), EMAD "MOTEAB" Mohamed Abd El
Naby Ibrahim (52 ELSAYED HAMDY Mahdy). (Coaches: HOSSAM EL BADRY &
MOHAMED YOUSSEF Abdul-Razak).
CF Monterrey: Jonathan Emmanuel OROZCO Martínez, Severo Efraín MEZA Mayorga,
Ricardo OSORIO Mendoza, Dárvin Francisco CHÁVEZ Ramírez, José María BASANTA
Pavone (ARG), Hiram Ricardo MIER Alanís, Walter Orlando AYOVÍ Corozo (ECU), Jesús
Manuel CORONA Ruiz (63' Abraham Darió CARREÑO Rohan), Neri Raúl CARDOZO
(ARG) (83' Edgar Iván Estuardo SOLÍS Castillón), César Fabián DELGADO Godoy (ARG)
(79' Héctor Miguel MORALES Llanas), Jesús Aldo DE NIGRIS Guajardo. (Coach: Víctor
Manuel VUCETICH Rojas).
Goals: CF Monterrey: 0-1 Jesús Manuel CORONA Ruiz (3'), 0-2 César Fabián DELGADO
Godoy (66').
Referee: Peter O'LEARY (NLZ)   Attendance: 56,301

FINAL

16-12-2012 International Stadium Yokohama, Yokohama:
SC Corinthians Paulista São Paulo – Chelsea FC London 1-0 (0-0)
SC Corinthians Paulista São Paulo: CÁSSIO Roberto Ramos, ALESSANDRO Mori Nunes, Anderson Sebastião Cardoso "CHICÃO", FÁBIO SANTOS Romeu, PAULO ANDRÉ Cren Benini, RALF de Souza Teles, José Paulo Bezerra Maciel Júnior "PAULINHO", DANILO Gabriel de Andrade, José Paolo GUERRERO Gonzales (PER) (87' Juan Manuel MARTÍNEZ (ARG)), Marcio Passos de Albuquerque "EMERSON SHEIK" (QAT) (90' WALLACE REIS Silva), JORGE HENRIQUE de Souza (YC56). (Coach: Adenor Léonardo Bachi "TITE").
Chelsea FC London: Petr CECH (CZE), Branislav IVANOVIC (SRB) (83' César AZPILICUETA Tanco (ESP)), Ashley COLE, DAVID LUIZ Moreira Marinho (BRA) (YC72), Gary CAHILL (RC90), RAMIRES Santos do Nascimento (BRA), Frank LAMPARD, Juan Manuel MATA García (ESP), FERNANDO José TORRES Sanz (ESP), Victor MOSES (NGR) (73' OSCAR dos Santos Emboaba Junior (BRA)), Eden HAZARD (BEL) (87' Marko MARIN (GER)). (Coach: Rafael "RAFA" BENÍTEZ Maudes (ESP)).
Goal: SC Corinthians Paulista: 1-0 José Paolo GUERRERO Gonzales (69').
Referee: Cüneyt ÇAKIR (TUR) Attendance: 68,275

*** SC Corinthians Paulista won the Cup ***

2013 FIFA Club World Cup

The 2013 FIFA Club World Cup (officially, the 'FIFA Club World Cup Morocco 2013 presented by Toyota' for sponsorship reasons) was played between 11th and 21st December 2013. It was the tenth edition of the FIFA Club World Cup.

Four countries entered bids to host the 2013 and 2014 tournaments (the same host was to be selected for both tournaments) – Iran, Morocco, South Africa and the United Arab Emirates – but all withdrew from the process with the exception of the eventual hosts, Morocco.

The Champions of the six confederations entered the tournament as did the Moroccan champions Raja CA Casablanca who faced the Oceanian Champions, Auckland City FC, in an initial play-off.

With home advantage, the Moroccan team did exceedingly well, defeating not just the Oceania champions, but also the CONCACAF and South American Champions on the way to the Final. However, they were unable to overcome German giants FC Bayern München who won 2-0 for what was, notionally at least, their third world title following Intercontinental Cup successes in 1976 and 2001.

The clubs invited to play in the 2013 tournament were:

FC Bayern München (GER) - winners of the 2012-13 UEFA Champions League
Clube Atlético Mineiro (BRA) - winners of the 2013 Copa Libertadores
Al Ahly SC Cairo (EGY) - winners 2013 CAF Champions League
Guangzhou Evergrande FC (CHN) - winners 2013 AFC Champions League
CF Monterrey (MEX) - winners 2012-13 CONCACAF Champions League
Auckland City FC (NZL) - winners 2012-13 OFC Champions League
Raja CA Casablanca (MAR) - winners 2012-13 Botola (Host)

PLAY-OFF FOR QUARTER-FINALS

11-12-2013 Stade Adrar, Agadir:
Raja CA Casablanca – Auckland City FC 2-1 (1-0)
Raja CA Casablanca: Khalid ASKRI, Zakaria EL HACHIMI, Mohamed OULHAJ, Adil KARROUCHY, Ismaïl BENLAMALEM (YC57), Mouhssine MOUTOUALI, Chemseddine CHTIBI (73' Déo KANDA (DRC)), Kouko GUEHI (CIV), Issam ERRAKI, Abdelilah HAFIDI (90' Ahmed RAHMANI), Mouhcine IAJOUR (85' Vianney MABIDÉ (CAF)). (Coach: Faouzi BENZARTI (TUN)).
Auckland City FC: Tamati WILLIAMS, Takuya IWATA (JPN), ÁNGEL Luis Viña BERLANGA (ESP), John IRVING (ENG) (86' James PRITCHETT), Ivan VICELICH, Mario BILEN, Christopher BALE (WAL), Daniel KOPRIVIC (CRO) (82' David BROWNE (PNG)), CRISTÓBAL Márquez Crespo (ESP), Roy KRISHNA (FIJ), Adam DICKINSON (ENG) (64' Emiliano TADE (ARG)). (Coach: RAMON TRIBULIETX Santolaya (ESP)).
Goals: Raja CA Casablanca: 1-0 Mouhcine IAJOUR (39'), 2-1 Abdelilah HAFIDI (90+2').
Auckland City FC: 1-1 Roy KRISHNA (63').
Referee: Bakary Papa GASSAMA (GAM)   Attendance: 34,875

QUARTER-FINALS

14-12-2013 Stade Adrar, Agadir:
Guangzhou Evergrande FC – Al Ahly SC Cairo 2-0 (0-0)
Guangzhou Evergrande FC: Cheng ZENG, Linpeng ZHANG (YC55), Xiaoting FENG, KIM Young-gwon (KOR), Xiang SUN (YC45) (80' Xuri ZHAO), ELKESON (Ai Kesen) de Oliveira Cardoso (BRA), Zhi ZHENG, Darió Leonardo CONCA (ARG), Bowen HUANG, Luíz Guilherme da Conceição Silva "MURIQUI" (BRA), Lin GAO (64' Hao RONG). (Coach: Marcello LIPPI (ITA)).
Al Ahly SC Cairo: SHERIF EKRAMY Ahmed, AHMAD SHEDID Kenawi, MOHAMED NAGUIB Mohamed El Ghareeb, RAMI Hisham Abdel Aziz RABIA, SAAD Eldin SAMIR, WALID SOLIMAN Said, ABDALLAH Mahmoud EL SAID Mohamed Bekhit, MUHAMMAD ABU TARIKA (46' Dominique DA SILVA (MTN)), AHMED FATHI Abdelmonem, HOSSAM Mohamed ASHOUR Sanad (79' Mahmoud Ahmed Ibrahim Hassan "TREZEGUET"), EMAD "MOTEAB" Mohamed Abd El Naby Ibrahim (65' ELSAYED HAMDY Mahdy). (Coach: MOHAMED YOUSSEF Abdul-Razak).
Goals: Guangzhou Evergrande FC: 1-0 ELKESON (Ai Kesen) de Oliveira Cardoso (49'), 2-0 Darió Leonardo CONCA (67').
Referee: SANDRO Meira RICCI (BRA)   Attendance: 34,579

14-12-2013   Stade Adrar, Agadir:
Raja CA Casablanca – CF Monterrey 2-1 (1-0, 1-1) **(AET)**
Raja CA Casablanca: Khalid ASKRI (YC118), Zakaria EL HACHIMI, Mohamed OULHAJ, Adil KARROUCHY (YC57), Ismaïl BENLAMALEM, Mouhssine MOUTOUALI, Chemseddine CHTIBI (YC30) (67' Vianney MABIDÉ (CAF)), Kouko GUEHI (CIV), Issam ERRAKI, Abdelilah HAFIDI (81' Yassine SALHI), Mouhcine IAJOUR (109' Idrissa COULIBALY (MLI)). (Coach: Faouzi BENZARTI (TUN)).
CF Monterrey: Jonathan Emmanuel OROZCO Martínez, Severo Efraín MEZA Mayorga, Leobardo LÓPEZ García, Ricardo OSORIO Mendoza (YC24), José María BASANTA Pavone (ARG), Efraín JUÁREZ Valdez (101' Dárvin Francisco CHÁVEZ Ramírez), LUCAS António SILVA de Oliveira (BRA), Jesús Eduardo ZAVALA Castañeda (YC80) (99' Marlon Jonathan DE JESÚS Pabón (ECU)), Neri Raúl CARDOZO (ARG), César Fabián DELGADO Godoy (ARG) (76' Omar ARELLANO Riverón), Humberto Andrés SUAZO Pontivo (CHI) (YC86). (Coach: José Guadalupe CRUZ Núñez).
Goals: Raja CA Casablanca: 1-0 Chemseddine CHTIBI (24'), 2-1 Kouko GUEHI (95').
CF Monterrey: 1-1 José María BASANTA Pavone (53').
Referee: Alireza FAGHANI (IRN)   Attendance: 34,579

SEMI–FINALS

17-12-2013   Stade Adrar, Agadir:
Guangzhou Evergrande FC – FC Bayern München 0-3 (0-2)
Guangzhou Evergrande FC: Cheng ZENG, Linpeng ZHANG, Xiaoting FENG, KIM Young-gwon (KOR), Xiang SUN, ELKESON (Ai Kesen) de Oliveira Cardoso (BRA), Zhi ZHENG, Darió Leonardo CONCA (ARG), Bowen HUANG (46' Hao RONG), Xuri ZHAO (76' Junyan FENG), Luíz Guilherme da Conceição Silva "MURIQUI" (BRA) (72' Lin GAO). (Coach: Marcello LIPPI (ITA)).
FC Bayern München: Manuel NEUER, Daniel VAN BUYTEN (BEL), Márcio Rafael Ferreira de Souza "RAFINHA" (BRA), Jérôme BOATENG, Philipp LAHM, David ALABA (AUT), THIAGO Alcântara do Nascimento (ESP), Franck RIBÉRY (FRA) (72' Xherdan SHAQIRI (SUI)), Mario GÖTZE, Toni KROOS (58' Javier "JAVI" MARTÍNEZ Aginaga (ESP)), Mario MANDZUKIC (CRO) (75' Claudio Miguel PIZARRO Bossio (PER)). (Coach: Josep "PEP" GUARDIOLA i Sala (ESP)).
Goals: FC Bayern München: 0-1 Franck RIBÉRY (40'), 0-2 Mario MANDZUKIC (44'), 0-3 Mario GÖTZE (47').
Referee: Bakary Papa GASSAMA (GAM)   Attendance: 27,311

18-12-2013   Stade de Marrakech, Marrakesh:
Raja CA Casablanca – Clube Atlético Mineiro Belo Horizonte 3-1 (0-0)
Raja CA Casablanca: Khalid ASKRI, Zakaria EL HACHIMI, Mohamed OULHAJ, Adil KARROUCHY, Ismaïl BENLAMALEM, Mouhssine MOUTOUALI, Chemseddine CHTIBI (56' Vianney MABIDÉ (CAF)), Kouko GUEHI (CIV), Issam ERRAKI, Abdelilah HAFIDI (76' Déo KANDA (DRC)), Mouhcine IAJOUR (88' Idrissa COULIBALY (MLI)). (Coach: Faouzi BENZARTI (TUN)).
Clube Atlético Mineiro Belo Horizonte: VICTOR Leandro Bagy, MARCOS Luis ROCHA Aquino (63'LUAN Madson Gedeao de Paiva), LEONARDO Fabiano da SILVA e Silva, RÉVER Humberto Alves de Araujo (YC82), Lucas PIERRE Santos Oliveira, Ronaldo De Assis Moreira "RONALDINHO", LUCAS CÂNDIDO Silva (85' ALECSANDRO Barbosa Felisbino), JOSUÉ Anunciado de Oliveira (58' LEANDRO DONIZETE Gonçalves da Silva), João Alves de Assis Silva "JÔ", DIEGO TARDELLI Martins, Luiz Fernando Pereira da Silva "FERNANDINHO". (Coach: Alexi Stival "CUCA").
Goals: Raja CA Casablanca: 1-0 Mouhcine IAJOUR (51'), 2-1 Mouhssine MOUTOUALI (84' penalty), 3-1 Vianney MABIDÉ (90+4').
Clube Atlético Mineiro: 1-1 Ronaldo De Assis Moreira "RONALDINHO" (63').
Referee: Carlos VELASCO CARBALLO (ESP)   Attendance: 35,219

FIFTH PLACE PLAY–OFF

18-12-2013   Stade de Marrakech, Marrakesh:
Al Ahly SC Cairo – CF Monterrey 1-5 (1-4)
Al Ahly SC Cairo: SHERIF EKRAMY Ahmed, WAEL GOMAA Kamel El Hooty, AHMAD SHEDID Kenawi (46' SAAD Eldin SAMIR), MOHAMED NAGUIB Mohamed El Ghareeb, RAMI Hisham Abdel Aziz RABIA (YC81), SHEHAB Eldin AHMED, WALID SOLIMAN Said (66' AHMED SHOKRY Abdelraouf Ali Khalifa), Mahmoud Ahmed Ibrahim Hassan "TREZEGUET", ABDALLAH Mahmoud EL SAID Mohamed Bekhit, AHMED FATHI Abdelmonem (YC43), EMAD "MOTEAB" Mohamed Abd El Naby Ibrahim (68' AMR GAMAL Sayed). (Coach: MOHAMED YOUSSEF Abdul-Razak).
CF Monterrey: Juan De Dios IBARRA Corral, Severo Efraín MEZA Mayorga, Leobardo LÓPEZ García, Ricardo OSORIO Mendoza, Dárvin Francisco CHÁVEZ Ramírez, José María BASANTA Pavone (ARG), Efraín JUÁREZ Valdez (YC38) (86' Alejandro Arturo GARCÍA Ruíz), LUCAS António SILVA de Oliveira (BRA) (89' Jesús Eduardo ZAVALA Castañeda), Neri Raúl CARDOZO (ARG) (78' Omar ARELLANO Riverón), César Fabián DELGADO Godoy (ARG), Humberto Andrés SUAZO Pontivo (CHI). (Coach: José Guadalupe CRUZ Núñez).
Goals: Al Ahly SC Cairo: 1-1 EMAD "MOTEAB" Mohamed Abd El Naby Ibrahim (8').
CF Monterrey: 0-1 Neri Raúl CARDOZO (3'), 1-2 César Fabián DELGADO Godoy (22'), 1-3 Leobardo LÓPEZ García (27'), 1-4 Humberto Andrés SUAZO Pontivo (45' penalty), 1-5 César Fabián DELGADO Godoy (65').
Referee: Mark William GEIGER (USA)   Attendance: 35,219

THIRD PLACE PLAY-OFF

21-12-2013   Stade de Marrakech, Marrakesh:
Guangzhou Evergrande FC – Clube Atlético Mineiro Belo Horizonte 2-3 (2-2)
Guangzhou Evergrande FC: Shuai LI, Linpeng ZHANG, Xiaoting FENG, KIM Young-gwon (KOR), Xiang SUN (YC33) (64' Hao RONG), ELKESON (Ai Kesen) de Oliveira Cardoso (BRA) (77' Junyan FENG), Zhi ZHENG (85' Xuri ZHAO), Darió Leonardo CONCA (ARG), Bowen HUANG, Luíz Guilherme da Conceição Silva "MURIQUI" (BRA), Lin GAO. (Coach: Marcello LIPPI (ITA)).
Clube Atlético Mineiro Belo Horizonte: VICTOR Leandro Bagy, MARCOS Luis ROCHA Aquino, LEONARDO Fabiano da SILVA e Silva, RÉVER Humberto Alves de Araujo (YC89), Lucas PIERRE Santos Oliveira, Ronaldo De Assis Moreira "RONALDINHO" (RC87), LUCAS CÂNDIDO Silva (YC14) (33' JÚNIOR CÉSAR Eduardo Machado), JOSUÉ Anunciado de Oliveira (79' LEANDRO DONIZETE Gonçalves da Silva), João Alves de Assis Silva "JÔ" (60' LUAN Madson Gedeao de Paiva), DIEGO TARDELLI Martins, Luiz Fernando Pereira da Silva "FERNANDINHO". (Coach: Alexi Stival "CUCA").
Goals: Guangzhou Evergrande FC: 1-1 Luíz Guilherme da Conceição Silva "MURIQUI" (9'), 2-1 Darió Leonardo CONCA (15' penalty).
Clube Atlético Mineiro: 0-1 DIEGO TARDELLI Martins (2'), 2-2 Ronaldo De Assis Moreira "RONALDINHO" (45+1'), 2-3 LUAN Madson Gedeao de Paiva (90+1').
Referee: Alireza FAGHANI (IRN)   Attendance: 37,774

FINAL

21-12-2013   Stade de Marrakech, Marrakesh:
FC Bayern München – Raja CA Casablanca 2-0 (2-0)
FC Bayern München: Manuel NEUER, Bonfim Costa Santos DANTE (BRA), Márcio Rafael Ferreira de Souza "RAFINHA" (BRA), Jérôme BOATENG, Philipp LAHM, David ALABA (AUT), THIAGO Alcântara do Nascimento (ESP), Franck RIBÉRY (FRA), Xherdan SHAQIRI (SUI) (80' Mario GÖTZE), Toni KROOS (60' Javier "JAVI" MARTÍNEZ Aginaga (ESP)), Thomas MÜLLER (76' Mario MANDZUKIC (CRO)). (Coach: Josep "PEP" GUARDIOLA i Sala (ESP)).
Raja CA Casablanca: Khalid ASKRI, Zakaria EL HACHIMI, Mohamed OULHAJ (YC55), Adil KARROUCHY, Ismaïl BENLAMALEM, Mouhssine MOUTOUALI, Chemseddine CHTIBI (50' Vianney MABIDÉ (CAF)), Kouko GUEHI (CIV), Issam ERRAKI, Abdelilah HAFIDI (88' Badr KACHANI), Mouhcine IAJOUR (78' Rachid SOULAIMANI (YC79)). (Coach: Faouzi BENZARTI (TUN)).
Goals: FC Bayern München: 1-0 Bonfim Costa Santos DANTE (7'), 2-0 THIAGO Alcântara do Nascimento (22').
Referee: SANDRO Meira RICCI (BRA)   Attendance: 37,774

*** FC Bayern München won the Cup ***

2014 FIFA Club World Cup

The 2014 FIFA Club World Cup (officially, the 'FIFA Club World Cup Morocco 2014 presented by Toyota' for sponsorship reasons) was played between 10th to 20th December 2014. It was the eleventh edition of the FIFA Club World Cup and was hosted in Morocco.

Earlier in 2014, there were concerns that the tournament might need to be moved after Morocco decided to withdraw from hosting the 2015 Africa Cup of Nations following a serious outbreak of Ebola in West Africa. However, Morocco quickly confirmed that they still planned to host the Club World Cup as none of the entrants would be from the countries with the most severe outbreaks of the virus.

The Champions of the six confederations entered the tournament as did the Moroccan champions Moghreb Athlétic de Tétouan who faced the Oceanian Champions in an initial play-off.

Real Madrid CF defeated CA San Lorenzo de Almagro 2-0 in the Final to win a first FIFA Club World Cup to go with their victories in the 1960, 1998 and 2002 Intercontinental Cup victories. This equalled AC Milan's record of four world club titles.

The clubs invited to play in the 2014 tournament were:

Real Madrid CF (ESP) - winners of the 2013-14 UEFA Champions League
CA San Lorenzo de Almagro (ARG) - winners of the 2014 Copa Libertadores
ES Sétif (ALG) - winners of the 2014 CAF Champions League
Western Sydney Wanderers FC (AUS) - winners of the 2014 AFC Champions League
CF Cruz Azul (MEX) - winners of the 2013-14 CONCACAF Champions League
Auckland City FC (NZL) - winners of the 2013-14 OFC Champions League
Moghreb Atlético Tétouan (MAR) - winners of the 2013-14 Botola (Host)

PLAY-OFF FOR QUARTER-FINALS

10-12-2014   Prince Moulay Abdellah Stadium, Rabat:
             Moghreb Atlético Tétouan – Auckland City FC 0-0 **(AET)**
Moghreb Atlético Tétouan: Mohamed EL YOUSFI, Mohamed ABARHOUN, Mehdi KHALLATI, Mourtada FALL (SEN), Abdeladim KHADROUF, Nassir EL MIMOUNI (97' Said GRADA), Zouhair NAÏM, Ahmed JAHOUH, Mouhcine IAJOUR (46' Zaid KROUCH), Faouzi ABDELGHANI (94' Salman OUALD EL HAJ), Abdelmoula EL HARDOUMI. (Coach: Abdelaziz EL AMRI).
Auckland City FC: Tamati WILLIAMS, Marko DJORDJEVIC (SRB), Takuya IWATA (JPN), ÁNGEL Luis Viña BERLANGA (ESP) (YC102), John IRVING (ENG), Ivan VICELICH, Mario BILEN (CRO), Tim PAYNE, Ryan DE VRIES, Emiliano TADE (ARG) (68' Darren WHITE (ENG)), Enrico Fabrizio Vicenzo TAVANO Alonso (MEX) (107' Sanni ISSA (NGR)). (Coach: RAMON TRIBULIETX Santolaya (ESP)).
Referee: Walter Alexander LÓPEZ Castellanos (GUA)   Attendance: 35,247

Penalties: 1 Tim PAYNE   * Ahmed JAHOUH
             2 John IRVING   1 Zaid KROUCH
             3 Darren WHITE   2 Mourtada FALL
             * Mario BILEN   3 Zouhair NAÏM
             4 Sanni ISSA   * Mehdi KHALLATI

Auckland City FC won on penalties (4-3).

QUARTER-FINALS

13-12-2014   Prince Moulay Abdellah Stadium, Rabat:
             ES Sétifienne – Auckland City FC 0-1 (0-0)
ES Sétifienne: Sofiane KHEDAIRIA, Said ARROUSSI, Amine MEGATELI, Lyes BOUKRIA (YC90), Farid MELLOULI, Mohamed LAGRAÂ, El Hedi BELAMEIRI (69' Sofiane YOUNÈS), Toufik ZERARA, Eudes DAGOULOU (CAF) (YC42) (46' Akram DJAHNIT (YC48)), Ahmed GASMI (YC63) (65' Abdelmalek ZIAYA), Mohamed BENYETTOU. (Coach: Kheïreddine MADOUI).
Auckland City FC: Tamati WILLIAMS, Marko DJORDJEVIC (SRB), Takuya IWATA (JPN), ÁNGEL Luis Viña BERLANGA (ESP), John IRVING (ENG), Ivan VICELICH, Mario BILEN (CRO), Tim PAYNE, Ryan DE VRIES (90' Darren WHITE (ENG)), Emiliano TADE (ARG), Enrico Fabrizio Vicenzo TAVANO Alonso (MEX) (86' Sanni ISSA (NGR)). (Coach: RAMON TRIBULIETX Santolaya (ESP)).
Goal: Auckland City FC: 0-1 John IRVING (52').
Referee: PEDRO PROENÇA Oliveira Alves Garcia (POR)   Attendance: 22,153

13-12-2014   Prince Moulay Abdellah Stadium, Rabat:
CF Cruz Azul – Western Sydney Wanderers FC 3-1 (0-0, 1-1) **(AET)**
CF Cruz Azul Mexico City: José de Jesús CORONA Rodríguez Rodríguez, Fausto Manuel PINTO Rosas, Francisco Javier RODRÍGUEZ Pinedo "MAZA" (78' Ismael VALADÉZ Arce), Julio César DOMÍNGUEZ Juárez, Gerardo FLORES Zúñiga, Gerardo TORRADO Diéz de Bonilla, Marco Jhonfai FABIÁN de la Mora (106' Manuel Alejandro VELA Garrido), Christian Eduardo GIMÉNEZ (YC37), Xavier Iván BÁEZ Gamiño (69' Joao Robin ROJAS Mendoza (ECU)), Mauro Abel FÓRMICA (ARG), Hugo Mariano PAVONE (ARG). (Coach: Luis Fernando TENA Garduño).
Western Sydney Wanderers FC: Ante COVIC, Nikolai TOPOR-STANLEY (YC53,YC102), Brendan HAMILL (YC73), Matthew SPIRANOVIC (YC31,YC74), Iacopo LA ROCCA (ITA) (YC84), Seyi ADELEKE (NGR) (72' Antony GOLEC), Mateo POLJAK (CRO), Labinot HALITI (67' Tomi JURIC (YC88)), Nikita RUKAVYTSYA, Romeo CASTELEN (HOL) (78' Shannon COLE), Mark BRIDGE. (Coach: Tony POPOVIC).
Goals: CDSC Cruz Azul: 1-1 Gerardo TORRADO Diéz de Bonilla (89' penalty), 2-1 Hugo Mariano PAVONE (108'), 3-1 Gerardo TORRADO Diéz de Bonilla (118' penalty).
Western Sydney Wanderers FC: 0-1 Iacopo LA ROCCA (65').
Referee: Noumandiez Désiré DOUÉ (CIV)   Attendance: 22,153

SEMI–FINALS

16-12-2014   Stade de Marrakech, Marrakesh:
CF Cruz Azul Mexico City – Real Madrid CF 0-4 (0-2)
CF Cruz Azul Mexico City: José de Jesús CORONA Rodríguez Rodríguez, Fausto Manuel PINTO Rosas, Francisco Javier RODRÍGUEZ Pinedo "MAZA", Julio César DOMÍNGUEZ Juárez, Gerardo FLORES Zúñiga, Gerardo TORRADO Diéz de Bonilla, Christian Eduardo GIMÉNEZ (65' Pablo Edson BARRERA Acosta), Joao Robin ROJAS Mendoza (ECU) (76' Ismael VALADÉZ Arce), Hernán Darío BERNARDELLO (ARG), Mauro Abel FÓRMICA (ARG), Hugo Mariano PAVONE (ARG) (65' Marco Jhonfai FABIÁN de la Mora). (Coach: Luis Fernando TENA Garduño).
Real Madrid CF: IKER CASILLAS Fernández, Képler Laveran Lima Ferreira "PEPE" (POR), SERGIO RAMOS García (YC39) (64' Raphaël VARANE (FRA)), MARCELO Vieira da Silva Júnior (BRA), Daniel "DANI" CARVAJAL Ramos, Toni KROOS (GER) (73' Sami KHEDIRA (GER)), Francisco Román Alarcón Suárez "ISCO" (76' JESÉ Rodríguez Ruíz), Asier Illarramendi Andonegi "ILLARRA", CRISTIANO RONALDO dos Santos Aveiro (POR), Karim BENZEMA (FRA), Gareth BALE (WAL). (Coach: Carlo ANCELOTTI (ITA)).
Goals: Real Madrid CF: 0-1 SERGIO RAMOS García (15'), 0-2 Karim BENZEMA (36'), 0-3 Gareth BALE (50'), 0-4 Francisco Román Alarcón Suárez "ISCO" (72').
Referee: Enrique Roberto OSSES Zencovich (CHI)   Attendance: 34,862

Gerardo TORRADO Diéz de Bonilla missed a penalty kick (40').

17-12-2014   Stade de Marrakech, Marrakesh:
CA San Lorenzo de Almagro – Auckland City FC 2-1 (1-0, 1-1) **(AET)**
CA San Lorenzo de Almargro Buenos Aires: Sebastián Alberto TORRICO, Mario Alberto YEPES Diaz (COL), Walter KANNEMANN (YC40), Juan Ignacio MERCIER (YC24), Julio Alberto BUFFARINI (YC105), Enzo Maximiliano KALINSKI Martinez (77' Mauro MATOS), Pablo César BARRIENTOS (YC79), Néstor Ezequiel ORTIGOZA (PAR) (YC59) (109' Facundo Tomás QUIGNÓN), Emanuel Matías MAS, Gonzalo Alberto VERÓN (68' Leandro Atilio ROMAGNOLI), Martín CAUTERUCCIO Rodríguez (URU). (Coach: Edgardo BAUZA).
Auckland City FC: Tamati WILLIAMS, Marko DJORDJEVIC (SRB) (YC8) (96' Sanni ISSA (NGR)), Takuya IWATA (JPN), ÁNGEL Luis Viña BERLANGA (ESP) (YC64), John IRVING (ENG), Ivan VICELICH, Mario BILEN (CRO) (YC60), Tim PAYNE, Ryan DE VRIES, Emiliano TADE (ARG) (90' David BROWNE (PNG)), Enrico Fabrizio Vicenzo TAVANO Alonso (MEX) (100' Sam BURFOOT (ENG)). (Coach: RAMON TRIBULIETX Santolaya (ESP)).
Goals: CA San Lorenzo de Almagro: 1-0 Pablo César BARRIENTOS (45+2'), 2-1 Mauro MATOS (93').
Auckland City FC: 1-1 ÁNGEL Luis Viña BERLANGA (67').
Referee: Benjamin Jon (Ben) WILLIAMS (AUS)   Attendance: 18,458

FIFTH PLACE PLAY–OFF

17-12-2014   Stade de Marrakech, Marrakesh:
ES Sétifienne – Western Sydney Wanderers FC 2-2 (0-1, 2-2) **(AET)**
ES Sétifienne: Sofiane KHEDAIRIA, Said ARROUSSI (YC87), Amine MEGATELI, Farid MELLOULI, Akram DJAHNIT, Sid Ali EL AMRI (64' Mohamed LAGRAÂ), Benjamin ZÉ ONDO (GAB), Toufik ZERARA, Sofiane YOUNÈS (77' El Hedi BELAMEIRI), Ahmed GASMI, Abdelmalek ZIAYA. (Coach: Kheïreddine MADOUI).
Western Sydney Wanderers FC: Dean BOUZANIS, Daniel MULLEN (YC45), Antony GOLEC (YC13), Seyi ADELEKE (NGR), Daniel ALESSI, Mateo POLJAK (CRO) (YC54) (79' Alusine FOFANAH), Jason TRIFIRO, Kearyn BACCUS (YC47) (67' Vítor Rodrigues SABA (BRA)), Labinot HALITI, Jaushua SOTIRIO (67' Tomi JURIC), Romeo CASTELEN (HOL). (Coach: Tony POPOVIC).
Goals: ES Sétif: 1-1 Daniel MULLEN (50' own goal), 2-1 Abdelmalek ZIAYA (57').
Western Sydney Wanderers FC: 0-1 Romeo CASTELEN (5'), 2-2 Vítor Rodrigues SABA (89').
Referee: Norbert HAUATA (TAH)   Attendance: 18,458

Penalties:	1 Vítor Rodrigues SABA	* Akram DJAHNIT
	* Labinor HALITI	1 Ahmed GASMI
	2 Jason TRIFIRO	2 El Hedi BELAMEIRI
	3 Tomi JURIC	* Abdelmalek ZIAYA
	* Dean BOUZANIS	3 Farid MELLOULI
	* Daniel MULLEN	* Said ARROUSSI
	4 Alusine FOFANAH	4 Amine METATELI
	* Seyi ADELEKE	5 Toufik ZERARA

ES Sétif won on penalties (5-4).

THIRD PLACE PLAY–OFF

20-12-2014   Stade de Marrakech, Marrakesh:
CF Cruz Azul Mexico City – Auckland City FC 1-1 (0-1, 1-1) **(AET)**
CF Cruz Azul Mexico City: José de Jesús CORONA Rodríguez Rodríguez, Francisco Javier RODRÍGUEZ Pinedo "MAZA", Julio César DOMÍNGUEZ Juárez, Gerardo FLORES Zúñiga, Gerardo TORRADO Diéz de Bonilla, Marco Jhonfai FABIÁN de la Mora (85' Hugo Mariano PAVONE (ARG)), Joao Robin ROJAS Mendoza (ECU), Xavier Iván BÁEZ Gamiño (46' Christian Eduardo GIMÉNEZ), Mauro Abel FÓRMICA (ARG), Ismael VALADÉZ Arce, Manuel Alejandro VELA Garrido. (Coach: Luis Fernando TENA Garduño).
Auckland City FC: Jacob SPOONLEY, Takuya IWATA (JPN), John IRVING (ENG), Darren WHITE (ENG), Ivan VICELICH (80' Cameron LINDSAY), Mario BILEN (CRO), Tim PAYNE, Sam BURFOOT (ENG) (57' Sanni ISSA (NGR)), Ryan DE VRIES, Emiliano TADE (ARG) (90' James PRITCHETT), Enrico Fabrizio Vicenzo TAVANO Alonso (MEX). (Coach: RAMON TRIBULIETX Santolaya (ESP)).
Goals: CDSC Cruz Azul: 1-1 Joao Robin ROJAS Mendoza (57').
Auckland City FC: 0-1 Ryan DE VRIES (45+2').
Referee: PEDRO PROENÇA Oliveira Alves Garcia (POR)   Attendance: 22,153
Penalties:
1 Ryan DE VRIES   1 Christian Eduardo GIMÉNEZ
* John IRVING   * Mauro Abel FÓRMICA
2 Darren WHITE   2 Francisco Javier RODRÍGUEZ Pinedo "MAZA"
3 James PRITCHETT   * Ismael VALADÉZ Arce
4 Sanni ISSA

Auckland City FC won on penalties (4-2).

FINAL

20-12-2014   Stade de Marrakech, Marrakesh:
Real Madrid CF – SA San Lorenzo de Almagro Buenos Aires 2-0 (1-0)
Real Madrid CF: IKER CASILLAS Fernández, Képler Laveran Lima Ferreira "PEPE" (POR), SERGIO RAMOS García (YC22) (89' Raphaël VARANE (FRA)), MARCELO Vieira da Silva Júnior (BRA) (44' FÁBIO Alexandre da Silva COENTRÃO (POR)), Daniel "DANI" CARVAJAL Ramos (YC30) (73' Álvaro ARBELOA Coca), Toni KROOS (GER), James David RODRÍGUEZ Rubio (COL), Francisco Román Alarcón Suárez "ISCO", CRISTIANO RONALDO dos Santos Aveiro (POR), Karim BENZEMA (FRA), Gareth BALE (WAL). (Coach: Carlo ANCELOTTI (ITA)).
CA San Lorenzo de Almargro Buenos Aires: Sebastián Alberto TORRICO, Mario Alberto YEPES Diaz (COL) (61' Mauro Darío Jesús CETTO), Walter KANNEMANN (YC85), Juan Ignacio MERCIER, Julio Alberto BUFFARINI (YC55), Enzo Maximiliano KALINSKI Martinez, Pablo César BARRIENTOS (YC17), Néstor Ezequiel ORTIGOZA (PAR) (YC12), Emanuel Matías MAS, Gonzalo Alberto VERÓN (57' Leandro Atilio ROMAGNOLI), Martín CAUTERUCCIO Rodríguez (URU) (68' Mauro MATOS). (Coach: Edgardo BAUZA).
Goals: Real Madrid CF: 1-0 SERGIO RAMOS García (37'), 2-0 Gareth BALE (51').
Referee: Walter Alexander LÓPEZ Castellanos (GUA)   Attendance: 38,345

*** Real Madrid CF won the Cup ***

2015 FIFA Club World Cup

The 2015 FIFA Club World Cup (officially, the 'FIFA Club World Cup Japan 2015 presented by Alibaba E-Auto' for sponsorship reasons) was played between 10th and 20th December 2015. Just two countries, India and Japan showed any interest in bidding to be hosts of the 2015 and 2016 tournaments but India quickly withdrew from the process so this 12th edition of the FIFA Club World Cup was once again hosted by Japan.

The Champions of the six confederations entered the tournament as did the Japanese champions Sanfrecce Hiroshima who faced the Oceanian Champions in an initial play-off.

European Champions FC Barcelona defeated CA River Plate Buenos Aires 3-0 in the Final, to win a record third Club World Cup title.

The clubs invited to the 2015 tournament were:

FC Barcelona (ESP) - winners of the 2014-15 UEFA Champions League
CA River Plate Buenos Aires (ARG)
                                             - winners of the 2015 Copa Libertadores
TP Mazembe (DRC) - winners of the 2015 CAF Champions League
Guangzhou Evergrande FC (CHN)
                                             - winners of the 2015 AFC Champions League
CF América (MEX) - winners of the 2014-15 CONCACAF Champions League
Auckland City FC (NZL) - winners of the 2014-15 OFC Champions League
Sanfrecce Hiroshima (JPN) - winners of the 2015 J1 League (Host)

PLAY-OFF FOR QUARTER-FINALS

10-12-2015   International Stadium, Yokohama, Yokohama:
                    Sanfrecce Hiroshima – Auckland City FC 2-0 (1-0)
Sanfrecce Hiroshima: Takuto HAYASHI, Hiroki MIZUMOTO, Kazuhiko CHIBA (YC43), Tsukasa SHIOTANI, Toshihiro AOYAMA, Yoshifumi KASHIWA, Gakuto NOTSUDA (14' Kosei SHIBASAKI, 52' Dyanfres DOUGLAS Chagas Matos (BRA)), Takuya MARUTANI, Yusuke MINAGAWA, Kohei SHIMIZU (65' Sho SASAKI), Takuma ASANO. (Coach: Hajime MORIYASU).
Auckland City FC: Jacob SPOONLEY, Marko DJORDJEVIC (SRB), Takuya IWATA (JPN), ÁNGEL Luis Viña BERLANGA (ESP), KIM Dae-wook (KOR) (YC56) (78' Darren WHITE (ENG) (YC80)), Mario BILEN (CRO) (71' Emiliano TADE (ARG)), MIKEL ÁLVARO Salazar (ESP), Te Atawhai HUDSON-WIHONGI, Ryan DE VRIES, JOÃO Vítor Rocha de Carvalho MOREIRA (POR) (84' Clayton LEWIS), Micah LEA'ALAFA (SLM). (Coach: RAMON TRIBULIETX Santolaya (ESP)).
Goals: Sanfrecce Hiroshima: 1-0 Yusuke MINAGAWA (9'), 2-0 Tsykasa SHIOTANI (70').
Referee: Sidi ALIOUM (CMR)   Attendance: 19,421

QUARTER-FINALS

13-12-2015   Nagai Stadium, Osaka:
CF América Mexico City – Guangzhou Evergrande FC 1-2 (0-0)
CF América Mexico City: Moisés Alberto MUÑOZ Rodríguez, Paolo Duval GOLTZ (ARG), Miguel Angel Ramón SAMUDIO (PAR), Pablo César AGUILAR Benítez (PAR), Paul Nicolás AGUILAR Rojas, Andrés Felipe ANDRADE Torres (COL), Rubens Omar Óscar SAMBUEZA (ARG), José Daniel Octavio GUERRERO Rodríguez, Darío Ismael BENEDETTO (ARG) (81' Osvaldo David MARTÍNEZ Arce (PAR)), Oribe PERALTA Morones, Carlos Darwin QUINTERO Villalba (COL) (83' Michael Antonio ARROYO Mina (ECU)). (Coach: Marcos Ignacio AMBRIZ Espinoza).
Guangzhou Evergrande FC: Shuai LI, Linpeng ZHANG, Xiaoting FENG (YC88), Zheng ZOU, KIM Young-gwon (KOR), ELKESON (Ai Kesen) de Oliveira Cardoso (BRA) (79' Hanchao YU), Zhi ZHENG, RICARDO GOULART Pereira (BRA), Bowen HUANG (66' Lin GAO), José Paulo Bezerra Maciel Júnior "PAULINHO" (BRA), Robson de Souza "ROBINHO" (BRA) (46' Long ZHENG). (Coach: Luiz Felipe SCOLARI (BRA)).
Goals: CF América: 1-0 Oribe PERALTA Morones (55').
Guangzhou Evergrande FC: 1-1 Long ZHENG (80'), 1-2 José Paulo Bezerra Maciel Júnior "PAULINHO" (90+3').
Referee: Jonas ERIKSSON SWE)   Attendance: 18,772

13-12-2015   Nagai Stadium, Osaka:
TP Mazembe Lubumbashi – Sanfrecce Hiroshima 0-3 (0-1)
TP Mazembe Lubumbashi: Sylvain GBOHOUO (CIV), Joël KIMWAKI, Nathan SINKALA (ZAM) (YC13) (63' Rainford KALABA (ZAM)), Salif COULIBALY (MLI) (YC12), Yaw FRIMPONG (GHA), Richard BOATENG (GHA) (69' Jonathan BOLINGI (YC79)), Roger ASSALÉ (CIV), Boubacar DIARRA (MLI), Mbwana SAMATTA (TAN), Given SINGULUMA (ZAM) (46' Thomas ULIMWENGU (TAN)), Adama TRAORÉ (MLI). (Coach: Patrice CARTERON).
Sanfrecce Hiroshima: Takuto HAYASHI, Kazuhiko CHIBA, Sho SASAKI (YC80), Tsukasa SHIOTANI, Toshihiro AOYAMA, Kazuyuki MORISAKI, Mihael MIKIC (CRO) (82' Hiroki MIZUMOTO), Yoshifumi KASHIWA, Yusuke CHAJIMA, Dyanfres DOUGLAS Chagas Matos (BRA) (87' Yusuke MINAGAWA), Hisato SATO (74' Takuma ASANO). (Coach: Hajime MORIYASU).
Goals: Sanfrecce Hiroshima: 0-1 Tsukasa SHIOTANI (44'), 0-2 Kazuhiko CHIBA (56'), 0-3 Yakuma ASANO (78').
Referee: Wilmar Alexander ROLDÁN Pérez (COL)   Attendance: 23,609

FIFTH PLACE PLAY–OFF

16-12-2015   Nagai Stadium, Osaka:
                    CF América Mexico City – TP Mazembe Lubumbashi 2-1 (2-1)
CF América Mexico City: Moisés Alberto MUÑOZ Rodríguez, Érick Alan PIMENTEL Benavides (YC37), Osmar MARES Martínez (YC63), Ventura ALVARADO Aispuro (USA), Paul Nicolás AGUILAR Rojas, Andrés Felipe ANDRADE Torres (COL) (83' Paolo Duval GOLTZ (ARG)), José Daniel Octavio GUERRERO Rodríguez, Darío Ismael BENEDETTO (ARG) (21' Martín Eduardo ZÚÑIGA Barria), Osvaldo David MARTÍNEZ Arce (PAR), Michael Antonio ARROYO Mina (ECU) (YC67), Oribe PERALTA Morones (66' Rubens Omar Óscar SAMBUEZA (ARG)). (Coach: Marcos Ignacio AMBRIZ Espinoza).
TP Mazembe Lubumbashi: Sylvain GBOHOUO (CIV), Joël KIMWAKI, Salif COULIBALY (MLI), Bopé BOKADI (46' Boubacar DIARRA (MLI)), Yaw FRIMPONG (GHA) (61' Kabaso CHONGO (ZAM)), Daniel NII ADJEI (GHA), Patient MWEPU, Mbwana SAMATTA (TAN), Adama TRAORÉ (MLI), Rainford KALABA (ZAM), Thomas ULIMWENGU (TAN) (72' Roger ASSALÉ (CIV)). (Coach: Patrice CARTERON).
Goals: CF América: 1-0 Darío Ismael BENEDETTO (19'), 2-0 Martín Eduardo ZÚÑIGA Barria (28').
TP Mazembe: 2-1 Rainford KALABA (43').
Referee: Alireza FAGHANI (IRN)   Attendance: 11,686

SEMI–FINALS

16-12-2015   Nagai Stadium, Osaka:
                    Sanfrecce Hiroshima – CA River Plate Buenos Aires 0-1 (0-0)
Sanfrecce Hiroshima: Takuto HAYASHI, Kazuhiko CHIBA (YC18), Sho SASAKI, Tsukasa SHIOTANI (YC77), Toshihiro AOYAMA, Kazuyuki MORISAKI (YC90), Yoshifumi KASHIWA (YC36) (61' Mihael MIKIC (CRO)), Yusuke CHAJIMA (76' Hisato SATO), Dyanfres DOUGLAS Chagas Matos (BRA), Yusuke MINAGAWA (66' Takuma ASANO), Kohei SHIMIZU. (Coach: Hajime MORIYASU).
CA River Plate Buenos Aires: Marcelo Alberto BAROVERO, Jonatan Ramón MAIDANA, Éder Fabián ÁLVAREZ Balanta (COL) (YC61), Leonel Jesús VANGIONI Rangel, Gabriel Iván MERCADO (YC51) (85' Camilo Sebastián MAYADA Mesa (URU)), Claudio Matías KRANEVITTER, Carlos Andrés SÁNCHEZ Arcosa (URU), Leonardo Nicolás PISCULICHI (64' Tabaré Uruguay VIÚDEZ Mora (URU)), Leonardo Daniel PONZIO (57' Luis Oscar GONZÁLEZ), Rodrigo Nicanor MORA Núñez (URU), Lucas Nicolás ALARIO. (Coach: Marcelo Daniel GALLARDO).
Goal: CA River Plate Buenos Aires: 0-1 Lucas Nicolás ALARIO (72').
Referee: Jonas ERIKSSON SWE)   Attendance: 20,133

17-12-2015   International Stadium, Yokohama, Yokohama:
             FC Barcelona – Guangzhou Evergrande FC 3-0 (1-0)
FC Barcelona: Claudio Andrés BRAVO Muñoz (CHI), Gerard PIQUÉ i Bernabéu, Daniel "DANI" ALVES da Silva (BRA), Javier Alejandro MASCHERANO (ARG), JORDI ALBA Ramos (76' ADRIANO Correia Claro (BRA)), Ivan RAKITIC (CRO), Sergio BUSQUETS Burgos, Andrés INIESTA Luján (81' Sergi SAMPER Montaña), SERGI ROBERTO Carnicer (72' SANDRO Ramírez Castillo), Luis Alberto SUÁREZ Díaz (URU), MUNIR El Haddadi Mohamed. (Coach: LUIS ENRIQUE Martínez García).
Guangzhou Evergrande FC: Shuai LI, Linpeng ZHANG, Xiaoting FENG (YC16), Zheng ZOU (35' Xuepeng LI), KIM Young-gwon (KOR), ELKESON (Ai Kesen) de Oliveira Cardoso (BRA) (67' Lin GAO), Zhi ZHENG, RICARDO GOULART Pereira (BRA), Bowen HUANG, Long ZHENG (56' Hanchao YU), José Paulo Bezerra Maciel Júnior "PAULINHO" (BRA). (Coach: Luiz Felipe SCOLARI (BRA)).
Goals: FC Barcelona: 1-0 Luis Alberto SUÁREZ Díaz (39'), 2-0 Luis Alberto SUÁREZ Díaz (50'), 3-0 Luis Alberto SUÁREZ Díaz (67' penalty).
Referee: Joel Antonio AGUILAR Chicas (SAL)   Attendance: 63,870

THIRD PLACE PLAY–OFF

20-12-2015   International Stadium, Yokohama, Yokohama:
             Sanfrecce Hiroshima – Guangzhou Evergrande FC 2-1 (0-1)
Sanfrecce Hiroshima: Takuto HAYASHI, Hiroki MIZUMOTO, Tsukasa SHIOTANI (YC65), Kazuya MIYAHARA, Toshihiro AOYAMA, Mihael MIKIC (CRO) (67' Yoshifumi KASHIWA), Yusuke CHAJIMA, Takuya MARUTANI, Hisato SATO (YC30) (58' Dyanfres DOUGLAS Chagas Matos (BRA)), Kohei SHIMIZU (87' Sho SASAKI), Takuma ASANO (YC73). (Coach: Hajime MORIYASU).
Guangzhou Evergrande FC: Shuai LI, Fang MEI (YC60), Linpeng ZHANG, KIM Young-gwon (KOR) (YC88), Xuepeng LI, ELKESON (Ai Kesen) de Oliveira Cardoso (BRA) (46' Long ZHENG), Zhi ZHENG (YC35), RICARDO GOULART Pereira (BRA) (81' Jian LIU), Bowen HUANG (86' Hanchao YU), José Paulo Bezerra Maciel Júnior "PAULINHO" (BRA), Lin GAO. (Coach: Luiz Felipe SCOLARI (BRA)).
Goals: Sanfrecce Hiroshima: 1-1 Dyanfres DOUGLAS Chagas Matos (70'), 2-1 Dyanfres DOUGLAS Chagas Matos (83').
Guangzhou Evergrande FC: 0-1 José Paulo Bezerra Maciel Júnior "PAULINHO" (4').
Referee: Matthew (Matt) CONGER (NZL)   Attendance: 47,968

FINAL

20-12-2015 International Stadium, Yokohama, Yokohama:
CA River Plate Buenos Aires – FC Barcelona 0-3 (0-1)
CA River Plate Buenos Aires: Marcelo Alberto BAROVERO, Jonatan Ramón MAIDANA, Éder Fabián ÁLVAREZ Balanta (COL), Leonel Jesús VANGIONI Rangel, Gabriel Iván MERCADO, Claudio Matías KRANEVITTER (YC10), Carlos Andrés SÁNCHEZ Arcosa (URU), Tabaré Uruguay VIÚDEZ Mora (URU) (56' Sebastián DRIUSSI), Leonardo Daniel PONZIO (YC32) (46' Gonzalo Nicolás MARTÍNEZ), Rodrigo Nicanor MORA Núñez (URU) (46' Luis Oscar GONZÁLEZ), Lucas Nicolás ALARIO. (Coach: Marcelo Daniel GALLARDO).
FC Barcelona: Claudio Andrés BRAVO Muñoz (CHI), Gerard PIQUÉ i Bernabéu, Daniel "DANI" ALVES da Silva (BRA), Javier Alejandro MASCHERANO (ARG) (81' Thomas VERMAELEN (BEL)), JORDI ALBA Ramos (YC16), Ivan RAKITIC (CRO) (YC43) (67' SERGI ROBERTO Carnicer (YC72)), Sergio BUSQUETS Burgos, Andrés INIESTA Luján, Luis Alberto SUÁREZ Díaz (URU), Lionel Andrés MESSI Cuccitini (ARG), NEYMAR da Silva Santos Júnior (BRA) (YC61) (89' Jérémy MATHIEU (FRA)). (Coach: LUIS ENRIQUE Martínez García).
Goals: FC Barcelona: 0-1 Lionel Andrés MESSI Cuccitini (36'), 0-2 Luis Alberto SUÁREZ Díaz (49'), 0-3 Luis Alberto SUÁREZ Díaz (68').
Referee: Alireza FAGHANI (IRN)   Attendance: 66,853

*** **FC Barcelona won the Cup** ***

2016 FIFA Club World Cup

The 2016 FIFA Club World Cup (officially, the 'FIFA Club World Cup Japan 2016 presented by Alibaba YunOS Auto' for sponsorship reasons) was the 13th edition of the FIFA Club World Cup and the tournament was played between 8th and 18th December 2016 in Japan.

The Champions of the six confederations entered the tournament as did the Japanese champions Kashima Antlers FC who faced the Oceanian Champions in an initial play-off.

Kashima Antlers progressed to the Final, defeating both the African and South American Champions along the way, but Real Madrid CF proved too strong and won 4-2 after extra-time to lift their second Club World Cup. Added to the Intercontinental Cup victories from 1960, 1998 and 2002, this meant the Spanish team had won a record 5 world club titles.

The clubs invited to play in the 2016 tournament were:

Real Madrid CF (ESP)	- winners of the 2015-16 UEFA Champions League
Atlético Nacional SA (COL)	- winners of the 2016 Copa Libertadores
Mamelodi Sundowns FC (RSA)	- winners of the 2016 CAF Champions League
Jeonbuk Hyundai Motors (KOR)	- winners of the 2016 AFC Champions League
CF América (MEX)	- winners of the 2015-16 CONCACAF Champions League
Auckland City FC (NZL)	- winners of the 2016 OFC Champions League
Kashima Antlers FC (JPN)	- winners of the 2016 J1 League (Host)

PLAY-OFF FOR QUARTER-FINALS

08-12-2016 International Stadium Yokohama, Yokohama:
  Kashima Antlers FC – Auckland City FC 2-1 (0-0)
Kashima Antlers FC: Hitoshi SOGAHATA, Gen SHOJI, HWANG Seok-ho (KOR), Shuto YAMAMOTO, Ryota NAGAKI, Shoma DOI, Gaku SHIBASAKI, FABRÍCIO dos Santos Messias (BRA) (54' Shuhei AKASAKI), Daigo NISHI (YC45), Yasushi ENDO (83' Atsutaka NAKAMURA), Mitsuo OGASAWARA (63' Mu KANAZAKI). (Coach: Masatada ISHII).
Auckland City FC: Eñaut ZUBIKARAI Goñi (ESP), Takuya IWATA (JPN), ÁNGEL Luis Viña BERLANGA (ESP), Darren WHITE (ENG), KIM Dae-wook (KOR), ALBERT RIERA Vidal (ESP), Clayton LEWIS, Ryan DE VRIES (83' Micah LEA'ALAFA (SLM)), Enrico Fabrizio Vicenzo TAVANO Alonso (MEX), JOÃO Vítor Rocha de Carvalho MOREIRA (POR), Emiliano TADE (ARG) (90' Nicolai BERRY). (Coach: RAMON TRIBULIETX Santolaya (ESP)).
Goals: Kashima Antlers FC: 1-1 Shuhei AKASAKI (67'), 2-1 Mu KANAZAKI (88').
Auckland City FC: 0-1 KIM Dae-wook (50').
Referee: Janny SIKAZWE (ZAM) Attendance: 17,667

QUARTER-FINALS

11-12-2016 Suita City Football Stadium, Osaka:
Jeonbuk Hyundai Motors FC Jeonju – CF América Mexico City 1-2 (1-0)
Jeonbuk Hyundai Motors FC Jeonju: HONG Jeong-nam, LIM Jong-eun, PARK Won-jae, CHOI Chul-soon (YC62), KIM Chang-soo (77' KO Moo-yeol), SHIN Hyung-min (YC90), JEONG Hyuk (YC48) (66' LEONARDO Rodrigues Pereira (BRA)), KIM Bo-kyung, LEE Jae-sung, Eduardo Gonçalves de Oliveira "EDU" (BRA) (76' LEE Dong-gook), KIM Shin-wook. (Coach: CHOI Kang-hee).
CF América Mexico City: Moisés Alberto MUÑOZ Rodríguez, Paolo Duval GOLTZ (ARG) (YC15), Miguel Angel Ramón SAMUDIO (PAR), Pablo César AGUILAR Benítez (PAR), Bruno Amilcar VALDEZ Rojas (PAR) (YC71), Edson Omar ÁLVAREZ Velázquez (46' Michael Antonio ARROYO Mina (ECU)), WILLIAN Fernando Da Silva (BRA), Silvio Ezequiel ROMERO (ARG), Osvaldo David MARTÍNEZ Arce (PAR) (46' José Daniel Octavio GUERRERO Rodríguez), Oribe PERALTA Morones, Carlos Darwin QUINTERO Villalba (70' Ventura ALVARADO Aispuro (USA)). (Coach: Ricardo Antonio LA VOLPE Guarchioni (ARG)).
Goals: Jeonbuk Hyundai Motors: 1-0 KIM Bo-kyung (23').
CF América: 1-1 Silvio Ezequiel ROMERO (58'), 1-2 Silvio Ezequiel ROMERO (74').
Referee: Viktor KASSAI (HUN)   Attendance: 14,587

11-12-2016 Suita City Football Stadium, Osaka:
Mamelodi Sundowns FC – Kashima Antlers FC 0-2 (0-0)
Mamelodi Sundowns FC: Denis ONYANGO (UGA), Tebogo LANGERMAN, Wayne ARENDSE, RICARDO dos Santos NASCIMENTO (BRA), Hlompho KEKANA, Tiyani MABUNDA, Thapelo MORENA (71' Anthony LAFFOR (LBR)), Keagan DOLLY, Percy TAU, David Leonardo CASTRO Cortés (COL) (65' Siyanda ZWANE), Khama BILLIAT (ZIM) (79' Sibusiso VILAKAZI). (Coach: Pitso MOSIMANE).
Kashima Antlers FC: Hitoshi SOGAHATA, Gen SHOJI, Shuto YAMAMOTO, Naomichi UEDA, Ryota NAGAKI, Shoma DOI, Gaku SHIBASAKI, Atsutaka NAKAMURA (61' Mu KANAZAKI), Daigo NISHI, Yasushi ENDO (89' Taro SUGIMOTO), Shuhei AKASAKI (84' Yuma SUZUKI). (Coach: Masatada ISHII).
Goals: Kashima Antlers FC: 0-1 Yasushi ENDO (63'), 0-2 Mu KANAZAKI (88').
Referee: Roberto GARCÍA Orozco (MEX)   Attendance: 21,702

FIFTH PLACE PLAY-OFF

14-12-2016 Suita City Football Stadium, Osaka:
Jeonbuk Hyundai Motors FC Jeonju – Mamelodi Sundowns FC 4-1 (3-0)
Jeonbuk Hyundai Motors FC Jeonju: HONG Jeong-nam, LIM Jong-eun, PARK Won-jae, CHOI Chul-soon, KIM Young-chan, KIM Bo-kyung, LEE Jae-sung, JANG Yun-ho (72' LEE Ho), HAN Kyo-won, LEE Jong-ho (78' KIM Shin-wook), KO Moo-yeol (62' LEONARDO Rodrigues Pereira (BRA)). (Coach: CHOI Kang-hee).
Mamelodi Sundowns FC: Denis ONYANGO (UGA), Tebogo LANGERMAN, Wayne ARENDSE, RICARDO dos Santos NASCIMENTO (BRA), Hlompho KEKANA (YC51), Tiyani MABUNDA (YC56), Thapelo MORENA (81' Lucky MOHOMI), Keagan DOLLY, Percy TAU, David Leonardo CASTRO Cortés (COL) (46' Sibusiso VILAKAZI), Khama BILLIAT (ZIM) (75' Asavela MBEKILE). (Coach: Pitso MOSIMANE).
Goals: Jeonbuk Hyundai Motors: 1-0 KIM Bo-kyung (18'), 2-0 LEE Jong-ho (29'), 3-0 RICARDO dos Santos NASCIMENTO (41' own goal), 4-1 KIM Shin-wook (89').
Mamelodi Sundowns FC: 3-1 Percy TAU (48').
Referee: Nawaf Abdullah GHAYYATH SHUKRALLA (BRN)   Attendance: 5,938

SEMI-FINALS

14-12-2016 Suita City Football Stadium, Osaka:
Atlético Nacional SA Medellín – Kashima Antlers FC 0-3 (0-1)
Atlético Nacional SA Medellín: Franco ARMANI (ARG), Daniel Eduardo BOCANEGRA Ortíz, Felipe AGUILAR Mendoza, Andrés Mateus URIBE Villa (YC71), Alexis Hector HENRIQUEZ Charales (YC56), Farid Alfonso DÍAZ Rhenals, Diego Alejandro ARIAS Hincapié (60' Alejandro Abraham GUERRA Morales (VEN)), Macnelly TORRES Berrio, Jhon Edison MOSQUERA Rebolledo (67' Cristián Andrés DÁJOME Arboleda), Miguel Ángel BORJA Hernández, Orlando Enrique BERRÍO Meléndez (87' Arley José RODRÍGUEZ Henry). (Coach: Reinaldo RUEDA Rivera).
Kashima Antlers FC: Hitoshi SOGAHATA, Gen SHOJI, Shuto YAMAMOTO, Naomichi UEDA, Shoma DOI, Gaku SHIBASAKI, Atsutaka NAKAMURA (84' Yuma SUZUKI), Daigo NISHI, Yasushi ENDO, Mitsuo OGASAWARA (58' Ryota NAGAKI), Shuhei AKASAKI (54' Mu KANAZAKI). (Coach: Masatada ISHII).
Goals: Kashima Antlers FC: 0-1 Shoma DOI (33' penalty), 0-2 Yasushi ENDO (83'), 0-3 Yuma SUZUKI (85').
Referee: Viktor KASSAI (HUN)   Attendance: 15.050

15-12-2016   International Stadium Yokohama, Yokohama:
CF América Mexico City – Real Madrid CF 0-2 (0-1)
CF América Mexico City: Moisés Alberto MUÑOZ Rodríguez, Paolo Duval GOLTZ (ARG), Miguel Angel Ramón SAMUDIO (PAR), Pablo César AGUILAR Benítez (PAR), Ventura ALVARADO Aispuro (USA) (54' José Daniel Octavio GUERRERO Rodríguez), Bruno Amilcar VALDEZ Rojas (PAR), WILLIAN Fernando Da Silva (BRA), Rubens Omar Óscar SAMBUEZA (ARG) (YC22), Alex Renato IBARRA Mina (ECU) (61' Carlos Darwin QUINTERO Villalba (COL)), Silvio Ezequiel ROMERO (ARG) (70' Michael Antonio ARROYO Mina (ECU)), Oribe PERALTA Morones. (Coach: Ricardo Antonio LA VOLPE Guarchioni (ARG)).
Real Madrid CF: Keylor Antonio NAVAS Gamboa (CRC), Daniel "DANI" CARVAJAL Ramos, Raphaël VARANE (FRA), José Ignacio Fernández Iglesias "NACHO" (YC90), MARCELO Vieira da Silva Júnior (BRA), Toni KROOS (GER) (72' James David RODRÍGUEZ Rubio (COL)), Carlos Henrique CASEMIRO (BRA), Luka MODRIC (CRO), CRISTIANO RONALDO dos Santos Aveiro (POR), Karim BENZEMA (FRA) (80' Álvaro Borja MORATA Martín), LUCAS VÁZQUEZ Iglesias. (Coach: Zinédine ZIDANE (FRA)).
Goals: Real Madrid CF: 0-1 Karim BENZEMA (45+2'), 0-2 CRISTIANO RONALDO dos Santos Aveiro (90+3').
Referee: Enrique Patricio CÁCERES Villafañe (PAR)   Attendance: 50,117

THIRD PLACE PLAY–OFF

18-12-2016   International Stadium Yokohama, Yokohama:
CF América Mexico City – Atlético Nacional SA 2-2 (1-2, 2-2) **(AET)**
CF América Mexico City: Moisés Alberto MUÑOZ Rodríguez, Érick Alan PIMENTEL Benavides (YC67), Miguel Angel Ramón SAMUDIO (PAR), Pablo César AGUILAR Benítez (PAR) (YC57), Ventura ALVARADO Aispuro (USA) (46' Carlos Darwin QUINTERO Villalba (COL)), Bruno Amilcar VALDEZ Rojas (PAR), WILLIAN Fernando Da Silva (BRA), Rubens Omar Óscar SAMBUEZA (ARG) (70' Osvaldo David MARTÍNEZ Arce (PAR)), José Daniel Octavio GUERRERO Rodríguez, Silvio Ezequiel ROMERO (ARG) (59' Oribe PERALTA Morones), Michael Antonio ARROYO Mina (ECU). (Coach: Ricardo Antonio LA VOLPE Guarchioni (ARG)).
Atlético Nacional SA Medellín: Franco ARMANI (ARG), Daniel Eduardo BOCANEGRA Ortíz, Felipe AGUILAR Mendoza, Andrés Mateus URIBE Villa (70' Juan Pablo NIETO Salazar (YC77)), Alexis Hector HENRIQUEZ Charales (YC78), Farid Alfonso DÍAZ Rhenals (YC65), Diego Alejandro ARIAS Hincapié, Macnelly TORRES Berrio, Alejandro Abraham GUERRA Morales (VEN) (78' Miguel Ángel BORJA Hernández), Jhon Édison MOSQUERA Rebolledo, Orlando Enrique BERRÍO Meléndez (YC82) (89' Arley José RODRÍGUEZ Henry). (Coach: Reinaldo RUEDA Rivera).
Goals: CF América: 1-2 Michael Antonio ARROYO Mina (38'), 2-2 Oribe PERALTA Morones (66' penalty).
Atlético Nacional SA: 0-1 Miguel Angel Ramón SAMUDIO (6' own goal), 0-2 Alejandro Abraham GUERRA Morales (26').
Referee: Nawaf Abdullah GHAYYATH SHUKRALLA (BRN)   Attendance: 44,625
Penalties:
* Osvaldo David MARTÍNEZ Arce   1 Jhon Édison MOSQUERA Rebolledo
* Miguel Angel Ramón SAMUDIO   * Juan Pablo NIETO Salazar
1 Carlos Darwin QUINTERO Villalba   2 Daniel Eduardo BOCANEGRA Ortíz
2 Oribe PERALTA Morones   3 Macnelly TORRES Berrio
3 Michael Antonio ARROYO Mina   4 Miguel Ángel BORJA Hernández

Atlético Nacional SA Medellín won 4-3 on penalties.

FINAL

18-12-2016   International Stadium Yokohama, Yokohama:
Real Madrid CF – Kashima Antlers FC 4-2 (1-1, 2-2) **(AET)**
Real Madrid CF: Keylor Antonio NAVAS Gamboa (CRC), Daniel "DANI" CARVAJAL Ramos (YC102), SERGIO RAMOS García (YC55), Raphaël VARANE (FRA), MARCELO Vieira da Silva Júnior (BRA), Toni KROOS (GER), Carlos Henrique CASEMIRO (BRA) (YC100), Luka MODRIC (CRO) (106' Mateo KOVACIC (CRO)), CRISTIANO RONALDO dos Santos Aveiro (POR) (112' Álvaro Borja MORATA Martín), Karim BENZEMA (FRA), LUCAS VÁZQUEZ Iglesias (81' Francisco Román Alarcón Suárez "ISCO"). (Coach: Zinédine ZIDANE (FRA)).
Kashima Antlers FC: Hitoshi SOGAHATA, Gen SHOJI, Shuto YAMAMOTO (YC58), Naomichi UEDA, Ryota NAGAKI (114' Shuhei AKASAKI), Shoma DOI (89' Yuma SUZUKI), Gaku SHIBASAKI, Daigo NISHI, Yasushi ENDO (103' Yukitoshi ITO), Mu KANAZAKI, Mitsuo OGASAWARA (68' FABRÍCIO dos Santos Messias (BRA) (YC93)). (Coach: Masatada ISHII).
Goals: Real Madrid CF: 1-0 Karim BENZEMA (9'), 2-2 CRISTIANO RONALDO dos Santos Aveiro (60' penalty), 3-2 CRISTIANO RONALDO dos Santos Aveiro (98'), 4-2 CRISTIANO RONALDO dos Santos Aveiro (104').
Kashima Antlers FC: 1-1 Gaku SHIBASAKI (44'), 1-2 Gaku SHIBASAKI (52').
Referee: Janny SIKAZWE (ZAM)   Attendance: 68,742

*** Real Madrid CF won the Cup ***

2017 FIFA Club World Cup

The 2017 FIFA Club World Cup (officially, the 'FIFA Club World Cup UAE 2017 presented by Alibaba Cloud' for sponsorship reasons) was played between 6th and 16th December 2017. This tournament was the 14th edition of the FIFA Club World Cup and was hosted by the United Arab Emirates who beat Brazil and Japan with their bid.

The Champions of the six confederations entered the tournament as did the UAE champions Al Jazira Club who faced the Oceanian Champions in an initial play-off.

Unusually, the reigning champions Real Madrid CF were in attendance to defend their title after winning the 2016-17 UEFA Champions League. Their 1-0 victory over Grêmio Foot-Ball Porto Alegrense in the Final meant that they became the first team to successfully defend Club World Cup title. It was Real's third victory in the competition which also extended their record to 6 'world titles' including Intercontinental Cup victories.

The clubs invited to play in the 2017 tournament were:

Real Madrid CF (ESP) - winners of the 2016-17 UEFA Champions League
Grêmio Foot-Ball Porto Alegrense (BRA)
                                         - winners of the 2017 Copa Libertadores
Wydad AC Casablanca (MAR) - winners of the 2017 CAF Champions League
Urawa Red Diamonds (JPN) - winners of the 2017 AFC Champions League
CF Pachuca (MEX) - winners of the 2016-17 CONCACAF Champions League

Auckland City FC (NZL) - winners of the 2017 OFC Champions League
Al Jazira Club (UAE) - winners of the 2016-17 UAE Pro-League (Host)

FIRST ROUND

06-12-2017 Hazza bin Zayed Stadium, Al Ain:
 Al Jazira Club Abu Dhabi – Auckland City FC 1-0 (1-0)
Al Jazira Club Abu Dhabi: ALI KHASEIF Humaid Khaseif Housani, MOHAMMED Ali AYED Mutlaq Al Shemmari (YC39) (90+1' SAIF Khalfan Saeed AL MEQBALI), MUSALLEM FAYEZ Muftah Hamdan Al Hamdani, SALEM RASHID Obaid Sanad Obaid, EISA AL OTAIBAH (YC78) (80' YAQOUB Yousif Matouq Mohamed AL HOSANI), MOHAMMED OMAR Zain Mohsen Zain AL ATTAS, FARES JUMA Hasan Juma Al Saadi, Moubarak BOUSSOUFA (MAR) (YC87), ALI Ahmed MABKHOUT Mohsen Omaran Al Hajeri, KHALFAN MUBARAK Khalfan Obaid Alrezzi Al Shamsi (58' AHMED RABIA Al Ghilani), Romário Ricardo da Silva "ROMARINHO" (BRA) (YC57). (Coach: Henk TEN CATE (HOL)).
Auckland City FC: Eñaut ZUBIKARAI Goñi (ESP), Takuya IWATA (JPN) (84' Micah LEA'ALAFA (SLM)), ÁNGEL Luis Viña BERLANGA (ESP), Darren WHITE (ENG), KIM Dae-wook (KOR), Cameron HOWIESON, ALBERT RIERA Vidal (ESP) (YC82), Callum McCOWATT (60' Daniel MORGAN), Ryan DE VRIES, Enrico Fabrizio Vicenzo TAVANO Alonso (MEX), Emiliano TADE (ARG). (Coach: RAMON TRIBULIETX Santolaya (ESP)).
Goal: Al Jazira Club: 1-0 Romário Ricardo da Silva "ROMARINHO" (38').
Referee: Malang DIEDHIOU (SEN)   Attendance: 4,246

SECOND ROUND

09-12-2017 Zayed Sports City Stadium, Abu Dhabi:
 CF Pachuca – Wydad AC Casablanca 1-0 (0-0, 0-0) **(AET)**
CF Pachuca: Oscar PÉREZ Rojas, Emmanuel GARCÍA Vaca, José Joaquín MARTÍNEZ Valadez (106' Raúl LÓPEZ Gómez), Oscar Fabián MURILLO Murillo (COL), Robert Fabián HERRERA Rosas (URU), Keisuke HONDA (JPN), Víctor Alonso GUZMÁN Guzmán (118' Omar Alejandro GONZÁLEZ (USA)), Érick Germain AGUIRRE Tafolla (YC21) (79' Erick Daniel SÁNCHEZ Ocegueda (YC97)), Jorge Daniel HERNÁNDEZ Govea, Ángelo Nicolás SAGAL Tapia (CHI) (58' Franco Daniel JARA (ARG)), Jonathan Matías URRETAVISCAYA da Luz (URU). (Coach: Diego Martín ALONSO López (URU)).
Wydad AC Casablanca: Zouhair LAAROUBI, Amine ATOUCHI, Zakaria EL HACHIMI (YC120), Abdellatif NOUSSIR (YC116), Cheick COMARA (CIV) (YC39), Salaheddine SAIDI, Brahim NAKACH (YC45+2,YC69), Walid EL KARTI, Abdeladim KHADROUF (90' Reda HAJHOUJ (YC108)), Mohammed AOULAD (BEL) (62' Ismail EL HADDAD), Achraf BENCHARKI. (Coach: Hussein AMMOUTA).
Goal: CF Pachuca: 1-0 Víctor Alonso GUZMÁN Guzmán (112').
Referee: Ravshan Sayfiddinovich IRMATOV (UZB)   Attendance: 12,488

09-12-2017   Zayed Sports City Stadium, Abu Dhabi:
Al Jazira Club Abu Dhabi – Urawa Red Diamonds 1-0 (0-0)
Al Jazira Club Abu Dhabi: ALI KHASEIF Humaid Khaseif Housani, MOHAMMED Ali AYED Mutlaq Al Shemmari (90' SAIF Khalfan Saeed AL MEQBALI), MUSALLEM FAYEZ Muftah Hamdan Al Hamdani, SALEM RASHID Obaid Sanad Obaid (YC56), MOHAMMED OMAR Zain Mohsen Zain AL ATTAS (89' EISA AL OTAIBAH), FARES JUMA Hasan Juma Al Saadi, Moubarak BOUSSOUFA (MAR), YAQOUB Yousif Matouq Mohamed AL HOSANI (YC64) (84' AHMED RABIA Al Ghilani), SALEM ABDULLAH Omar Salem Ba Abdulla, ALI Ahmed MABKHOUT Mohsen Omaran Al Hajeri, Romário Ricardo da Silva "ROMARINHO" (BRA). (Coach: Henk TEN CATE (HOL)).
Urawa Red Diamonds: Shusaku NISHIKAWA, Tomoaki MAKINO (YC42), Wataru ENDO (72' Ryota MORIWAKI), Tomoya UGAJIN, Yosuke KASHIWAGI, Takuya AOKI, Yuki ABE, Shinya YAJIMA (76' Zlatan LJUBIJANKIC (SVN)), RAFAEL da SILVA (BRA), Yuki MUTO (YC62) (67' Toshiyuki TAKAGI), Shinzo KOROKI. (Coach: Takafumi HORI).
Goal: Al Jazira Club: 1-0 ALI Ahmed MABKHOUT Mohsen Omaran Al Hajeri (52').
Referee: César Arturo RAMOS Palazuelos (MEX)   Attendance: 15,593

FIFTH PLACE PLAY–OFF

12-12-2017   Hazza bin Zayed Stadium, Al Ain:
Wydad AC Casablanca – Urawa Red Diamonds 2-3 (1-2)
Wydad AC Casablanca: Badreddine BENACHOUR, Badr GADDARINE, Youssef RABEH, Mouhamed OUATTARA (BKF), Mohammed EL NAHIRI (YC36), Walid EL KARTI (YC80), Jamel AÏT BEN IDIR, Abdeladim KHADROUF (74' Salaheddine SAIDI), Mohammed AOULAD (BEL) (76' Amin TIGHAZOUI), Ismail EL HADDAD (88' Guillaume Nicaise DAHO (CIV)), Reda HAJHOUJ. (Coach: Hussein AMMOUTA).
Urawa Red Diamonds: Shusaku NISHIKAWA, MAURÍCIO de Carvalho ANTÔNIO (BRA), Tomoaki MAKINO, Ryota MORIWAKI, Yosuke KASHIWAGI, Kazuki NAGASAWA, Takuya AOKI, Yuki ABE, RAFAEL da SILVA (BRA) (58' Tsukasa UMESAKI, 77' Zlatan LJUBIJANKIC (SVN)), Yuki MUTO, Shinzo KOROKI (90+5' Daisuke KIKUCHI). (Coach: Takafumi HORI).
Goals: Wydad AC Casablanca: 1-1 Ismail EL HADDAD (21'), 2-3 Reda HAJHOUJ (90+4' penalty).
Urawa Red Diamonds: 0-1 MAURÍCIO de Carvalho ANTÔNIO (18'), 1-2 Yosuke KASHIWAGI (26'), 1-3 MAURÍCIO de Carvalho ANTÔNIO (60').
Referee: Matthew (Matt) CONGER (NZL)   Attendance: 4,281

SEMI–FINALS

12-12-2017   Hazza bin Zayed Stadium, Al Ain:
Grêmio Foot-Ball Porto Alegrense – CF Pachuca 1-0 (0-0, 0-0) **(AET)**
Grêmio Foot-Ball Porto Alegrense: MARCELO GROHE, EDÍLSON Mendes Guimarães (90' Leonardo da Silva "LEO" MOURA), Pedro Tonon GEROMEL, Walter KANNEMANN (ARG) (YC23), BRUNO CORTES Barbosa, MICHEL Ferreira dos Santos (72' ÉVERTON Sousa Soares), RAMIRO Moschen Benetti (YC51), JAÍLSON Marques Siqueira, LUAN Guilherme de Jesús Vieira, Lucas Ramón BARRIOS Cáceres (PAR) (55' JAEL Ferreira Vieira (YC113)), Luiz Fernando Pereira da Silva "FERNANDINHO" (118' RAFAEL THYERE de Albuquerque Marques). (Coach: RENATO "GAÚCHO" Portaluppi).
CF Pachuca: Oscar PÉREZ Rojas, Omar Alejandro GONZÁLEZ (USA), Emmanuel GARCÍA Vaca (YC84) (101' Ángelo Nicolás SAGAL Tapia (CHI)), José Joaquín MARTÍNEZ Valadez, Oscar Fabián MURILLO Murillo (COL), Keisuke HONDA (JPN), Víctor Alonso GUZMÁN Guzmán (YC34,YC110), Érick Germain AGUIRRE Tafolla (67' Erick Daniel SÁNCHEZ Ocegueda), Jorge Daniel HERNÁNDEZ Govea (YC105), Jonathan Matías URRETAVISCAYA da Luz (URU) (106' Germán Ezequiel CANO (ARG)), Franco Daniel JARA (ARG) (91' Robert Fabián HERRERA Rosas (URU)). (Coach: Diego Martín ALONSO López (URU)).
Goal: Grêmio Foot-Ball Porto Alegrense: 1-0 ÉVERTON Sousa Soares (95').
Referee: Dr.Felix BRYCH (GER)   Attendance: 6,428

13-12-2017   Zayed Sports City Stadium, Abu Dhabi:
Al Jazira Club Abu Dhabi – Real Madrid CF 1-2 (1-0)
Al Jazira Club Abu Dhabi: ALI KHASEIF Humaid Khaseif Housani (51' KHALED Saif Hamad Ali AL SENANI), MOHAMMED Ali AYED Mutlaq Al Shemmari (YC68), MUSALLEM FAYEZ Muftah Hamdan Al Hamdani, SALEM RASHID Obaid Sanad Obaid, MOHAMMED OMAR Zain Mohsen Zain AL ATTAS, FARES JUMA Hasan Juma Al Saadi, KHALIFA Mubarak Khalfan Khairi AL HAMMADI (60' EISA AL OTAIBAH), Moubarak BOUSSOUFA (MAR), YAQOUB Yousif Matouq Mohamed AL HOSANI (72' AHMED RABIA Al Ghilani), ALI Ahmed MABKHOUT Mohsen Omaran Al Hajeri, Romário Ricardo da Silva "ROMARINHO" (BRA). (Coach: Henk TEN CATE (HOL)).
Real Madrid CF: Keylor Antonio NAVAS Gamboa (CRC), Raphaël VARANE (FRA), José Ignacio Fernández Iglesias "NACHO", MARCELO Vieira da Silva Júnior (BRA), Achraf HAKIMI Mouh (MAR), Luka MODRIC (CRO), Carlos Henrique CASEMIRO (BRA), Francisco Román Alarcón Suárez "ISCO" (68' Marco ASENSIO Willemsen), Mateo KOVACIC (CRO) (68' LUCAS VÁZQUEZ Iglesias), CRISTIANO RONALDO dos Santos Aveiro (POR), Karim BENZEMA (FRA) (81' Gareth BALE (WAL)). (Coach: Zinédine ZIDANE (FRA)).
Goals: Al Jazira Club: 1-0 Romário Ricardo da Silva "ROMARINHO" (41').
Real Madrid CF: 1-1 CRISTIANO RONALDO dos Santos Aveiro (52'), 1-2 Gareth BALE (81').
Referee: SANDRO Meira RICCI (BRA)   Attendance: 36,650

THIRD PLACE PLAY-OFF

16-12-2017 Zayed Sports City Stadium, Abu Dhabi:
Al Jazira Club Abu Dhabi – CF Pachuca 1-4 (0-1)
Al Jazira Club Abu Dhabi: KHALED Saif Hamad Ali AL SENANI, MUSALLEM FAYEZ Muftah Hamdan Al Hamdani, SAIF Khlafan Saeed AL MEQBALI, SALEM RASHID Obaid Sanad Obaid, MOHAMMED OMAR Zain Mohsen Zain AL ATTAS (46' SALIM ALI IBRAHIM Hassan Al-Hammadi), FARES JUMA Hasan Juma Al Saadi (YC50), Moubarak BOUSSOUFA (MAR) (YC30), YAQOUB Yousif Matouq Mohamed AL HOSANI (67' ABDALLA RAMADAN Bakheet Sulaiman (YC71)), ALI Ahmed MABKHOUT Mohsen Omaran Al Hajeri, KHALFAN MUBARAK Khalfan Obaid Alrezzi Al Shamsi (78' AHMED RABIA Al Ghilani), Romário Ricardo da Silva "ROMARINHO" (BRA). (Coach: Henk TEN CATE (HOL)).
CF Pachuca: Alfonso BLANCO Antúnez, Omar Alejandro GONZÁLEZ (USA), Raúl LÓPEZ Gómez, Emmanuel GARCÍA Vaca, Oscar Fabián MURILLO Murillo (COL), Érick Germain AGUIRRE Tafolla, Jorge Daniel HERNÁNDEZ Govea (85' Pablo César LÓPEZ Martínez), Erick Daniel SÁNCHEZ Ocegueda, Ángelo Nicolás SAGAL Tapia (CHI), Jonathan Matías URRETAVISCAYA da Luz (URU) (86' Francisco Antonio FIGUEROA Díaz), Franco Daniel JARA (ARG) (YC50) (78' Roberto Carlos DE LA ROSA González). (Coach: Diego Martín ALONSO López (URU)).
Goals: Al Jazira Club: 1-1 KHALFAN MUBARAK Khalfan Obaid Alrezzi Al Shamsi (57').
CF Pachuca: 0-1 Jonathan Matías URRETAVISCAYA da Luz (37'), 1-2 Franco Daniel JARA (60'), 1-3 Roberto Carlos DE LA ROSA González (79'), 1-4 Ángelo Nicolás SAGAL Tapia (84' penalty).
Referee: Malang DIEDHIOU (SEN)   Attendance: 11,785

FINAL

16-12-2017 Zayed Sports City Stadium, Abu Dhabi:
Real Madrid CF – Grêmio Foot-Ball Porto Alegrense 1-0 (0-0)
Real Madrid CF: Keylor Antonio NAVAS Gamboa (CRC), Daniel "DANI" CARVAJAL Ramos, SERGIO RAMOS García, Raphaël VARANE (FRA), MARCELO Vieira da Silva Júnior (BRA), Toni KROOS (GER), Luka MODRIC (CRO), Carlos Henrique CASEMIRO (BRA) (YC27), Francisco Román Alarcón Suárez "ISCO" (73' LUCAS VÁZQUEZ Iglesias), CRISTIANO RONALDO dos Santos Aveiro (POR), Karim BENZEMA (FRA) (80' Gareth BALE (WAL)). (Coach: Zinédine ZIDANE (FRA)).
Grêmio Foot-Ball Porto Alegrense: MARCELO GROHE, EDÍLSON Mendes Guimarães, Pedro Tonon GEROMEL, Walter KANNEMANN (ARG), BRUNO CORTES Barbosa, MICHEL Ferreira dos Santos (84' MAICON Thiago Pereira de Souza Nascimento), RAMIRO Moschen Benetti (71' ÉVERTON Sousa Soares), JAÍLSON Marques Siqueira, LUAN Guilherme de Jesús Vieira, Lucas Ramón BARRIOS Cáceres (PAR) (63' JAEL Ferreira Vieira), Luiz Fernando Pereira da Silva "FERNANDINHO". (Coach: RENATO "GAÚCHO" Portaluppi).
Goal: Real Madrid CF: 1-0 CRISTIANO RONALDO dos Santos Aveiro (53').
Referee: César Arturo RAMOS Palazuelos (MEX)   Attendance: 41,094

*** **Real Madrid CF won the Cup** ***

2018 FIFA Club World Cup

The 2018 FIFA Club World Cup (officially, the 'FIFA Club World Cup UAE 2018 presented by Alibaba Cloud' for sponsorship reasons) was played between 12th and 22nd December 2018 in the United Arab Emirates. It was the 15th edition of the FIFA Club World Cup.

The Champions of the six confederations entered the tournament as did the UAE champions Al-Ain FC who faced the Oceanian champions in an initial play-off.

Al-Ain FC performed extremely well in the tournament, defeating the African and South American Champions on the way to the Final. However, they were unfortunate enough to have to face defending champions Real Madrid CF whose remarkable run continued as they won 4-1 to earn a third consecutive Club World Cup title. This was a record fourth victory in the competition and further extended the Madrid team's number of club world titles (including the Intercontinental Cup) to seven.

The clubs invited to play in the 2018 tournament were:

Real Madrid CF (ESP)	- winners of the 2017-18 UEFA Champions League
CA River Plate Buenos Aires (ARG)	
	- winners of the 2018 Copa Libertadores
ES Tunis (TUN)	- winners of the 2018 CAF Champions League
Kashima Antlers FC (JPN)	- winners of the 2018 AFC Champions League
CD Guadalajara SA (MEX)	- winners of the 2018 CONCACAF Champions League
Team Wellington FC (NZL)	- winners of the 2018 OFC Champions League
Al-Ain FC (UAE)	- winners of the 2017-18 UAE Pro-League (Host)

FIRST ROUND

12-12-2018 Hazza bin Zayed Stadium, Al Ain:
Al-Ain FC – Team Wellington FC 3-3 (1-3, 3-3) **(AET)**
Al-Ain FC: KHALID EISA Mohamed Bilal Saeed, ISMAIL AHMED Ismail Mohamed, MOHANNAD SALEM Ghazy Marzuk Al Amin (YC31) (38' BANDAR Mohamed Mohamed Saeed Mahdi AL AHBABI), MOHAMED AHMED Ali Gharib Juma, Tsukasa SHIOTANI (JPN), Tongo Hamed DOUMBIA (MLI) (YC54) (63' Ibrahim Amuah DIAKY (CIV)), AHMED BARMAN Ali Barman Shamroukh Al Hamoudi (118' RAYAN YASLAM Mohamad Aboudan Al Jaberi), MOHAMMED ABDULRAHMAN Ahmed Al Raqi Al Amoudi (YC55,YC120+1), HUSSEIN EL SHAHAT (EGY), CAIO Lucas Fernandes (BRA), JAMAL Ibrahim Hussain MAROOF Al Blooshi (78' Marcus BERG (SWE)). (Coach: Zoran MAMIC (CRO)).
Team Wellington FC: Scott BASALAJ, Justin GULLEY, Scott HILLIAR, Mario ILICH, Taylor SCHRIJVERS, Henry CAMERON (57' Eric MOLLOY (IRL), 120' Ross ALLEN (GGY)), Mario Alberto BARCIA (ARG) (YC108), Jack-Henry SINCLAIR (80' Angus KILKOLLY), Aaron CLAPHAM (74' Nathaniel HAILEMARIAM), Andrew BEVIN, Hamish WATSON. (Coach: José Manuel FIGUEIRA (ENG)).
Goals: Al-Ain FC: 1-3 Tsukasa SHIOTANI (45'), 2-3 Tongo DOUMBIA (49'), 3-3 Marcus BERG (85').
Team Wellington FC: 0-1 Mario BARCIA (11'), 0-2 Aaron CLAPHAM (15'), 0-3 Mario ILICH (44').
Referee: Ryuji SATO (JPN)   Attendance: 15,279
Penalties: 1 Ibrahim Amuah DIAKY   1 Ross ALLEN
              * Marcus BERG   * Angus KILKOLLY
              2 HUSSEIN EL SHAHAT   2 Mario ILICH
              3 Tsukasa SHIOTANI   3 Hamish WATSON
              4 CAIO Lucas Fernandes   * Justin GULLEY

Al-Ain FC won on penalties (4-3).

SECOND ROUND

15-12-2018 Hazza bin Zayed Stadium, Al Ain:
Kashima Antlers FC – CD Guadalajara SA 3-2 (0-1)
Kashima Antlers FC: KWOUN Sun-tae (KOR), Atsuto UCHIDA, Gen SHOJI, Shuto YAMAMOTO, JUNG Seung-hyun (KOR) (YC42), Hugo Leonardo "LÉO" Da SILVA Serejo (BRA), Ryota NAGAKI, Shoma DOI (80' Koki ANZAI), Sergio Antonio Soler de Oliveira Junior "SERGINHO" (BRA), Yasushi ENDO (87' Daigo NISHI), Weverson LEANDRO Oliveira Moura (BRA) (YC45+1) (46' Hiroke ABE (YC83)). (Coach: Go OIWA).
CD Guadalajara SA: Raúl Manolo GUDIÑO Vega, Josecarlos VAN RANKIN Galland, Jair PEREIRA Rodríguez (YC23), Hedgardo MARÍN Arroyo, Miguel Ángel PONCE Briseño, Orbelín PINEDA Alvarado (85' José de Jesús GODÍNEZ Navarro), Javier Eduardo LÓPEZ Ramírez (71' Walter Gael SANDOVAL Contreras), Isaác BRIZUELA Muñoz, Ángel ZALDÍVAR Caviedes, Michael PÉREZ Ortiz (YC73), Alan PULIDO Izaguirre. (Coach: José Saturnino CARDOZO Otazú (PAR)).
Goals: Kashima Antlers FC: 1-1 Ryota NAGAKI (49'), 2-1 Sergio Antonio Soler de Oliveira Junior "SERGINHO" (69' penalty), 3-1 Hiroki ABE (84').
CD Guadalajara SA: 0-1 Ángel ZALDÍVAR Caviedes (3'), 3-2 Hugo Leonardo "LÉO" Da SILVA Serejo (90+4' own goal).
Referee: Bamlak TESSEMA WEYESA (ETH)   Attendance: 3,997

Alan PULIDO Izaguirre missed a penalty kick (90+4').

15-12-2018   Hazza bin Zayed Stadium, Al Ain: ES Tunis – Al-Ain FC 0-3 (0-2)
ES Tunis: Moez BEN CHÉRIFIA, Chamseddine DHAOUADI, Khalil CHEMMAM (70' Ali MACHANI), Ayman BEN MOHAMED, Sameh DERBALI, Fousseny COULIBALY (CIV), Ghaylène CHAALALI (46' Amine MESKINI), Franck KOM (CMR) (64' Adem REJAIBI), Anice BADRI, Youcef BELAÏLI (ALG) (YC69), Yassine KHENISSI. (Coach: Moïne CHAÂBANI).
Al-Ain FC: KHALID EISA Mohamed Bilal Saeed, ISMAIL AHMED Ismail Mohamed, MOHAMMED FAYEZ Sbait Khalifa Al Alawi, MOHAMED AHMED Ali Gharib Juma, Tsukasa SHIOTANI (JPN), Tongo Hamed DOUMBIA (MLI) (85' YAHYA NADER Mostafa El Sharif), BANDAR Mohamed Mohamed Saeed Mahdi AL AHBABI (80' Marcus BERG (SWE)), AHMED BARMAN Ali Barman Shamroukh Al Hamoudi, RAYAN YASLAM Mohamad Aboudan Al Jaberi (67' AMER ABDULRAHMAN Abdulla Husain Al Hammadi), HUSSEIN EL SHAHAT (EGY), CAIO Lucas Fernandes (BRA). (Coach: Zoran MAMIC (CRO)).
Goals: Al-Ain FC: 0-1 MOHAMED AHMED Ali Gharib (2'), 0-2 HUSSEIN EL SHAHAT (16'), 0-3 BANDAR Mohamed Mohamed Saeed Mahdi AL AHBABI (60').
Referee: Jair Antonio MARRUFO (USA)   Attendance: 21,333

FIFTH PLACE PLAY–OFF

18-12-2018   Hazza bin Zayed Stadium, Al Ain:
            ES Tunis – CD Guadalajara SA 1-1 (1-1, 1-1) **(AET)**
ES Tunis: Rami JRIDI, Chamseddine DHAOUADI (YC87), Khalil CHEMMAM, Ayman BEN MOHAMED (90+3' Saâd BGUIR), Sameh DERBALI (YC80), Houcine RABII (RC90+6), Fousseny COULIBALY (CIV), Franck KOM (CMR) (YC51) (90+5' Ali MACHANI), Anice BADRI (YC63,YC79), Bilel MEJRI (90+3' Yassine KHENISSI), Youcef BELAÏLI (ALG) (YC60). (Coach: Moïne CHAÂBANI).
CD Guadalajara SA: Raúl Manolo GUDIÑO Vega (90+5' Miguel JIMÉNEZ Ponce), Josecarlos VAN RANKIN Galland (YC37), Jair PEREIRA Rodríguez, Hedgardo MARÍN Arroyo, Miguel Ángel PONCE Briseño, Isaác BRIZUELA Muñoz (YC79), Walter Gael SANDOVAL Contreras (64' Orbelín PINEDA Alvarado), Ángel ZALDÍVAR Caviedes, Michael PÉREZ Ortiz, Alan Jhosué CERVANTES Martín del Campo (46' Carlos Arnoldo SALCIDO Flores), José de Jesús GODÍNEZ Navarro. (Coach: José Saturnino CARDOZO Otazú (PAR)).
Goals: ES Tunis: 1-1 Youcef BELAÏLI (38' penalty).
CD Guadalajara SA: 0-1 Walter Gael SANDOVAL Contreras (5' penalty).
Referee: Matthew (Matt) CONGER (NZL)   Attendance: 5,883

Penalties:
1 Ángel ZALDÍVAR Caviedes   * Youcef BELAÏLI
* Hedgardo MARÍN Arroyo   1 Ali MACHANI
2 José de Jesús GODÍNEZ Navarro   2 Khalil CHEMMAM
* Josecarlos VAN RANKIN Galland   * Saâd BGUIR
3 Carlos Arnoldo SALCIDO Flores   3 Yassine KHENISSI
4 Orbelín PINEDA Alvarado   4 Sameh DERBALI
5 Miguel Ángel PONCE Briseño   5 Fousseny COULIBALY
* Isaác BRIZUELA Muñoz   6 Chamseddine DHAOUADI
ES Tunis won on penalties (6-5).

SEMI–FINALS

18-12-2018   Hazza bin Zayed Stadium, Al Ain:
CA River Plate Buenos Aires – Al-Ain FC 2-2 (2-1, 2-2) **(AET)**
CA River Plate Buenos Aires: Franco ARMANI, Jonatan Ramón MAIDANA, Milton Óscar CASCO (YC89), Horacio Javier PINOLA (YC9), Gonzalo Ariel MONTIEL, Gonzalo Nicolás MARTÍNEZ (91' Ignacio Martín SCOCCO), Ignacio Martín FERNÁNDEZ Lobbe (56' Juan Fernando QUINTERO Paniagua (COL)), Exequiel Alejandro PALACIOS (55' Enzo Nicolás PÉREZ), Leonardo Daniel PONZIO (87' Diego Nicolás DE LA CRUZ Arcosa (URU) (YC112)), Rafael Santos BORRÉ Maury (COL) (YC54), Lucas David PRATTO. (Coach: Marcelo Daniel GALLARDO).
Al-Ain FC: KHALID EISA Mohamed Bilal Saeed, ISMAIL AHMED Ismail Mohamed, MOHAMMED FAYEZ Sbait Khalifa Al Alawi, MOHAMED AHMED Ali Gharib Juma (YC80), Tsukasa SHIOTANI (JPN), Tongo Hamed DOUMBIA (MLI) (107' YAHYA NADER Mostafa El Sharif), AHMED BARMAN Ali Barman Shamroukh Al Hamoudi (82' AMER ABDULRAHMAN Abdulla Husain Al Hammadi), MOHAMMED ABDULRAHMAN Ahmed Al Raqi Al Amoudi (64' RAYAN YASLAM Mohamad Aboudan Al Jaberi), HUSSEIN EL SHAHAT (EGY) (YC50), CAIO Lucas Fernandes (BRA) (YC61), Marcus BERG (SWE) (75' BANDAR Mohamed Mohamed Saeed Mahdi AL AHBABI). (Coach: Zoran MAMIC (CRO)).
Goals: CA River Plate Buenos Aires: 1-1 Rafael Santos BORRÉ Maury (11'), 2-1 Rafael Santos BORRÉ Maury (16').
Al-Ain FC: 0-1 Marcus BERG (3'), 2-2 CAIO Lucas Fernandes (51').
Referee: Gianluca ROCCHI (ITA)   Attendance: 21,383

Penalties:
1 CAIO Lucas Fernandes   1 Ignacio Martín SCOCCO
2 Tsukasa SHIOTANI   2 Juan Fernando QUINTERO Paniagua
3 BANDAR Mohamed Mohamed Saeed Mahdi AL AHBABI
                                  3 Lucas David PRATTO
4 AMER ABDULRAHMAN Abdulla Husain Al Hammadi
                                  4 Rafael Santos BORRÉ Maury
5 RAYAN YASLAM Mohamad Aboudan Al Jaberi
                                  * Enzo Nicolás PÉREZ
Gonzalo Nicolás MARTÍNEZ missed a penalty kick (69').

Al-Ain FC won on penalties (5-4).

19-12-2018 Zayed Sports City Stadium, Abu Dhabi:
Kashima Antlers FC – Real Madrid CF 1-3 (0-1)
Kashima Antlers FC: KWOUN Sun-tae (KOR), Gen SHOJI, Shuto YAMAMOTO (YC52), JUNG Seung-hyun (KOR), Hugo Leonardo "LÉO" Da SILVA Serejo (BRA), Ryota NAGAKI (46' Atsuto UCHIDA), Shoma DOI, Sergio Antonio Soler de Oliveira Junior "SERGINHO" (BRA), Daigo NISHI (56' Koki ANZAI), Yasushi ENDO (81' Weverson LEANDRO Oliveira Moura (BRA)), Hiroke ABE. (Coach: Go OIWA).
Real Madrid CF: Thibaut COURTOIS (BEL), Daniel "DANI" CARVAJAL Ramos (YC42), SERGIO RAMOS García, Raphaël VARANE (FRA), MARCELO Vieira da Silva Júnior (BRA), Toni KROOS (GER), Luka MODRIC (CRO), MARCOS LLORENTE Moreno, Karim BENZEMA (FRA), Gareth BALE (WAL) (60' Marco ASENCIO Willemsen, 74' Carlos Henrique CASEMIRO (BRA)), LUCAS VÁZQUEZ Iglesias (68' Francisco Román Alarcón Suárez "ISCO"). (Coach: Santiago Hernán SOLARI Poggio (ARG)).
Goals: Kashima Antlers FC: 1-3 Shoma DIO (78').
Real Madrid CF: 0-1 Gareth BALE (44'), 0-2 Gareth BALE (53'), 0-3 Gareth BALE (55').
Referee: WILTON Pereira SAMPAIO (BRA)   Attendance: 30,554

THIRD PLACE PLAY–OFF

22-12-2018 Zayed Sports City Stadium, Abu Dhabi:
Kashima Antlers FC – CA River Plate Buenos Aires 0-4 (0-1)
Kashima Antlers FC: KWOUN Sun-tae (KOR) (23' Hitoshi SOGAHATA), Atsuto UCHIDA (76' Mitsuo OGASAWARA), Koki ANZAI, JUNG Seung-hyun (KOR), Tomoya INUKAI (YC32), Hugo Leonardo "LÉO" Da SILVA Serejo (BRA), Ryota NAGAKI, Shoma DOI, Sergio Antonio Soler de Oliveira Junior "SERGINHO" (BRA), Yasushi ENDO (65' Daigo NISHI), Hiroke ABE (YC71). (Coach: Go OIWA).
CA River Plate Buenos Aires: Germán Darío LUX, Milton Óscar CASCO (YC36), Horacio Javier PINOLA (YC54), Lucas MARTÍNEZ Quarta (YC77), Jorge Luís MOREIRA Ferreira (PAR) (46' Juan Fernando QUINTERO Paniagua (COL)), Bruno ZUCULINI, Diego Nicolás DE LA CRUZ Arcosa (URU) (69' Gonzalo Nicolás MARTÍNEZ), Exequiel Alejandro PALACIOS (46' Ignacio Martín FERNÁNDEZ Lobbe), Camilo Sebastián MAYADA Mesa (URU), Julián ÁLVAREZ, Rafael Santos BORRÉ Maury (COL). (Coach: Marcelo Daniel GALLARDO).
Goals: CA River Plate Buenos Aires: 0-1 Bruno ZUCULINI (24'), 0-2 Gonzalo Nicolás MARTÍNEZ (73'), 0-3 Rafael Santos BORRÉ Maury (89' penalty), 0-4 Gonzalo Nicolás MARTÍNEZ (90+3').
Referee: Gianluca ROCCHI (ITA)   Attendance: 13,550

FINAL

22-12-2018   Zayed Sports City Stadium, Abu Dhabi:
Real Madrid CF – Al-Ain FC 4-1 (1-0)
Real Madrid CF: Thibaut COURTOIS (BEL), Daniel "DANI" CARVAJAL Ramos, SERGIO RAMOS García (YC45), Raphaël VARANE (FRA), MARCELO Vieira da Silva Júnior (BRA), Toni KROOS (GER) (70' Daniel "DANI" CEBALLOS Fernández), Luka MODRIC (CRO), MARCOS LLORENTE Moreno (82' Carlos Henrique CASEMIRO (BRA)), Karim BENZEMA (FRA), Gareth BALE (WAL), LUCAS VÁZQUEZ Iglesias (84' VINÍCIUS José Paixão de Olveira JÚNIOR (BRA)). (Coach: Santiago Hernán SOLARI Poggio (ARG)).
Al-Ain FC: KHALID EISA Mohamed Bilal Saeed, ISMAIL AHMED Ismail Mohamed, MOHAMMED FAYEZ Sbait Khalifa Al Alawi, MOHAMED AHMED Ali Gharib Juma (64' BANDAR Mohamed Mohamed Saeed Mahdi AL AHBABI), Tsukasa SHIOTANI (JPN), Tongo Hamed DOUMBIA (MLI), MOHAMMED ABDULRAHMAN Ahmed Al Raqi Al Amoudi (67' AMER ABDULRAHMAN Abdulla Husain Al Hammadi), RAYAN YASLAM Mohamad Aboudan Al Jaberi, HUSSEIN EL SHAHAT (EGY), CAIO Lucas Fernandes (BRA), Marcus BERG (SWE) (75' YAHYA NADER Mostafa El Sharif). (Coach: Zoran MAMIC (CRO)).
Goals: Real Madrid CF: 1-0 Luka MODRIC (14'), 2-0 MARCOS LLORENTE Moreno (60'), 3-0 SERGIO RAMOS García (79'), 4-1 YAHYA NADER Mostafa El Sharif (90+1' own goal).
Al-Ain FC: 3-1 Tsukasa SHIOTANI (86').
Referee: Jair Antonio MARRUFO (USA)   Attendance: 21,333

*** Real Madrid CF won the Cup ***

2019 FIFA Club World Cup

The 2019 FIFA Club World Cup (officially the 'FIFA Club World Cup Qatar 2019 presented by Alibaba Cloud' for sponsorship reasons) was played between 11th and 21st December 2018. It was the 16th edition of the FIFA Club World Cup and was hosted by Qatar for the first time, the Gulf state being selected in so that the tournament (along with the 2020 competition) could serve as test events ahead of the 2022 World Cup.

The Champions of the six confederations entered the tournament as did the Qatari champions Al-Sadd SC Doha who faced the Oceanian Champions in an initial play-off.

European Champions Liverpool FC won the Final 1-0 after extra time against South American Champions CR Flamengo to earn their first FIFA Club World Cup title.

The clubs invited to play in the 2019 tournament were:

Liverpool FC (ENG)	- winners of the 2018-19 UEFA Champions League
CR Flamengo (BRA)	- winners of the 2019 Copa Libertadores
ES Tunis (TUN)	- winners of the 2018-19 CAF Champions League
Al-Hilal Saudi FC Riyadh (KSA)	- winners of the 2019 AFC Champions League
CF Monterrey (MEX)	- winners of the 2019 CONCACAF Champions League
Hienghène Sport (NCL)	- winners of the 2019 OFC Champions League
Al-Sadd SC Doha (QAT)	- winners of the 2018-19 Qatar Stars League (Host)

FIRST ROUND

11-12-2019 Jassim bin Hamad Stadium, Doha:
Al Sadd SC Doha – Hienghène Sport 3-1 (1-0, 1-1) **(AET)**
Al Sadd SC Doha: SAAD Abdullah AL SHEEB, Pedro Miguel Carvalho Deus Correia "RÓ-RÓ", ABDELKARIM HASSAN Al Haj Fadlalla, Boualem KHOUKHI, SALEM Ali AL HAJRI (118' TAREK SALMAN Suleiman Odeh), JUNG Woo-young (KOR), ABDULAZIZ Rashid AL ANSARI (25' HASAN Khailad AL HAYDOS), Gabriel Fernández Arenas "GABI" (ESP), NAM Tae-hee (KOR) (106' ALI ASSADALLA Thaimn Qambar), Baghdad BOUNEDJAH (ALG), AKRAM Hassan AFIF Yahya Afif (116' HASHIM ALI Abdullatif Ali). (Coach: Xavier Hernández i Creus "XAVI" (ESP)).
Hienghène Sport: Rocky NYIKEINE (YC98), Jordan DINET, Joseph ATHALÉ, Emile BÉARUNÉ (YC115), Cédric SANSOT, Geordy GONY, Jefferson DAHITE, Roy KAYARA (112' Bruno HAYNEM), Pedro LUIS Sousa Vilela (POR) (55' Miguel KAYARA), Bertrand KAÏ (80' Antony KAI), Antoine ROÏNÉ (70' Kohei MATSUMOTO (JPN)). (Coach: Félix TAGAWA (TAH)).
Goals: Al Sadd SC Doha: 1-0 Baghdad BOUNEDJAH (26'), 2-1 ABDELKARIM HASSAN Al Haj Fadlalla (100'), 3-1 Pedro Miguel Carvalho Deus "RÓ-RÓ" (114').
Hienghène Sport: 1-1 Antoine ROÏNÉ (46').
Referee: Mustapha GHORBAL (ALG) Attendance: 7,047

SECOND ROUND

14-12-2019 Jassim bin Hamad Stadium, Doha:
Al-Hilal Saudi FC Riyadh – ES Tunis 1-0 (0-0)
Al-Hilal Saudi FC Riyadh: ABDULLAH Ibrahim AL MAYOOF, MOHAMMED Ibrahim AL BURAYK (87' ABDULLAH Fareed AL HAFITH), ALI Hadi AL BULAYHI, YASIR Gharsan Seed Al Mohammadi AL SHAHRANI, JANG Hyun-soo (KOR), CARLOS EDUARDO de Oliveira Alves (BRA), Gustavo Leonardo CUÉLLAR Gallego (COL) (YC39) (65' Bafétimbi GOMIS (FRA)), André Martín CARRILLO Díaz (PER), MOHAMMED Ibrahim KANNO (YC83,YC85), SALEM Mohammed AL DAWSARI, OMAR Maher KHRBIN (SYR) (78' ABDULLAH Ibrahim OTAYF). (Coach: Razvan LUCESCU (ROM)).
ES Tunis: Moez BEN CHÉRIFIA, Mohamed YACOUBI, Sameh DERBALI (YC60), Ilyes CHETTI (ALG), Abdelkader BEDRANE (ALG), Kwame BONSU (GHA) (80' Yassine KHENISSI), Foussény COULIBALY (CIV), Raouf BENGUIT (ALG) (76' Raed FEDAA), Anice BADRI, Ibrahim OUATTARA (CIV), HAMDOU Mohamed El Houni AL MASRY (LBA) (87' Billel BENSAHA (ALG)). (Coach: Moïne CHAÂBANI).
Goal: Al-Hilal Saudi FC Riyadh: 1-0 Bafétimbi GOMIS (73').
Referee: Roberto TOBAR Vargas (CHI) Attendance: 7,726

14-12-2019   Jassim bin Hamad Stadium, Doha:
             CF Monterrey – Al Sadd SC Doha 3-2 (2-0)
CF Monterrey: Marcelo Alberto BAROVERO (ARG), César Jasib MONTES Castro (86' José María BASANTA Pavone (ARG)), Nicolás Gabriel SÁNCHEZ (ARG) (YC61), Leonel Jesús VANGIONI Rangel (ARG), Jesús Daniel GALLARDO Vasconcelos, John Stefan MEDINA Ramírez (COL), Jonathan Alexander GONZÁLEZ Mendoza (YC55), Carlos Alberto RODRÍGUEZ Gómez, Rogelio Gabriel FUNES Mori, Dorlan Mauricio PABÓN Ríos (COL) (73' Maximiliano Eduardo MEZA (ARG)), Rodolfo Gilbert PIZARRO Thomas (80' Miguel Arturo LAYÚN Prado). (Coach: Antonio Ricardo MOHAMED Matijevich (ARG)).
Al Sadd SC Doha: SAAD Abdullah AL SHEEB (85' MESHAAL Aissa BARSHAM), Pedro Miguel Carvalho Deus Correia "RÓ-RÓ" (YC41), ABDELKARIM HASSAN Al Haj Fadlalla, TAREK SALMAN Suleiman (YC75), Boualem KHOUKHI (YC37), SALEM Ali AL HAJRI (71' JUNG Woo-young (KOR)), HASAN Khailad AL HAYDOS, Gabriel Fernández Arenas "GABI" (ESP), NAM Tae-hee (KOR), Baghdad BOUNEDJAH (ALG) (YC32), AKRAM Hassan AFIF Yahya Afif. (Coach: Xavier Hernández i Creus "XAVI" (ESP)).
Goals: CF Monterrey: 1-0 Leonel Jesús VANGIONI Rangel (23'), 2-0 Rogelio Gabriel FUNES Mori (45+1'), 3-1 Carlos Alberto RODRÍGUEZ Gómez (77').
Al Sadd SC Doha: 2-1 Baghdad BOUNEDJAH (66'), 3-2 ABDELKARIM HASSAN Al Haj Fadlalla (89').
Referee: Ovidiu Alin HATEGAN (ROM)   Attendance: 4,878

FIFTH PLACE PLAY–OFF

17-12-2019   Khalifa International Stadium, Doha:
             Al Sadd SC Doha – ES Tunis 2-6 (1-4)
Al Sadd SC Doha: MESHAAL Aissa BARSHAM, ABDELKARIM HASSAN Al Haj Fadlalla (RC24), TAREK SALMAN Suleiman, Boualem KHOUKHI, JUNG Woo-young (KOR), ALI ASSADALLA Thaimn Qambar, HASAN Khailad AL HAYDOS, HAMID ISMAIL Khaleefa (46' Pedro Miguel Carvalho Deus Correia "RÓ-RÓ"), Gabriel Fernández Arenas "GABI" (ESP) (58' SALEM Ali AL HAJRI), Baghdad BOUNEDJAH (ALG), AKRAM Hassan AFIF Yahya Afif (79' HASHIM ALI Abdullatif Ali). (Coach: Xavier Hernández i Creus "XAVI" (ESP)).
ES Tunis: Moez BEN CHÉRIFIA, Khalil CHEMMAM, Sameh DERBALI, Ilyes CHETTI (ALG), Abdelkader BEDRANE (ALG), Kwame BONSU (GHA) (82' Raed FEDAA), Fousseny COULIBALY (CIV), Mohamed Ali BEN ROMDHANE (57' Raouf BENGUIT (ALG)), Anice BADRI, Ibrahim OUATTARA (CIV) (72' Yassine KHENISSI), HAMDOU Mohamed El Houni AL MASRY (LBA). (Coach: Moïne CHAÂBANI).
Goals: Al Sadd SC Doha: 1-3 Baghdad BOUNEDJAH (32' penalty), 2-4 HASAN Khailad AL HAYDOS (49' penalty).
ES Tunis: 0-1 HAMDOU Mohamed El Houni AL MASRY (6'), 0-2 Anice BADRI (13'), 0-3 Anice BADRI (25' penalty), 1-4 HAMDOU Mohamed El Houni AL MASRY (42'), 2-5 HAMDOU Mohamed El Houni AL MASRY (74'), 2-6 Sameh DERBALI (87').
Referee: Abdelkader ZITOUNI (TAH)   Attendance: 15,037

SEMI–FINALS

17-12-2019   Khalifa International Stadium, Doha:
CR Flamengo Rio de Janeiro – Al-Hilal Saudi FC Riyadh 3-1 (0-1)
CR Flamengo Rio de Janeiro: DIEGO ALVES Carreira, RODRIGO CAIO Coquette Russo, Márcio Rafael Ferreira de Souza "RAFINHA", FILIPE LUÍS Kasmirski, PABLO MARÍ Villar (ESP) (YC45+1), WILLIAM Souza ARÃO da Silva, ÉVERTON Augusto de Barros RIBEIRO, Giorgian Daniel DE ARRASCAETA Benedetti (URU) (90+3' Robert Ayrton PIRIS DA MOTTA Mendoza (PAR)), GERSON Santos da Silva (74' DIEGO Ribas da Cunha (YC87)), GABRIEL BARBOSA Almeida, BRUNO HENRIQUE Pinto (YC20) (89' Victor Vinícius Coelho dos Santos "VITINHO"). (Coach: JORGE Fernando Pinheiro de JESUS (POR)).
Al-Hilal Saudi FC Riyadh: ABDULLAH Ibrahim AL MAYOOF, MOHAMMED Ibrahim AL BURAYK, ALI Hadi AL BULAYHI (YC45+2), YASIR Gharsan Seed Al Mohammadi AL SHAHRANI, JANG Hyun-soo (KOR), CARLOS EDUARDO de Oliveira Alves (BRA), Gustavo Leonardo CUÉLLAR Gallego (COL), André Martín CARRILLO Díaz (PER) (RC83), SALEM Mohammed AL DAWSARI (YC69) (83' NAWAF Shaker AL ABID), Sebastian GIOVINCO (ITA) (YC44) (71' OMAR Maher KHRBIN (SYR)), Bafétimbi GOMIS (FRA) (90+2' ABDULLAH Ibrahim OTAYF). (Coach: Razvan LUCESCU (ROM)).
Goals: CR Flamengo: 1-1 Giorgian Daniel DE ARRASCAETA Benedetti (49'), 2-1 BRUNO HENRIQUE Pinto (78'), 3-1 ALI Hadi AL BULAYHI (82' own goal).
Al-Hilal Saudi FC Riyadh: 0-1 SALEM Mohammed AL DAWSARI (18').
Referee: Ismail ELFATH (USA)   Attendance: 21,588

18-12-2019   Khalifa International Stadium, Doha:
CF Monterrey – Liverpool FC 1-2 (1-1)
CF Monterrey: Marcelo Alberto BAROVERO (ARG), César Jasib MONTES Castro (79' Miguel Arturo LAYÚN Prado), Nicolás Gabriel SÁNCHEZ (ARG), Leonel Jesús VANGIONI Rangel (ARG) (YC47), Jesús Daniel GALLARDO Vasconcelos (YC78), John Stefan MEDINA Ramírez (COL), Celso Fabián ORTÍZ Gamarra (PAR), Carlos Alberto RODRÍGUEZ Gómez, Rogelio Gabriel FUNES Mori, Dorlan Mauricio PABÓN Ríos (COL) (82' Maximiliano Eduardo MEZA (ARG)), Rodolfo Gilbert PIZARRO Thomas (90' Jonathan Alexander GONZÁLEZ Mendoza). (Coach: Antonio Ricardo MOHAMED Matijevich (ARG)).
Liverpool FC: ALISSON Ramses Becker (BRA), Joe GOMEZ (YC58), Andrew ROBERTSON (SCO), James MILNER (75' Trent ALEXANDER-ARNOLD), Naby KEÏTA (GUI), Jordan HENDERSON, Alex OXLADE-CHAMBERLAIN, Adam LALLANA, Mohamed SALAH (EGY), Xherdan SHAQIRI (SUI) (68' Sadio MANÉ (SEN)), Divock ORIGI (BEL) (85' Roberto FIRMINO Barbosa de Oliveira (BRA)). (Coach: Jürgen KLOPP (GER)).
Goals: CF Monterrey: 1-1 Rogelio Gabriel FUNES Mori (14').
Liverpool FC: 0-1 Naby KEÏTA (12'), 1-2 Roberto FIRMINO Barbosa de Oliveira (90+1').
Referee: Roberto TOBAR Vargas (CHI)   Attendance: 45,416

THIRD PLACE PLAY-OFF

21-12-2019 Khalifa International Stadium, Doha:
CF Monterrey – Al-Hilal Saudi FC Riyadh 2-2 (0-1, 2-2) **(AET)**
CF Monterrey: Luis Alberto CÁRDENAS López, Edson Antonio GUTIÉRREZ Moreno, José María BASANTA Pavone (ARG), Miguel Arturo LAYÚN Prado, Johan Felipe VÁSQUEZ Ibarra, Arturo Alfonso GONZÁLEZ González (85' John Stefan MEDINA Ramírez (COL)), Jonathan Alexander GONZÁLEZ Mendoza, Maximiliano Eduardo MEZA (ARG) (YC90), William Sergio MEJÍA Castillo (YC64) (72' Rodolfo Gilbert PIZARRO Thomas), Jonathan Matías URRETAVISCAYA da Luz (URU) (YC31), Ángel ZALDÍVAR Caviedes (68' Rogelio Gabriel FUNES Mori). (Coach: Antonio Ricardo MOHAMED Matijevich (ARG)).
Al-Hilal Saudi FC Riyadh: ABDULLAH Ibrahim AL MAYOOF, MOHAMMED Ibrahim AL BURAYK, ALI Hadi AL BULAYHI, YASIR Gharsan Seed Al Mohammadi AL SHAHRANI, JANG Hyun-soo (KOR), CARLOS EDUARDO de Oliveira Alves (BRA), Gustavo Leonardo CUÉLLAR Gallego (COL) (63' HATTAN Sultan BAHEBRI), ABDULLAH Ibrahim OTAYF (74' MOHAMMED Ibrahim KANNO), SALEM Mohammed AL DAWSARI, Sebastian GIOVINCO (ITA), OMAR Maher KHRBIN (SYR) (60' Bafétimbi GOMIS (FRA)). (Coach: Razvan LUCESCU (ROM)).
Goals: CF Monterrey: 1-1 Arturo Alfonso GONZÁLEZ González (55'), 2-1 Maximiliano Eduardo MEZA (60').
Al-Hilal Saudi FC Riyadh: 0-1 CARLOS EDUARDO de Oliveira Alves (35'), 2-2 Bafétimbi GOMIS (66').
Referee: Ovidiu Alin HATEGAN (ROM) Attendance: 19,318

Penalties:
1 Bafétimbi GOMIS   1 Jonathan Alexander GONZÁLEZ Mendoza
2 Sebastian GIOVINCO   2 John Stefan MEDINA Ramírez
* CARLOS EDUARDO de Oliveira Alves
                               3 Rogelio Gabriel FUNES Mori
3 JANG Hyun-soo   * Johan Felipe VÁSQUEZ Ibarra
* MOHAMMED Ibrahim KANNO
                               4 Luis Alberto CÁRDENAS López

CF Monterrey won 4-3 on penalties.

FINAL

21-12-2019   Khalifa International Stadium, Doha:
Liverpool FC – CR Flamengo Rio de Janeiro 1-0 (0-0, 0-0) **(AET)**
Liverpool FC: ALISSON Ramses Becker (BRA), Virgil VAN DIJK (HOL), Joe GOMEZ, Andrew ROBERTSON (SCO), Trent ALEXANDER-ARNOLD, Naby KEÏTA (GUI) (100' James MILNER (YC105)), Jordan HENDERSON, Alex OXLADE-CHAMBERLAIN (75' Adam LALLANA), Roberto FIRMINO Barbosa de Oliveira (BRA) (YC100) (106' Divock ORIGI (BEL)), Sadio MANÉ (SEN) (YC45+1), Mohamed SALAH (EGY) (YC81) (120+1' Xherdan SHAQIRI (SUI)). (Coach: Jürgen KLOPP (GER)).
CR Flamengo Rio de Janeiro: DIEGO ALVES Carreira, RODRIGO CAIO Coquette Russo, Márcio Rafael Ferreira de Souza "RAFINHA", FILIPE LUÍS Kasmirski, PABLO MARÍ Villar (ESP), WILLIAM Souza ARÃO da Silva (120' Orlando Enrique BERRÍO Meléndez (COL)), ÉVERTON Augusto de Barros RIBEIRO (82' DIEGO Ribas da Cunha (YC112)), Giorgian Daniel DE ARRASCAETA Benedetti (URU) (77' Victor Vinícius Coelho dos Santos "VITINHO" (YC90)), GERSON Santos da Silva (102' LINCOLN Corrêa dos Santos), GABRIEL BARBOSA Almeida, BRUNO HENRIQUE Pinto. (Coach: JORGE Fernando Pinheiro de JESUS (POR)).
Goal: Liverpool FC: 1-0 Roberto FIRMINO Barbosa de Oliveira (99').
Referee: Abdulrahman Ibrahim Al-JASSIM (QAT)   Attendance: 45,416

*** Liverpool FC won the Cup ***

2020 FIFA Club World Cup

The 2020 FIFA Club World Cup (officially the 'FIFA Club World Cup Qatar 2020 presented by Alibaba Cloud' for sponsorship reasons) was played between 1st and 11th February 2021. It was the 17th edition of the FIFA Club World Cup and was again hosted by Qatar.

The effects of the COVID-19 pandemic meant that the tournament had to be postponed to 2021, as the AFC, CONMEBOL, and CONCACAF champions would not have been decided in time for the original tournament date which was set for December 2020.

Originally, seven teams were to compete in the tournament. However, the OFC's representatives Auckland City FC were forced to withdraw from the competition due to the effects of the pandemic and the strict quarantine measures enforced by the New Zealand authorities. Therefore, only six teams competed, and the First Round match was awarded as a 3-0 win to Auckland's planned opponents, Al-Duhail SC, the representatives of the Qatari hosts.

European Champions FC Bayern München won the Final 1-0 against the Mexican team CF Tigres UANL for their second FIFA Club World Cup title. In winning this trophy, FC Bayern München became only the second club in European football history to win all six titles on offer in a single calendar year, duplicating the achievement of FC Barcelona in 2009.

The clubs invited to play in the 2020 tournament were:

FC Bayern München (GER)	- winners of the 2019-20 UEFA Champions League
SE Palmeiras (BRA)	- winners of the 2020 Copa Libertadores
Al Ahly SC Cairo (EGY)	- winners of the 2019-20 CAF Champions League
Ulsan Hyundai FC (KOR)	- winners of the 2020 AFC Champions League
CF Tigres UANL (MEX)	- winners of the 2020 CONCACAF Champions League
Auckland City FC (NZL)	- nominated by OFC
Al-Duhail SC (QAT)	- winners of the 2019-20 Qatar Stars League (Host)

The Oceania Football Confederation abandoned the 2020 OFC Champions League due to border and travel restrictions caused by the COVID-19 pandemic. Auckland City FC were selected as the confederation's representatives by the OFC Executive Committee based on the OFC Champions League regulations. However, as noted above, on 15th January 2021, FIFA confirmed that Auckland City FC had withdrawn from the competition due to the effects of the pandemic and the strict quarantine measures required by the New Zealand authorities.

FIRST ROUND

01-02-2021   Ahmed bin Ali Stadium, Al Rayyan:
Al-Duhail SC Doha – Auckland City FC 3-0 **(awarded)**

SECOND ROUND

04-02-2021   Ahmed bin Ali Stadium, Al Rayyan:
CF Tigres UANL San Nicolás de los Garza – Ulsan Hyundai FC 2-1 (2-1)
CF Tigres UANL: Nahuel Ignacio GUZMÁN Palomeque (ARG), Carlos Joel SALCEDO Hernández, Diego Antonio REYES Rosales, Francisco Javier MEZA Palma (COL) (46' Carlos Gabriel GONZÁLEZ Espínola (PAR)), Luis Alfonso RODRÍGUEZ Alanís (YC69), RAFAEL "CARIOCA" de Souza Pereira (BRA), Guido Hernán PIZARRO Demestri (ARG), Javier Ignacio AQUINO Carmona (65' Raymundo de Jesús FULGENCIO Román), Jesús Alberto DUEÑAS Manzo (YC81) (83' Hugo AYALA Castro), André-Pierre GIGNAC (FRA), Luis Enrique QUIÑÓNES García (COL) (YC84) (90' Jordan Steeven SIERRA Flores (ECU)). (Coach: RICARDO FERRETTI de Oliveira (BRA)).
Ulsan Hyundai FC: JO Hyeon-woo, Dave BULTHUIS (HOL), WON Du-jae, KIM Kee-hee (YC45+4), SEOL Young-woo, YOON Bit-garam, LEE Dong-jun, SHIN Hyung-min (79' KANG Yun-gu), KIM Tae-hwan, KIM In-sung (66' KIM Seong-jun), KIM Ji-hyeon (73' Lukas HINTERSEER (AUT) (YC90+1)). (Coach: HONG Myung-bo).
Goals: CF Tigres UANL: 1-1 André-Pierre GIGNAC (38'), 2-1 André-Pierre GIGNAC (45+5' penalty).
Ulsan Hyundai FC: 0-1 KIM Kee-hee (24').
Referee: Esteban Daniel OSTOJICH Vega (URU)   Attendance: 866

04-02-2021   Education City Stadium, Al Rayyan:
Al-Duhail SC Doha – Al Ahly SC Cairo 0-1 (0-1)
Al-Duhail SC Doha: SALAH ZAKARIA Hassan Moussa, MOHAMMED MUSA Abbas Ali, Medhi Amine El Moutaqui BENATIA (MAR) (YC85), AHMED YASSER Mohammedi Abdelrahman (72' ISMAIL MOHAMMED Mohammed), SULTAN Hussain AL BRAKE, BASSAM Hisham Ali AL RAWI (46' ALMOEZ ALI Zainalabiddin Abdulla), Karim BOUDIAF, Ali KARIMI (IRN) (82' LUIZ "CEARÁ" Mairton Carlos Júnior), EDMILSON Junior Paulo da Silva (BRA), Michael OLUNGA Ogada (KEN) (46' Mohammed MUNTARI), Eduardo Pereira Rodrigues "DUDU" (BRA). (Coach: Sabri LAMOUCHI (FRA)).
Al Ahly SC Cairo: MOHAMED Elsayed Mohamed EL SHENAWY, AYMAN ASHRAF El Sayed, Badr BANOUN (MAR), Ali MAÂLOUL (TUN), MOHAMED HANY Gamal El Demerdash (YC89), HAMDY FATHY Abdelhalim Fattah (YC27) (54' Aliou DIENG (MLI)), HUSSEIN EL SHAHAT (82' SALAH MOHSEN Shalaby), AMR Mohamed AL SULAYA, Mohamed Magdy Mohamed Moursy "AFSHA", TAHER MOHAMED Taher (70' AKRAM TAWFIK Mohamed Hassan), WALTER Binene Sabwa BWALYA (DRC) (70' MARWAN MOHSEN Fahmy Tharwat Gamaleldin Mahmoud Fahmy). (Coach: Pitso John MOSIMANE (RSA)).
Goal: Al Ahly SC Cairo: 0-1 HUSSEIN EL SHAHAT (30').
Referee: Mario Alberto ESCOBAR Toca (GUA)

FIFTH PLACE PLAY–OFF

07-02-2021   Ahmed bin Ali Stadium, Al Rayyan:
Ulsan Hyundai FC – Al-Duhail SC Doha 1-3 (0-1)
Ulsan Hyundai FC: JO Hyeon-woo, Jason DAVIDSON (AUS) (46' KIM In-sung), Dave BULTHUIS (HOL), WON Du-jae, KIM Kee-hee, SEOL Young-woo (YC83), YOON Bit-garam, LEE Dong-jun (76' KIM Min-jun), KIM Seong-jun (66' SHIN Hyung-min), KIM Tae-hwan (YC74), Lukas HINTERSEER (AUT) (46' KIM Ji-hyeon). (Coach: HONG Myung-bo).
Al-Duhail SC Doha: SALAH ZAKARIA Hassan Moussa, Medhi Amine El Moutaqui BENATIA (MAR), BASSAM Hisham Ali AL RAWI, ISMAIL MOHAMMED Mohammed (90+4' ALI MALOLAH Karami), ABDULLAH Abdulsalam Ali AL AHRAK (75' ASSIM Omer Al Haj MADIBO), Ali KARIMI (IRN), EDMILSON Junior Paulo da Silva (BRA), ALMOEZ ALI Zainalabiddin Abdulla (YC90+1), ALI Hasan AFIF Yahya, Michael OLUNGA Ogada (KEN) (61' Mohammed MUNTARI), Eduardo Pereira Rodrigues "DUDU" (BRA) (90+4' KHALED MOHAMMED Mohammed Saleh). (Coach: Sabri LAMOUCHI (FRA)).
Goals: Ulson Hyundai FC: 1-1 YOON Bit-garam (62').
Al-Duhail SC: 0-1 EDMILSON Junior Paulo da Silva (21'), 1-2 Mohammed MUNTARI (66'), 1-3 ALMOEZ ALI Zainalabiddin Abdulla (82').
Referee: EDINA ALVES Batista (BRA)   Attendance: 920

SEMI–FINALS

07-02-2021   Education City Stadium, Al Rayyan:
SE Palmeiras São Paulo – CF Tigres UANL San Nicolás de los Garza 0-1 (0-0)
SE Palmeiras: WÉVERTON Pereira da Silva, MARCOS Luis ROCHA Aquino (72' MAYKE Rocha de Oliveira), LUAN Garcia Teixeira (YC52), Gustavo Raúl GÓMEZ Portillo (PAR), Matías Nicolás VIÑA Susperreguy (URU), José "ZÉ" RAFAEL Vivian (57' PATRICK DE PAULA Carreiro), RAPHAEL Cavalcante VEIGA (73' GUSTAVO Henrique Furtado SCARPA), GABRIEL Vinicius MENINO (YC32) (62' WILLIAN Gomes de Siqueira), DANILO dos Santos de Oliveira (57' FELIPE MELO de Carvalho), Ronielson da Silva Barbosa "RONY", LUIZ ADRIANO Souza da Silva. (Coach: ABEL Fernando Moreira FERREIRA (POR)).
CF Tigres UANL: Nahuel Ignacio GUZMÁN Palomeque (ARG) (YC84), Carlos Joel SALCEDO Hernández, Diego Antonio REYES Rosales, Luis Alfonso RODRÍGUEZ Alanís, RAFAEL "CARIOCA" de Souza Pereira (BRA), Guido Hernán PIZARRO Demestri (ARG), Javier Ignacio AQUINO Carmona (YC45) (90+2' Jordan Steeven SIERRA Flores (ECU)), Jesús Alberto DUEÑAS Manzo (86' Francisco Javier MEZA Palma (COL)), André-Pierre GIGNAC (FRA), Luis Enrique QUIÑONES García (COL) (87' Raymundo de Jesús FULGENCIO Román), Carlos Gabriel GONZÁLEZ Espínola (PAR). (Coach: RICARDO FERRETTI de Oliveira (BRA)).
Goal: CF Tigres UANL: 0-1 André-Pierre GIGNAC (54' penalty).
Referee: Danny Desmond MAKKELIE (HOL)   Attendance: 1,854

08-02-2021   Ahmed bin Ali Stadium, Al Rayyan:
Al Ahly SC Cairo – FC Bayern München 0-2 (0-1)
Al Ahly SC Cairo: MOHAMED Elsayed Mohamed EL SHENAWY, AYMAN ASHRAF El Sayed, Badr BANOUN (MAR), Ali MAÂLOUL (TUN) (28' YASSER IBRAHIM El Hanafi), MOHAMED HANY Gamal El Demerdash, HAMDY FATHY Abdelhalim Fattah, HUSSEIN EL SHAHAT (69' SALAH MOHSEN Shalaby), AMR Mohamed AL SULAYA, Mohamed Magdy Mohamed Moursy "AFSHA" (70' Aliou DIENG (MLI)), Mahmoud Abdul Monem Abdelhamid Soliman "KAHRABA" (69' WALTER Binene Sabwa BWALYA (DRC)), TAHER MOHAMED Taher (83' MOHAMED SHERIF Mohamed). (Coach: Pitso John MOSIMANE (RSA)).
FC Bayern München: Manuel NEUER, Benjamin PAVARD (FRA), Jérôme BOATENG (77' Niklas SÜLE), Alphonse DAVIES (CAN), David ALABA (AUT), Joshua KIMMICH, MARC ROCA Junqué (ESP) (69' Corentin TOLISSO (FRA)), Serge GNABRY (62' Leroy SANÉ), Robert LEWANDOWSKI (POL), Thomas MÜLLER (62' Eric Maxim CHOUPO-MOTING (CMR)), Kingsley COMAN (FRA) (78' Jamal MUSIALA). (Coach: Hansi FLICK).
Goals: FC Bayern München: 0-1 Robert LEWANDOWSKI (17'), 0-2 Robert LEWANDOWSKI (86').
Referee: MOHAMMED Abdulla HASSAN Mohamed (UAE)   Attendance: 7,982

THIRD PLACE PLAY–OFF

11-02-2021   Education City Stadium, Al Rayyan:
Al Ahly SC Cairo – SE Palmeiras São Paulo 0-0 **(AET)**
Al Ahly SC Cairo: MOHAMED Elsayed Mohamed EL SHENAWY, YASSER IBRAHIM El Hanafi, AYMAN ASHRAF El Sayed, Badr BANOUN (MAR), MOHAMED HANY Gamal El Demerdash, HAMDY FATHY Abdelhalim Fattah, AMR Mohamed AL SULAYA, Mohamed Magdy Mohamed Moursy "AFSHA" (59' MOHAMED SHERIF Mohamed), AKRAM TAWFIK Mohamed Hassan (76' Aliou DIENG (MLI)), TAHER MOHAMED Taher (76' MARWAN MOHSEN Fahmy Tharwat Gamaleldin Mahmoud Fahmy), WALTER Binene Sabwa BWALYA (DRC) (58' Junior Oluwafemi AJAYI (NGR)). (Coach: Pitso John MOSIMANE (RSA)).
SE Palmeiras: WÉVERTON Pereira da Silva (YC27), MAYKE Rocha de Oliveira, LUAN Garcia Teixeira, Gustavo Raúl GÓMEZ Portillo (PAR), Matías Nicolás VIÑA Susperreguy (URU), PATRICK DE PAULA Carreiro (YC69) (81' DANILO dos Santos de Oliveira), RAPHAEL Cavalcante VEIGA (80' GUSTAVO Henrique Furtado SCARPA), FELIPE MELO de Carvalho, Ronielson da Silva Barbosa "RONY", LUIZ ADRIANO Souza da Silva, WILLIAN Gomes de Siqueira (YC45+2) (81' GABRIEL Vinicius MENINO). (Coach: ABEL Fernando Moreira FERREIRA (POR)).
Referee: Maguette N'DIAYE (SEN)   Attendance: 5,606

Penalties:
1 Badr BANOUN   * Ronielson da Silva Barbosa "RONY"
* AMR Mohamed AL SULAYA   * LUIZ ADRIANO Souza da Silva
* MARWAN MOHSEN Fahmy Tharwat Gamaleldin Mahmoud Fahmy
                                      1 GUSTAVO Henrique Furtado SCARPA
2 MOHAMED HANY Gamal El Demerdash
                                      2 Gustavo Raúl GÓMEZ Portillo
3 Junior Oluwafemi AJAYI   * FELIPE MELO de Carvalho

Al Ahly SC Cairo won 3-2 on penalties.

FINAL

11-02-2021 Education City Stadium, Al Rayyan:
FC Bayern München – CF Tigres UANL San Nicolás de los Garza 1-0 (0-0)
FC Bayern München: Manuel NEUER, Niklas SÜLE, Benjamin PAVARD (FRA), Alphonse DAVIES (CAN), Lucas François Bernard HERNÁNDEZ Pi (FRA), David ALABA (AUT), Joshua KIMMICH, Serge GNABRY (64' Corentin TOLISSO (FRA)), Robert LEWANDOWSKI (POL) (73' Eric Maxim CHOUPO-MOTING (CMR)), Leroy SANÉ (73' Jamal MUSIALA), Kingsley COMAN (FRA) (73' DOUGLAS COSTA de Souza (BRA)). (Coach: Hansi FLICK).
CF Tigres UANL: Nahuel Ignacio GUZMÁN Palomeque (ARG), Carlos Joel SALCEDO Hernández, Diego Antonio REYES Rosales, Luis Alfonso RODRÍGUEZ Alanís (YC69) (80' Julián Andrés QUIÑONES Quiñones (COL)), RAFAEL "CARIOCA" de Souza Pereira (BRA) (YC90), Guido Hernán PIZARRO Demestri (ARG), Javier Ignacio AQUINO Carmona, Jesús Alberto DUEÑAS Manzo (YC42), André-Pierre GIGNAC (FRA), Luis Enrique QUIÑÓNES García (COL), Carlos Gabriel GONZÁLEZ Espínola (PAR). (Coach: RICARDO FERRETTI de Oliveira (BRA)).
Goal: FC Bayern München: 1-0 Benjamin PAVARD (59').
Referee: Esteban Daniel OSTOJICH Vega (URU)   Attendance: 7,411

*** FC Bayern München won the Cup ***

2021 FIFA Club World Cup

The 2021 FIFA Club World Cup (officially, the 'FIFA Club World Cup UAE 2021 presented by Alibaba Cloud' for sponsorship reasons) was played between 3rd and 12th February 2022 in the United Arab Emirates. It was the 18th edition of the FIFA Club World Cup.

It had originally been planned that an expanded Club World Cup would be held in China in June and July 2021 but fixture congestion caused by the postponement of the 2020 Summer Olympics and the impact of COVID-19 on football around the world meant this would be impossible. FIFA instead announced that the competition would be hosted in the previous format in Japan with the tournament to be played in late 2021. However, the Japanese Football Association dropped its commitment to host the tournament in September 2021 due to the likelihood of restrictions for attending fans because of the ongoing pandemic. The bidding process resumed and countries including Brazil, Egypt, Qatar, Saudi Arabia, South Africa and the United Arab Emirates all offered to host the tournament. FIFA chose the United Arab Emirates as hosts and postponed the event until early 2022.

The Champions of 5 of the 6 confederations entered the tournament as did AS Pirae of Tahiti, who were nominated as the representative of the Oceania Football Confederation and they faced the UAE champions Al Jazira Club in the initial play-off.

In the Final, the European Champions Chelsea FC required extra time to defeat the South American Champions 2-1 to win their first FIFA Club World Cup title.

The clubs invited to play in the 2021 tournament were:

Chelsea FC (ENG)	- winners of the 2020-21 UEFA Champions League
SE Palmeiras (BRA)	- winners of the 2021 Copa Libertadores
Al Ahly SC Cairo (EGY)	- winners of the 2020-21 CAF Champions League
Al Hilal Saudi FC (KSA)	- winners of the 2021 AFC Champions League
CF Monterrey (MEX)	- winners of the 2021 CONCACAF Champions League
AS Pirae (TAH)	- Nominated by OFC
Al Jazira Club (UAE)	- winners of the 2020-21 UAE Pro League (Host)

The 2021 OFC Champions League was cancelled due to border closures throughout the Pacific caused by the COVID-19. Auckland City FC were selected as the OFC representative under the sporting merit principles which looked back at past performances but they were forced to withdraw from the competition due to the delayed reopening of the New Zealand borders. As a result, AS Pirae were nominated as the OFC's representative in their place.

FIRST ROUND

03-02-2022 Mohammed bin Zayed Stadium, Abu Dhabi:
Al Jazira Club Abu Dhabi – AS Pirae 4-1 (3-0)
Al Jazira Club Abu Dhabi: ALI KHASEIF Humaid Khaseif Al Housani (46' ABDULLRAHMAN Abdulla Khamis Mubarak AL AMERI), Milos KOSANOVIC (SRB) (85' NAWAF Salem DHAWI Jumaa Alharthi), ABDULLAH IDREES Saqar Mubarak Alhammadi (YC90+3), KHALIFA Mubarak Khalfan Khairi AL HAMMADI (46' ZAYED SULTAN Ahmed Jassim Ibrahim Al Zaabi), Mohammed RABII (MAR) (YC58), Thulani Caleb SERERO (RSA) (YC34) (46' Mamadou COULIBALY (CIV)), MOHAMMED JAMAL Nasser Mubarak Badhafari, JOÃO VICTOR Santos Sá (BRA), Abdoulay DIABY (MLI), AHMED Mohamed Ahmed Husain AL HASHMI, ZAYED Abdulla Braik Saeed AL AMERI (61' ALI Ahmed MABKHOUT Mohsen Omran Al Hajeri). (Coach: Marcel KEIZER (HOL)).
AS Pirae: Teva DUROT, Dylan Terahitiarii Matatia Tearaa PAAMA, Heimano Donovan BOUREBARE, Alvin TEHAU, Jonathan TEHAU, Benoît MATHON (FRA), Heirauarii SALEM (57' Jimmy Patrick TEPA), Avearii BENNETT (87' Jay WARREN), Yohann TIHONI (46' Sylvain GRAGLIA), Roonui TINIRAUARII (79' Teimanaiterai Karel Teariki PATER), Louis Tehotu GITTON (87' Nehemia Harrisson TERIITAHI). (Coach: Naea BENNETT).
Goals: Al Jazira Club: 1-0 ZAYED Abdulla Braik Saeed AL AMERI (5'), 2-0 AHMED Mohamed Ahmed Husain AL HASHMI (25'), 3-0 Milos KOSANOVIC (41'), 4-1 Abdoulay DIABY (63').
AS Pirae: 3-1 Mohammed RABII (48' own goal).
Referee: Mustapha GHORBAL (ALG)   Attendance: 4,970

SECOND ROUND

05-02-2022 Al Nahyan Stadium, Abu Dhabi:
Al Ahly SC Cairo – CF Monterrey 1-0 (0-0)
Al Ahly SC Cairo: ALY LOTFY Ibrahim Moustafa Ibrahim (YC77), Ali MAÂLOUL (TUN), RAMI Hisham Abdel Aziz RABIA, YASSER IBRAHIM El Hanafi, MOHAMED HANY Gamal El Demerdash, MOHAMED EL MAGHRABY (YC31) (64' KARIM FOUAD), Mohamed Magdy Mohamed Moursy "AFSHA" (YC66), Aliou DIENG (MLI) (YC90+2), HUSSEIN EL SHAHAT (79' WALID SOLIMAN Said), AHMED Mohamed ABDELKADER Radwan (74' Luís José MIQUISSONE (MOZ)), TAHER MOHAMED Taher. (Coach: Pitso John MOSIMANE (RSA)).
CF Monterrey: Esteban Maximiliano ANDRADA (ARG), Luis Francisco ROMO Barrón, Héctor Alfredo MORENO Herrera, Sebastián Ignacio VEGAS Orellana (CHI) (57' Jesús Daniel GALLARDO Vasconcelos), Celso Fabián ORTÍZ Gamarra (PAR), Arturo Alfonso GONZÁLEZ González (57' Vincent JANSSEN (HOL)), Maximiliano Eduardo MEZA (ARG), Claudio Matías KRANEVITTER (ARG), Rodolfo Gilbert PIZARRO Thomas (68' Joel Nathaniel CAMPBELL Samuels (CRC)), Érick Germain AGUIRRE Tafolla, Rogelio Gabriel FUNES MORI. (Coach: Javier AGUIRRE Onandía).
Goal: Al Ahly SC Cairo: 1-0 MOHAMED HANY Gamal El Demerdash (53').
Referee: Christopher James BEATH (AUS)   Attendance: 9,396

06-02-2022 Mohammed bin Zayed Stadium, Abu Dhabi:
Al Hilal Saudi FC Riyadh – Al Jazira Club Abu Dhabi 6-1 (2-1)
Al Hilal Saudi FC Riyadh: ABDULLAH Ibrahim AL MAIOUF, YASIR Gharsan AL SHAHRANI (83' MOHAMMED Ibrahim AL BURAYK), JANG Hyun-Soo (KOR) (87' MUTEB Abdullah AL MUFARRIJ), ALI Hadi AL BULAIHI, SAUD Abdullah Salim ABDUL HAMID, Gustavo Leonardo CUÉLLAR Gallego (COL), SALEM Mohammed AL DAWSARI (83' MICHAEL Richard Delgado de Oliveira (BRA)), MOHAMMED Ibrahim KANNO (84' MOHAMMED Yahya JAHFALI), MATHEUS Fellipe Costa PEREIRA (BRA), Odion Jude IGHALO (NGR) (75' André Martín CARRILLO Díaz (PER)), Moussa MAREGA (MLI). (Coach: José LEONARDO Nunes Alves Sousa JARDIM (POR)).
Al Jazira Club Abu Dhabi: ALI KHASEIF Humaid Khaseif Al Housani, Milos KOSANOVIC (SRB) (YC46), MOHAMMED Omar Zain Mohsen Zain AL ATTAS, ABDULLAH IDREES Saqar Mubarak Alhammadi (60' ZAYED Abdulla Braik Saeed AL AMERI), KHALIFA Mubarak Khalfan Khairi AL HAMMADI, Mohammed RABII (MAR) (YC89), Thulani Caleb SERERO (RSA), JOÃO VICTOR Santos Sá (BRA) (60' ALI Ahmed MABKHOUT Mohsen Omran Al Hajeri), ABDALLA RAMADAN Bekheet Soliman Bekheet, Abdoulay DIABY (MLI), AHMED Mohamed Ahmed Husain AL HASHMI (61' Oumar TRAORÉ (MLI)). (Coach: Marcel KEIZER (HOL)).
Goals: Al Hilal Saudi FC: 1-1 Odion Jude IGHALO (36'), 2-1 MATHEUS Fellipe Costa PEREIRA (40'), 3-1 MOHAMMED Ibrahim KANNO (57'), 4-1 SALEM Mohammed AL DAWSARI (77'), 5-1 Moussa MAREGA (88'), 6-1 André Martín CARRILLO Díaz (90+2' penalty).
Al Jazira Club: 0-1 Abdoulay DIABY (14').
Referee: César Arturo RAMOS Palazuelos (MEX) Attendance: 12,538

SEMI–FINALS

08-02-2022 Al Nahyan Stadium, Abu Dhabi:
SE Palmeiras São Paulo – Al Ahly SC Cairo 2-0 (1-0)
SE Palmeiras: WÉVERTON Pereira da Silva, MARCOS Luis ROCHA Aquino, Gustavo Raúl GÓMEZ Portillo (PAR), LUAN Garcia Teixeira, Joaquín PIQUEREZ Moreira (URU), José "ZÉ" RAFAEL Vivian (86' Eduard Andrés ATUESTA Velasco (COL)), GUSTAVO Henrique Furtado SCARPA (89' BRENO Henrique Vasconcelos LOPES), RAPHAEL Cavalcante VEIGA (79' JAÍLSON Marques Siqueira), DANILO dos Santos de Oliveira, Eduardo Pereira Rodrigues "DUDU" (78' WESLEY Ribeiro Silva), Ronielson da Silva Barbosa "RONY" (88' DEYVERSON Brum Silva Acosta). (Coach: ABEL Fernando Moreira FERREIRA (POR)).
Al Ahly SC Cairo: ALY LOTFY Ibrahim Moustafa Ibrahim, AYMAN ASHRAF Elsayed Elsembeskany (RC81), Ali MAÂLOUL (TUN), RAMI Hisham Abdel Aziz RABIA (54' HAMDI FATHI Abdel Halim Abdul Fattah), YASSER IBRAHIM El Hanafi, MOHAMED HANY Gamal El Demerdash, AMR Mohamed Eid EL SOLEYA (54' AHMED Mohamed ABDELKADER Radwan), Mohamed Magdy Mohamed Moursy "AFSHA" (YC90+1), Aliou DIENG (MLI), HUSSEIN EL SHAHAT (54' MOHAMED SHERIF Mohamed Ragaei Bakr), TAHER MOHAMED Taher (74' WALID SOLIMAN Said). (Coach: Pitso John MOSIMANE (RSA)).
Goals: SE Palmeiras: 1-0 RAPHAEL Cavalcante VEIGA (39'), 2-0 Eduardo Pereira Rodrigues "DUDU" (49').
Referee: Clément TURPIN (FRA) Attendance: 11,902

09-02-2022   Mohammed bin Zayed Stadium, Abu Dhabi:
Al Hilal Saudi FC Riyadh – Chelsea FC London 0-1 (0-1)
Al Hilal Saudi FC Riyadh: ABDULLAH Ibrahim AL MAIOUF, YASIR Gharsan AL SHAHRANI, JANG Hyun-Soo (KOR), MOHAMMED Ibrahim AL BURAYK, ALI Hadi AL BULAIHI (YC84), Gustavo Leonardo CUÉLLAR Gallego (COL) (YC66), SALEM Mohammed AL DAWSARI (81' André Martín CARRILLO Díaz (PER)), MOHAMMED Ibrahim KANNO, MATHEUS Fellipe Costa PEREIRA (BRA) (82' MICHAEL Richard Delgado de Oliveira (BRA)), Odion Jude IGHALO (NGR), Moussa MAREGA (MLI). (Coach: José LEONARDO Nunes Alves Sousa JARDIM (POR)).
Chelsea FC London: KEPA Arrizabalaga Revuelta (ESP), THIAGO Emiliano da SILVA (BRA), César AZPILICUETA Tanco (ESP), MARCOS ALONSO Mendoza (ESP) (87' Malang SARR (FRA)), Antonio RÜDIGER (GER), Andreas Bødtker CHRISTENSEN (DEN), Mateo KOVACIC (CRO) (YC81), Jorge Luiz Frello Filho "JORGINHO" (ITA) (46' N'Golo KANTÉ (FRA)), Hakim ZIYECH (MAR) (72' Mason MOUNT), Kai Lukas HAVERTZ (GER), Romelu LUKAKU Menama (BEL). (Coach: Thomas TUCHEL (GER)).
Goal: Chelsea FC: 0-1 Romelu LUKAKU Menama (32').
Referee: César Arturo RAMOS Palazuelos (MEX)   Attendance: 19,175

FIFTH PLACE PLAY-OFF

09-02-2022   Al Nahyan Stadium, Abu Dhabi:
CF Monterrey – Al Jazira Club Abu Dhabi 3-1 (3-0)
CF Monterrey: Esteban Maximiliano ANDRADA (ARG), Héctor Alfredo MORENO Herrera (46' Sebastián Ignacio VEGAS Orellana (CHI) (YC81)), John Stefan MEDINA Ramírez (COL), César Jasib MONTES Castro, Arturo Alfonso GONZÁLEZ González (46' Rodolfo Gilbert PIZARRO Thomas (YC56)), Maximiliano Eduardo MEZA (ARG) (YC73) (75' José Alfonso ALVARADO Pérez), Claudio Matías KRANEVITTER (ARG), Érick Germain AGUIRRE Tafolla, Jesús Daniel GALLARDO Vasconcelos (YC41) (46' Joel Nathaniel CAMPBELL Samuels (CRC) (YC54)), Luis Francisco ROMO Barrón, Rogelio Gabriel FUNES MORI (58' Vincent JANSSEN (HOL)). (Coach: Javier AGUIRRE Onandía).
Al Jazira Club Abu Dhabi: ALI KHASEIF Humaid Khaseif Al Housani, ABDULLAH IDREES Saqar Mubarak Alhammadi (88' NAWAF Salem DHAWI Jumaa Alharthi), KHALIFA Mubarak Khalfan Khairi AL HAMMADI, Thulani Caleb SERERO (RSA), SALEM RASHID Obaid Sanad Rashid, ABDALLA RAMADAN Bekheet Soliman Bekheet (86' Mamadou COULIBALY (CIV)), Oumar TRAORÉ (MLI) (73' BRUNO Conçeicão de Oliveira (BRA)), ZAYED SULTAN Ahmed Jassim Ibrahim Al Zaabi, Abdoulay DIABY (MLI), AHMED Mohamed Ahmed Husain AL HASHMI (73' YOUSEF AYMAN Yousef Ali Al Mansoori), ZAYED Abdulla Braik Saeed AL AMERI. (Coach: Marcel KEIZER (HOL)).
Goals: CF Monterrey: 1-0 ZAYED SULTAN Ahmed Jassim Ibrahim Al (4' own goal), 2-0 Rogelio Gabriel FUNES MORI (11'), 3-0 César Jasib MONTES Castro (25').
Al Jazira Club: 3-1 BRUNO Conçeicão de Oliveira (90+1').
Referee: Mustapha GHORBAL (ALG)   Attendance: 892

THIRD PLACE PLAY-OFF

12-02-2022 Al Nahyan Stadium, Abu Dhabi:
Al Hilal Saudi FC Riyadh – Al Ahly SC Cairo 0-4 (0-3)
Al Hilal Saudi FC Riyadh: MOHAMMED Khalil Ibrahim AL OWAIS, YASIR Gharsan AL SHAHRANI (72' MOHAMMED Ibrahim AL BURAYK), JANG Hyun-Soo (KOR) (72' MUSAB Fahz AL JUWAYR), MUTEB Abdullah AL MUFARRIJ, SAUD Abdullah Salim ABDUL HAMID, Gustavo Leonardo CUÉLLAR Gallego (COL) (46' MOHAMMED Yahya JAHFALI), André Martín CARRILLO Díaz (PER) (46' SALMAN Mohammed AL FARAJ (YC58)), SALEM Mohammed AL DAWSARI (84' MICHAEL Richard Delgado de Oliveira (BRA)), MOHAMMED Ibrahim KANNO (RC28), MATHEUS Fellipe Costa PEREIRA (BRA) (RC14), Moussa MAREGA (MLI). (Coach: José LEONARDO Nunes Alves Sousa JARDIM (POR)).
Al Ahly SC Cairo: ALY LOTFY Ibrahim Moustafa Ibrahim, Ali MAÂLOUL (TUN) (87' MAHMOUD WAHEED Elsayed Mohamed), YASSER IBRAHIM El Hanafi, MOHAMED HANY Gamal El Demerdash (YC32) (46' KARIM FOUAD Abdelhamid Mahmoud), MOHAMED ABDELMONEM Elsayed Mohamed Ahmed, AMR Mohamed Eid EL SOLEYA, Aliou DIENG (MLI) (66' WALID SOLIMAN Said), HAMDI FATHI Abdel Halim Abdul Fattah, AHMED Mohamed ABDELKADER Radwan (87' Luís Jose MIQUISSONE (MOZ)), TAHER MOHAMED Taher (YC45+6) (46' HUSSEIN EL SHAHAT), MOHAMED SHERIF Mohamed Ragaei Bakr (YC55). (Coach: Pitso John MOSIMANE (RSA)).
Goals: Al Ahly SC Cairo: 0-1 HAMDI FATHI Abdel Halim Abdul Fattah (8'), 0-2 YASSER IBRAHIM El Hanafi (17'), 0-3 AHMED Mohamed ABDELKADER Radwan (40'), 0-4 AMR Mohamed Eid EL SOLEYA (64').
Referee: Clément TURPIN (FRA)   Attendance: 9,008

FINAL

12-02-2022 Mohammed bin Zayed Stadium, Abu Dhabi:
Chelsea FC London – SE Palmeiras São Paulo 2-1 (0-0, 1-1) **(AET)**
Chelsea FC London: Édouard MENDY (SEN), THIAGO Emiliano da SILVA (BRA), César AZPILICUETA Tanco (ESP), Antonio RÜDIGER (GER), Andreas Bødtker CHRISTENSEN (DEN) (91' Malang SARR (FRA)), Mateo KOVACIC (CRO) (91' Hakim ZIYECH (MAR)), N'Golo KANTÉ (FRA), Mason MOUNT (31' Christian PULISIC (USA)), Kai Lukas HAVERTZ (GER) (YC118), Romelu LUKAKU Menama (BEL) (76' Timo WERNER (GER)), Callum HUDSON-ODOI (76' SAÚL Ñíguez Esclapez (ESP)). (Coach: Thomas TUCHEL (GER)).
SE Palmeiras São Paulo: WÉVERTON Pereira da Silva, MARCOS Luis ROCHA Aquino (118' DEYVERSON Brum Silva Acosta), Gustavo Raúl GÓMEZ Portillo (PAR), LUAN Garcia Teixeira (YC116,RC120+6), Joaquín PIQUEREZ Moreira (URU), José "ZÉ" RAFAEL Vivian (59' JAÍLSON Marques Siqueira), GUSTAVO Henrique Furtado SCARPA, RAPHAEL Cavalcante VEIGA (78' Eduard Andrés ATUESTA Velasco (COL) (YC116)), DANILO dos Santos de Oliveira, Eduardo Pereira Rodrigues "DUDU" (103' RAFAEL NAVARRO Leal), Ronielson da Silva Barbosa "RONY" (77' WESLEY Ribeiro Silva (YC105)). (Coach: ABEL Fernando Moreira FERREIRA (POR) (YC120)).
Goals: Chelsea FC: 1-0 Romelu LUKAKU Menama (54'), 2-1 Kai Lukas HAVERTZ (117' penalty).
SE Palmeiras: 1-1 RAPHAEL Cavalcante VEIGA (64' penalty).
Referee: Christopher James BEATH (AUS)   Attendance: 32,871

*** Chelsea FC won the Cup ***